FINANCIAL SECTOR REFORM AND PRIVATIZATION IN TRANSITION ECONOMIES

ADVANCES IN FINANCE, INVESTMENT AND BANKING

SERIES EDITOR: ELROY DIMSON

FINANCIAL SECTOR REFORM AND PRIVATIZATION IN TRANSITION ECONOMIES

Edited by
John Doukas

Department of Finance
College of Business and Public Administration
Old Dominion University
Norfolk, VA 23529 0218, U.S.A.

Victor Murinde

Department of Accounting and Finance
The Birmingham Business School
The University of Birmingham
Edgbaston, Birmingham, B15 2TT, UK

Clas Wihlborg

Department of Economics
School of Economics and Commercial Law
Göteborg University
Vasagatan 1, S 4111 80, Göteborg, Sweden

1998
ELSEVIER
Amsterdam – Lausanne – New York – Oxford – Shannon – Singapore – Tokyo

ELSEVIER SCIENCE B.V.
Sara Burgerhartstraat 25
P.O. Box 211, 1000 AE Amsterdam, The Netherlands

Library of Congress Cataloging-in-Publication Data

Financial sector reform and privatization in transition economies /
edited by John Doukas, Victor Murinde, Clas Wihlborg.
        p.   cm. -- (Advances in finance, investment, and banking ; v.
7)
   "A selection of the best papers presented at various conferences
and workshops held in Estonia, Poland, and the Netherlands, as well
as several invited papers, in the period 1994-97"--Pref.
   Includes index.
   ISBN 0-444-82653-X
   1. Finance--Europe, Eastern--Congresses.   2. Europe, Eastern-
-Economic policy--1989- --Congresses.   3. Privatization--Europe,
Eastern--Congresses.   I. Doukas John.   II. Murinde, Victor.
III. Wihlborg, Clas.   IV. Series.
HG186.E8F57   1998
336.47--dc21   98-15131
                                                              CIP

ISBN: 0 444 82653 X

Printed in The Netherlands.

Introduction to the Series

This series presents a number of hitherto unpublished studies on a variety of financial themes.

The subjects covered by the *Advances in Finance, Investment and Banking* (AFIB) book series include financial institutions and markets, corporate finance, portfolio investment, regulatory issues in banking and finance, comparative surveys, international taxation and accounting issues, and relevant macro-economics and asset pricing research studies. Books in this series include contributed volumes and edited conference proceedings, as well as single authored monographs. The attributes which bind these contributions together into a series are the focus on theoretical, empirical and applied issues within the field of finance.

Contributions stem from authors all over the world; their focus is consistently international. The editors of the AFIB series join me in hoping that the publication of these studies will help to stimulate international efforts in achieving advances within the fields covered by the series.

Elroy Dimson

Preface
and acknowledgements

This volume brings together a collection of research papers on financial sector reform and privatization in the transition economies of Eastern Europe and related issues in other transforming economies. Unlike a conference volume, the papers were not presented at a single conference; rather, the volume represents a selection of the best papers presented at various conferences and workshops held in Estonia, Poland and the Netherlands, as well as several invited papers, in the period 1994-97. Specifically, the origins of the research effort on the theme of this volume can be traced in a conference on "Restructuring Financial Institutions in Emerging Economies" held at Tallin-Lohusalu in Estonia on 17-18 October 1994. The conference brought together an international group of leading researchers, government (especially Ministry of Finance) and central bank officials from transition economies and representatives of international organisations to share experience and insights on financial sector reforms in transition economies. Immediately following the conference, a team of leading researchers from Estonia, The Netherlands, Poland, Sweden, and United Kingdom embarked on a joint research project on "Coping with financial sector reforms in transition economies" under the financial auspices of the European Commission's Phare/ACE Programme 1994, contract number 94-0685-R. Subsequently, a conference on "Financial Reform in Emerging Market Economies" was held at Poznan University of Economics in Poland on 20-21 January 1996, followed by another conference on "Financial Sector Reform" held at Tallinn Technical University on 18-20 September 1996. A number of papers were also presented, in a special forum, at the European Financial Management Association (EFMA) Annual Meetings, June 24-29, 1996 in Innsbruck, Austria.

In this context, the editors would like to thank the organisers of the above mentioned conferences (notably Vello Vensel, Alfred Janc and Tadeusz Kowalski) for making possible the preliminary dissemination of research results. Many conference participants, academics as well as practitioners, provided useful comments and insights on the transition process in Eastern Europe. The editors therefore acknowledge financial support from the European Commission's Phare / ACE Programme 1994 under contract number 94-0685-R for Christopher Green, Niels Hermes, Robert Lensink, Victor Murinde, Vello Vensel and Clas Wihlborg; and under contract number 94-0772-R for Andy Mullineux. For conferences held in Estonia and Poland, the local organisers acknowledge additional financial and moral support from the respective central banks and universities. Funding for research by Clas Wihlborg and Vello Vensel from HSFR, Sweden, and the Royal Swedish Academy of Sciences is also acknowledged.

Special thanks go to Heather Rowlands for her competence and patience in typesetting the volume to a perfect finish; we are indebted to Göteborg University which partly funded the production of the book. For the reproduction of technical drawings in the volume, we thank The Birmingham Business School for financial support and Geraldine Bousie for her expertise and commitment. The staff at Elsevier Science Publishers B.V., especially Sabine Plantevin and Treja van den Heuvel, deserve a lot of credit for their patience and support during the gestation period for this final product.

We are greatly indebted to the contributing authors for availing us their original and previously unpublished papers rather than opting for the recent tendency to send the papers to top-rated journals. The editorial work was made particularly easy by the co-operation of the authors in revising their drafts as well as proof-reading the galleys.

Finally, we are very grateful to Elroy Dimson who, as the editor of the series in *Advances in Finance, Investment and Banking*, offered constructive comments on the manuscript and generally encouraged the development of the book.

John Doukas
Norfolk

Victor Murinde
Birmingham

Clas Wihlborg
Göteborg

November 1997

Notes on the contributors

J. Kimball Dietrich is Professor of Finance, University of Southern California, Los Angeles.

John Doukas is Professor of Finance and International Finance at the College of Business and Public Administration, Old Dominion University.

Gunnar Eliasson is Professor of Industrial Economics, The Royal Institute of Technology (KTH), Stockholm.

Subhashis Gangopadhyay is Professor of Economics at the Indian Statistical Institute, New Delhi.

Michael A. Goldstein is Assistant Professor of Finance at the Graduate School of Business Administration, University of Colorado at Boulder.

Christopher J. Green is Professor of Economics and Finance, Loughborough University.

N. Bulent Gultekin is Associate Professor of Finance at The Wharton School and Associate Director of the Wharton Center for Quantitative Finance, the Wharton School, University of Pennsylvania. Formerly, he was Governor of the Central Bank of the Republic of Turkey, President of the Privatization Agency in Turkey, and Chief Advisor to the Minister of Privatization in Poland.

Niels Hermes is Assistant Professor, Department of Economics, University of Groningen, The Netherlands.

Dwight M. Jaffee is Professor of Finance at the Haas School of Business, University of California Berkeley. Within the Haas School, he is also a co-Chairman of the Fisher Center for Real Estate and Urban Economics and the Academic Director of the St. Petersburg (Russia) -- UC Berkeley School of Management Progam.

John D. Knopf is an Assistant Professor of Finance at the Lubin School of Business at Pace University, New York.

Robert Lensink is Associate Professor in Macroeconomics, Department of Economics, University of Groningen, The Netherlands.

Andy Mullineux is Professor of Money and Banking and Head of The School of Social Sciences, The University of Birmingham.

Victor Murinde is Senior Lecturer in Finance and Director of Corporate Finance Research, The Birmingham Business School, The University of Birmingham.

Kelvin Pan is Research Fellow at the School of Economics and Commercial Law, Göteborg University.

Betrand Renaud is Housing Finance Advisor in the Financial Sector Development Department, The World Bank, Washington D.C.

Anthony M. Santomero is the Richard K. Mellon Professor of Finance and the Director of the Wharton Financial Institutions Center at the Wharton School of the University of Pennsylvania.

Richard J. Sweeney is the Sullivan/Dean Professor of International Finance at the Georgetown School of Business, Georgetown University.

Vello Vensel is Professor of Statistics and Head of the Department of Economics, Faculty of Economics and Business Administration, Tallinn Technical University.

Ingo Walter is the Charles Simon Professor of Applied Financial Economics at the Stern School of Business, New York University, and the Director of the New York University Salomon Centre.

Clas Wihlborg is the Felix Neubergh Professor of Banking and Financial Economics at the School of Economics and Commercial Law, Göteborg University.

About the Editors

John Doukas earned his PhD in Financial Economics at Stern School of Business, New York University, in 1982, and is currently Professor of Finance and International Finance at Old Dominion University. His current research interests are in the areas of international financial management, foreign exchange markets, and international asset pricing. Professor Doukas has published over forty articles in many journals including the *Journal of Finance, Journal of Financial and Quantitative Analysis, Journal of Banking and Finance, Journal of International Money and Finance, Journal of International Business Studies, Journal of Futures Markets, Journal of Applied Corporate Finance, Financial Management and Financial Review.* He is the founding editor of the *European Financial Management (EFM) Journal* and founder of the *European Financial Management Association (EFMA).* He is the co-editor of the JAI Press Annual Research Series in *International Business and Finance.*

Victor Murinde is Senior Lecturer in Finance and Director of Corporate Finance Research at the University of Birmingham. He completed his PhD in Financial Economics at Cardiff Business School, University of Wales Cardiff in 1990 and joined the staff as Lecturer in Banking. Dr Murinde has also worked as a consultant to the World Bank, the United Nations and several governments of developing and transition economies. He has published widely in mainstream journals and his recent research monographs include *Macroeconomic Policy Modelling for Developing Countries* (Avebury, 1993; reprinted 1995), *Development Banking and Finance* (Avebury, 1996; reprinted 1997) and, co-authored with Charles L. Chanthunya, *Trade Regime and Economic Growth* (Ashgate Publishing Ltd, 1998). His current research focuses on corporate finance and financial sector development.

Clas Wihlborg is the Felix Neubergh Professor of Banking and Financial Economics at the School of Economics and Commercial Law, Göteborg University, since 1988. He received his PhD in economics from Princeton University in 1977. Thereafter he held positions as Assistant and Associate Professor of Finance and International Business at New York University and Associate Professor of Finance and Business Economics at the University of Southern California. During 1993 he was the Harry Reynolds International Visiting Professor of the Wharton School of the University of Pennsylvania. Professor Wihlborg has published journal articles and books in the areas of international finance and monetary economics. He is currently conducting research on bank and financial sector regulation with special emphasis on emerging market economies and the EU, and on the implications of a European monetary union for intra-European policy conflicts. He is a member of the Royal Swedish Academy of Engineering Sciences.

Table of Contents

List of Exhibits and Figures

List of Tables

Financial Sector Reform and
Privatization in Transition Economies
J. Doukas, V. Murinde and C. Wihlborg (Editors)
© 1998 Elsevier Science Publishers B. V. All rights reserved

/— 18

1

Chapter 1

$L33$ $\overline{o}16$

$P31$ $P21$

MAIN ISSUES IN FINANCIAL SECTOR REFORM
AND PRIVATIZATION IN TRANSITION ECONOMIES: $P34$
INTRODUCTION AND OVERVIEW

$F21$

John Doukas
Department of Finance, College of Business and Public Administration, Old
Dominion University, Norfolk, VA 23529-0218, USA

Victor Murinde
Department of Accounting and Finance, The Birmingham Business School, The
University of Birmingham, Edgbaston, Birmingham B15 2TT, UK

Clas Wihlborg
Department of Economics, School of Economics and Commercial Law, Göteborg
University, Vasagatan 1, S-411 80, Göteborg, Sweden

1.1 The transition economies

The transition from central planning has been going on for several years.
Some countries are quite clearly successful and approaching functioning
market economies. Poland, Hungary, the Czech Republic and Slovenia are
generally counted in this group. Others are still struggling to come out of
the period of falling output, increasing poverty and social despair. Russia
and Ukraine, the two most populous countries, must be counted in this
group although reform has by no means come to a standstill. There are also
countries that seem to have simply stagnated in the reform process. Slovakia
may be one of them in contrast to its former partner. It seems as if the
former Soviet Republics have great difficulties although there are
exceptions in the Baltic states in particular. The former republics have
much in common in that their economies were more interdependent than
other central and eastern European countries. However, Albania is a tragedy
of its own and it can only be hoped that other countries currently in
stagnation will not follow in Albania's path.

It is by now obvious that transition economies are not a homogenous group. Considering initial differences in, for example, the use of market oriented incentives during the communist days, and the extent of private property rights, it is no surprise that the transition has met with difficulties to various degrees among the countries. Poland, for example, allowed private ownership of farm-land, while Soviet farming was completely collectivized. There was a capitalist parallel economy in Poland during the communist era. This economy was expanding or contracting depending on how hard the Soviet leaders were leaning ideologically on the Polish leaders. The slowly increasing market orientation of the Hungarian economy through the 1960s and 1970s is also well-known. Other differentiating factors among the transition economies are the length of the communist period, and what existed before. The Baltic states became Soviet Republics during the Second World War after having developed like other capitalist economies, while Russia went from a largely feudal society to communism in 1917.

One feature that all transition economies had in common during the communist period, was the almost complete absence of a market oriented financial system. Naturally, some informal financing arrangements must have existed but, in general, the allocation of financial resources was highly centralized in all countries. The so-called monobanks of the communist states did not have a credit allocating role, but they were primarily accounting and disbursement units that carried out directives from the central planning agencies. Thus, when the monobanks were to be transformed to market oriented, credit allocating banks, the knowledge and culture gaps within the banking systems were enormous. The first step in the transformation was to create a two-tier banking system with a central bank responsible for monetary policy and banking supervision, and one or more commercial banks accepting deposits and lending. The second step was to privatize some or all of the commercial banks, and to allow the establishment of private commercial banks. As will be discussed, these steps do not, by any means, guarantee a functioning banking system. One reason is the inheritance of loans to the state-owned enterprises (SOEs) of the communist days. Another reason is the political fall-out that comes from a sudden and drastic change of the principles for credit allocation.

A second common feature of the communist countries now in transition was the domination of state ownership of manufacturing and real property. The inherited credits of the commercial banking systems were, as noted, loans to the SOEs. Thus, the quality of the assets of the commercial banks at the beginning of the transition depended on the quality of the SOEs as generators of future cash flows to repay loans. Clearly, the process of privatization of SOEs and reform of the banking system had to be intertwined. Herein lay great difficulties of economic and political nature both to privatize and to reform the financial sector. Fundamentally, the problem was to be found in the low quality of the manufacturing sector in terms of its ability to generate future cash flows. The products supplied by the SOEs were generally not competitive in a market economy and the economic organization of the manufacturing sector was so poor that both the level and the growth suffered greatly. The most telling evidence of the low productivity is the experiences in East Germany after unification with West Germany. East Germany was probably the communist country with the highest level of productivity. Nevertheless, very few East German firms remained competitive after unification in spite of substantial wage differences. West Germany has transfered enormous subsidies to West German firms to induce them to buy East German units and to induce individuals with skills to remain in the eastern part of the new Germany.

1.2 Issues in financial sector reform

The important role of financial markets and the role of ownership in capitalist countries seemed forgotten by most western economists in the early days of the transition. Portes (1994) argues that "the single most important error in sequencing ... was not to have implemented urgently a financial clean-out". This error cannot be blamed on leaders of transition countries alone, but the advice of Western economists focused on macroeconomic stabilization for several years.

The sequencing of banking reform relative to macroeconomic stabilization programs has become an issue of debate. In the early stages of transition a monetary contraction would force either the state-owned banks to cut off credit to the SOEs with immediate unemployment as a consequence, or the banks would impose a credit crunch on the emerging private sector. Because the financial sector was not restructured, macroeconomic stabilization became less politically acceptable in many transition economies. Thus, inflation rates remained high and the subsidization of SOEs continued.

It could be argued that the restructuring of the banking system should occur before severe monetary contraction is imposed on the economy. The incentives of the banking sector to direct credit away from the emerging private sector consisting of small enterprises are then lessened at the time contraction occurs.

In general, the design of reform packages under uncertainty remains on top of the policy agenda in the transition economies in Eastern and Central Europe (see Dewatripond and Roland, 1995). The micro aspects of these reforms are considered in this volume with respect to banks, firms and financial markets; the macro aspects are discussed with respect to the general economic policy framework.

The two bad loan problems

It is by now widely recognized among economists that an effective system of corporate governance plays a major role in economic growth. The corporate governance system depends on the structure of incentives for managers, board members, and owners of enterprises. These incentives are determined by the contracts among managers, owners, and lenders, financial institutions, and corporate law. The banking system may play a major role in the system of corporate governance because it enforces lending contracts and monitors and sometimes influences management.

In countries with a legacy of loss-making enterprises supported by credits from banks, reform of the banking system can enhance economic efficiency substantially. Banks can contribute to the hardening of the budget constraint of firms by monitoring and enforcing loan-contracts. In order to accomplish this task effectively the incentive structure of banks must be drastically changed.

The legacy facing the reformers of banking systems is a combination of bad loans on the balance sheets, and state ownership or at least strong government guarantees of the suppliers of funds to the banks leading to inefficient corporate governance in banks, and weak incentives to allocate credit according to sound risk-return criteria. In this context, the bad debt problem is actually a double one: banks have been settled with bad loans originating in the history of the SOEs but the prevention of future bad loans is just as important. The latter problem is one of creating a structure of incentives for the management of banks to allocate credit to borrowers with successful projects in terms of risk and return. The former problem involves removing a drag of historical losses on current operations of a bank. It is almost inevitable, however, that the method of dealing with historical losses influences the banks' incentives when allocating credit, and therefore, future losses. Governments in almost all countries considering either the "cleaning of balance sheets" or more fundamental reform with the objective of changing the incentives of bank-managers, must be aware that the future behaviour of bank-managers depends on the government's strategy for dealing with any acute banking crisis. Sweden provides an interesting example: A blanket guarantee of all bank-liabilities was issued by the government in 1992 in order to enable the banks to raise funds in international markets at rates that would keep their competitiveness intact. By the end of 1994, the government discussed withdrawing the guarantee, because the financial health of the banks had been restored. Formally the guarantee could be abolished with the stroke of a pen, but if it is expected that the government will intervene again in times of crisis then the formal removal of the guarantee will not affect banks' behaviour.

As noted the two bad loan problems are not independent. It is therefore of great importance how recapitalizaiton and reform is carried out. Furthermore, the legislative framework for the economy, and the ownership of enterprises are important for the incentives of corporate managers of borrowing firms. In 1992 with the regulatory framework essentially in place, in most Eastern European countries, the policy problems with respect to the banking sector could be summarized by the following points:

1. For the sake of the long-run efficiency of market economies, the banking system should contribute to effective corporate governance by imposing hard budget constraints on borrowers.

2. In the short-run, imposing hard budget constraints on borrowers would lead to wide-spread failures of many SOEs and, as a consequence, worsen unemployment.

3. Without imposition of hard budget constraints on SOEs, attempts to reduce inflation by reducing monetary growth would lead to a credit crunch for the aspiring new enterprises in the private sector.

4. Privatization of the banks or inducing banks in other ways to function as commercially oriented firms would lead to "perverse" lending incentives as long as the net worth of many banks are negative or near zero. The reason is that a bank that has lent to loss-making firms and has a zero net worth has nothing to loose and can only gain by keeping the firms afloat with new loans.

5. Cleaning the balance sheets of the banks would entail large fiscal costs.

6. Cleaning the balance sheets and the recapitalization of banks with low or negative net worths could create expectations of similar bail-outs in the future. Such expectations would reduce the incentives of bank-managers to impose hard budget constraints on firms and encourage excessive risk-taking.

7. The legislative framework for dealing with distressed firms was incomplete or lacking leading to uncertainty about claims in case of liquidation of firms.

8. The legislative framework for property rights, registration of, and trade in, property was incomplete leading to a lack of assets for entrepreneurs to offer as collateral against loans.

9. Privatization of SOEs had progressed slowly with the consequence that the political pressures to cover losses remained substantial, and the incentives of managers were strongly affected by the political sector.

Several papers in this volume deal with these problems in principle or assessing the experiences of attempts to address them as part of the reform process in different countries.

Regulatory issues for the financial system

Before discussing specific regulatory issues a discussion of the financial system is worthwhile. A useful starting point is the following list of functions according to Rybczynski (1991):

1. organize the payment system

2. collect new savings and allocate them to projects according to market participants' preferences for risk and return

3. reallocate accumulated old savings to projects and firms according to market participants' preferences for risk and return

4. provide liquidity of claims and securities

5. provide a system of corporate governance influencing managerial incentives, and mechanisms for changing management.

The first two functions are widely known and accepted. The third function of allocating old savings puts the emphasis on transactions and information costs, and on dynamic aspects of the financial system. As new information appears, accumulated savings must be reallocated at the lowest possible cost. A low cost reallocation requires market liquidity so that an asset can be sold fast at the market price. Furthermore, the reallocation of old savings requires that financial resources must be withdrawn from the control of managers of poorly performing projects in order to be made available for other managers. Managers are in control of financial resources under specific contractual arrangements as specified, for example, in company law. Thus, the reallocation function depends on a set of legal and contractual arrangements between managers and wealth-holders. We enter here into the area of corporate governance. Taking dynamic aspects into account two more functions of the financial system are added to the first three (payment system, consumption smoothing, and risk-sharing), namely the fourth and fifth functions.

Traditional welfare oriented economic models analyze optimal consumption smoothing and risk-sharing without consideration of costs of transactions and information and under the assumption of homogeneous information. Liquidity of securities cannot be obtained without substantial volume of trading, however. A high volume of trade requires heterogeneity of information and/or risk-preferences at any time. Since risk-preferences are nearly constant over time, it is the heterogeneity of information, causing trading activity based on differences in expectations, that must be relied upon to create liquidity in securities markets. Lacking liquid securities markets, financial institutions may serve as intermediaries, issuing highly liquid assets for depositors, while managing the depositors' funds in such a way that depositors' preferences for return, risk, and liquidity are satisfied.

Corporate governance issues have increasingly gained economists' attention during recent years and they were touched upon above in connection with the bad loan problem. Financial economists in particular study this issue, because most financial contracts more or less explicitly include rights to control or influence management under some conditions, besides the rights to a stream of cash flows. Equity in firms has obvious control rights as specified by a vote or a fraction of a vote in shareholder meetings.

Banks and corporate bond-holders lending funds to a firm are usually able to obtain direct control rights under specific conditions when the firm does not meet its financial obligations. Lending contracts often include specific rights of monitoring or conditions with respect to the financial performance of the borrower. The latter solution is common when there is direct lending, i.e. when a firm issues securities to the public most commonly within the Anglo-Saxon countries. Monitoring rights, on the other hand, are associated with indirect lending from households to banks, and from banks to firms.

Clearly, financial institutions matter for the effectiveness of corporate governance structures. In a bank-oriented system monitoring of managers by banks on behalf of wealth-holders play a major role, as already noted. In financial systems dominated by direct lending through securities markets, information about management must either be publicly available or individual buyers of securities must themselves monitor for the quality of management to affect firms' capital costs.

In order to analyze the effectiveness of financial systems with respect to corporate governance, it is common to start from the premise that managers and wealth-holders are asymmetrically informed about available projects as well as about managers' characteristics and actions.

The financial system must solve two problems. First, as a result of asymmetric information about managers' and projects' characteristics wealth-holders and lenders in general face the so called adverse selection problem. This problem arises, for example, when borrowers/managers of different quality face the same price of loans. The relatively low quality borrowers/managers have stronger incentive to take loans than the high-quality borrowers/managers and lenders must act to avoid being saddled with bad loans. The adverse selection problem is often called the lemon problem.

The second problem arising with asymmetric information is the moral hazard problem also called the hidden action, or the principal agent problem. An example is that managers' objectives may differ from shareholders' and lenders' objectives with the possible consequence that the manager's unobservable actions may be contrary to the interests of shareholders and other lenders. Managers' incentives are then possibly contrary to share-holders' wealth-maximization.

The term agency costs is often used to describe the efficiency costs caused by both the adverse selection and the moral hazard problems. By incurring, for example monitoring costs and costs of creating and enforcing contracts influencing managers' incentives agency costs can be decreased.

Varying institutional set-ups differ with respect to these costs. For example, the Anglo-Saxon financial system dominated by securities markets rely on the threat of hostile take-overs to align the incentives of managers and shareholders. If this threat is weak managers become "entrenched" and agency costs rise. The European and the Japanese financial systems are more bank-oriented. They rely on bank-monitoring and few dominating shareholders to influence managerial incentives and to fire inefficient managers. It is not obvious, however, that the banks and the dominating shareholders always serve the interests of the many smaller shareholders.

There are necessarily conflicts and trade-offs among the five functions of the financial system described here. For example, optimal risk-sharing and consumption-smoothing in securities markets require that all relevant information about projects and securities is quickly reflected in prices. However, if prices quickly incorporate information from various sources, then the threat of hostile take-overs is reduced and management entrenchment becomes pervasive.

The regulatory framework behind a financial system affects the trade-offs among the five functions. For example, a trade-off may exist between payment system efficiency and efficiency of corporate governance. It is often argued that without government protection of depositors the payment system is subject to the risk of bank-runs that could be contagious. Government protection of the banking system reduces the incentives of bankers to devote resources to credit evaluation and monitoring, and the protection induces excessive risk-taking in limited liability banks. Thus, the extent of explicit and implicit deposit insurance is an important regulatory issue and the desirable degree of insurance may very well be different in transition economies as opposed to western industrialized economies.

Another regulatory issue affecting the safety of the payment system is capital adequacy rules. By requiring that shareholders must bear a substantial share of a bank's risk, the shareholders' incentive to take excessive risk with depositors' funds is reduced.

If the government protection of the banking system extends to protection of the banks' shareholders, as well as the banks' depositors, the incentives of banks to monitor, evaluate credit, and to enforce loan-contracts are naturally reduced further. Banks cannot be expected to contribute to effective corporate governance then.

The functions of the financial system discussed so far refer to a market economy, where economic efficiency and growth are the main objectives. Governments in most countries "use" the financial system to achieve a multitude of objectives, however. For example, in Western Europe and the USA governments have long used their influence over the financial system to subsidize housing construction and, indirectly, housing costs.

Many governments in both industrialized and developing economies conduct industrial policy by trying to influence the allocation of credit among industries or between exporting firms and firms oriented towards the domestic market.

The intervention in the credit allocation process becomes even more pervasive when a government conducts labor market and employment policies using the financial system. In this case, it is nearly inevitable that the government forces banks to favor firms with a high likelihood of being non-profitable. Such policies necessitate that loan losses are covered by the government in order to ensure the survival of financial institutions. Consequently, both depositors and shareholders are "freed" from responsibility for loan losses.

The more the financial system is used by governments to achieve other objectives than those related to economic efficiency in the sense described above, the stronger becomes the conflict of interest between efficiency in terms of the above five functions of the financial system and other policy objectives. For example, if certain industries are favored without regard to profitability and risk it is clear that the ability of financial institutions to function effectively is reduced in terms of each of the five functions. The payment system is threatened by loan losses and consumption smoothing and risk-sharing have to be restricted. Liquidity is reduced by a reduction of speculative activity in financial markets. By definition, the hard budget constraint is not imposed by the bank on favored industries.

The government can intervene in the financial system further to protect one or more of the functions. Most often it is the payment system that ends up being protected by guarantees of depositors' and shareholders' claims on financial institutions. These guarantees have the effect of reducing the effectiveness of the banking system with respect to the other functions. Increased supervision of banks is often suggested as a remedy for, for example, excessive risk-taking. It is highly questionable, however, whether supervision alone can hinder banks from allocating credits according to incentives. One reason is that supervisory authorities depend on information from banks.

There has been much debate whether the transition economies should try to encourage the creation of Anglo-Saxon type financial systems relying heavily on decentralized securities markets for corporate bonds and equity. This can be done by restricting the permissible activities of commercial banks as in the USA where investment banking and commercial banking must be separated. Another way to encourage securities markets is for the government to set up, subsidize, and protect trading and traders in securities in, for example, a stock-exchange.

An alternative regulatory strategy is to allow, banks, stock-markets and other institutions to develop freely. If so, it seems that the financial systems develop as banking oriented system initially with a relatively small role for securities markets.

Securities markets can also be encouraged by various forms of legislation protecting the investors in financial assets. Insider trading rules and information disclosure requirements can be considered aspects of such investor protection. The issue of whether such protection actually encourages trading in securities is debatable and academic research does not provide clear cut answers.

The arguments for encouraging securities markets are that the trading in and diversification of risk can be more efficient, and that the liquidity of various securities is enhanced, if sufficient trading takes place. Small shareholders would also be better protected against a few large shareholders "cutting deals". These arguments are far from controversial, however. One reason is that the liquidity in a security must be high before benefits are realized. Another is that the "cutting of deals" among a few large shareholders may benefit all shareholders in the longer-run, because the large shareholders are typically relatively well-informed about the prospects of the firm. Furthermore, if they cut deals against the interest of small shareholders, the prices of affected securities would fall once the deals were discovered. Thereby, the cost of raising capital would increase for firms controlled by "deal-cutters".

Most of the regulatory issues mentioned here - the extent of deposit insurance, capital adequacy rules, the separation of investment and commercial banking, the subsidisation of securities markets, and legislation for investor protection - will be discussed in one or several of the chapters in this volume. Academic research has not produced any definitive results with respect to many of the issues discussed in this section, while there is more agreement among economists of the importance of the bad loan problem and privatization.

1.3 The contents of this volume

This volume brings together some extant research results on the mainstream issues relating to financial sector reform and privatization in transition economies. The volume is motivated to contribute to the recent growth in the corpus of analytical findings in the belief that while at the onset of economic transition the initial financial reform experiments lacked some blueprint, any new analytical findings should be useful in informing the policy debates highlighted in Sections 1.1 and 1.2.

The volume is divided into four thematic but well linked parts, altogether consisting of 13 chapters. Part 1 contains micro studies on the financial sector. Four papers are presented including a general assessment of progress with financial sector reforms in six transforming countries by Andy Mullineux, an empirical study of financial constraints on entreprenuership in Estonia by Vello Vensel and Clas Wihlborg, an analytical study on strategies to develop mortgage markets in transition economies by Dwight Jaffee and Bertrand Renaud, and a case study based on India on dividends and conflicts between equityholders and debtholders with a weak bank monitoring system (as seem to exist in most transition economies) by Shubhashis Gangopadhyay and John Knopf. Part 2 is concerned with issues relating to the development process in the financial sector as market economies emerge, thus highlighting the analytical and policy aspects of financial development during the transition process. There are four papers, including a study on the design of financial systems and economic transformation by Ingo Walter, an analysis of the regulation and public policy agenda for effective financial intermediation in the post-socialist economies by Anthony Santomero, an analysis of arguments for and against universal banking with equity ownership by banks in emerging market economies by J. Kimball Dietrich, Kelvin Pan and Clas Wihlborg, and a study of emerging stock markets in view of the lessons that could be learned from the history of industrialised countries by Richard J. Sweeney. Part 3 deals with analytical and policy issues that overarch the financial sector and the macroeconomy. Two papers are presented. The first one, by Niels Hermes and Robert Lensink deals with the role of business conglomerates in financing investment during macroeconomic adjustment in Chile in 1983-1992; and the second one, by Christopher J. Green and Victor Murinde, addresses flow-of-funds and the macroeconomic policy framework for financial restructuring in transition economies. Finally, Part 4 focuses on privatization and foreign investment, and consists of two papers. The first paper by Michael A. Goldstein and N. Bulent Gultekin delves into the main issues relating to privatization in post-communist economies, while the second paper by Gunnar Eliasson suggests a specific insurance mechanism that could be instituted with the objectives of increasing the flow of investment into emerging market economies and creating incentives for reducing political risk associated with investment in these economies.

Micro-studies of the financial sector

The focus on micro-studies of the financial sector begins with an evaluation of progress with financial sector reforms in six transforming countries. Andy Mullineux, in Chapter 2, draws lessons for economies at an early stage in transition from the experiences of other formerly centrally planned economies at a later stage in their transition. Emphasis is placed on financial sector reform, stabilisation, banking sector restructuring, debt consolidation, and small and medium-sized enterprise financing in these economies.

Against this general background, Chapter 3 by Vello Vensel and Clas Wihlborg is more specific; it analyzes investments, financing, and institutions in Estonia's manufacturing sector based on a relatively detailed survey of firms' relations with suppliers, employees, and lenders. The paper focuses on relations with lenders in order to analyze sources of financing for new and ongoing projects. The stated objective is to discover whether financial markets, or the lack thereof, hinder investments and enterprise development in Estonia; if so, the issue is whether hindrances depend on deficient institutions. It is also investigated whether informal financing and trade credits substitute for formal loans when firms are unable to obtain loans in banks. Because of its history as a part of the former Soviet Union, Estonia is used as an interesting target for the survey and detailed study. For example, the financial structure and the financing of investments of manufacturing firms are discussed with a focus on firm-size as a determinant of access to various sources of financing, and managers' perceptions of regulatory and legal constraints on investments are explored. The survey data are also used to analyze whether access to financing can be explained by those firm characteristics that could proxy for riskiness and information availability. The findings suggest that the financial system is undersupplying financial resources to firms; for example, firms holding financial assets showed a higher likelihood of being an investor and a borrower in a bank, and more financial assets were associated with larger investments in 1996. It is also found that many firms have borrowed from the informal sector although the share of these loans in total financing is quite small. In general, however, Estonia does not seem to differ much from most countries, including western industrialized countries, with respect to financing of entrepreneurship; own savings is the primary source of an entrepreneur's start-up financing with some help from family and friends.

The focus then shifts to the micro-study of the housing finance market in Chapter 4. The paper, by Dwight Jaffee and Betrand Renaud, analyzes the factors that hinder the development of mortgage markets in economies that are in transition from central planning to a market system, and proposes a strategy to expedite this development. It is shown that banks in transition economies are reluctant to make mortgage loans due to the risks in mortgage lending (credit, interest rate, and liquidity risk). It is argued that a secondary mortgage market (SMM) is likely to help solve this problem in the sense that a SMM separates the act of making mortgage loans (which can still be carried out by banks) from the act of holding mortgage loans (which can be carried out more effectively by capital market investors).

Some important corporate finance issues earlier introduced in Section 1.2, especially bank monitoring and corporate governance, are taken up in a paper by Shubhashis Gangopadhyay and John Knopf (Chapter 5) with respect to India, but with implications for transition economies. The paper studies the dividend policy of Indian firms, facing barriers to exit and laws that do not permit firms to fire labour for economic reasons (for example during economic downturn). It is argued that given the absence of any conflicts between managers and shareholders regarding the capital structure of Indian firms, equityholders are able to withdraw resources, through the payment of dividends, at the expense of debtholders from firms with a potential for financial distress. It is noted that this is possible because the institutional environment in India discourages monitoring by banks, a point that has much relevance to the current debate on agency theory and bank monitoring issues in the transition economies in Eastern Europe.

The financial sector in the development of market economies

The initial paper in the analytical and policy aspects of financial development during the transition process, in Part 2 (Chapters 6 - 9), focuses on the design of financial systems and economic transformation. The paper, by Ingo Walter, begins by making an observation that the structure, conduct and performance of a nation's financial system is crucial in setting the agenda for economic growth and development, most important of all because high-performance financial systems are central to the transactions and resource allocation process domestically as well as internationally. In this context, the paper outlines the framework parameters of high-performance financial systems that can be applied in a transition-economy context. Beginning with an intuitive structural model of financial intermediation, and then discussing the various stages of its evolution in terms of static and dynamic efficiency characteristics, the paper continues with an emphasis on the critical role of regulation as a major factor affecting the performance of the financial system itself, both in the context of national economic growth and competitiveness, and as a factor in defining the role of various types of financial firms. A critical and controversial dimension in the design of the financial system is then considered, namely the relationship between the structure of financial institutions, and the linkages to ownership and the control process in industry. It is argued that the way countries deal with this issue can have dramatic effects on both the financial system and the fundamentals of economic performance; that, for example, in the case of the transition economies of Eastern Europe and Asia, a choice has had to be made as to the type of financial system that is likely to deliver the best economic performance over the long term, while at the same time being adequately capable of dealing with the kinds of crises and market inefficiencies that are characteristic of the transition process.

The regulation and public policy agenda for effective financial intermediation in the post-socialist economies is then taken up by Anthony Santomero in Chapter 7. In this paper, Santomero argues that the advent of a market economy in formerly centralized economies has led to dramatic change in their financial sector, and the behaviour of banking institutions; these firms must convert from de facto government agencies to credit evaluators, borrower monitors, and loan collectors. It is further argued that just as substantial change has begun to transform the accounting, legal and property/bankruptcy laws in the these economies, an equal change needs to occur in financial institution regulation. A number of suggestions are offered. For example, it is suggested that financial system reforms must include a set of functions, procedures, and controls which collectively are referred to as a safety net for the system as a whole. It is further suggested that a carefully constructed set of regulations is necessary which will offset market imperfections without replacing them with a new bureaucratic structure; these regulations, therefore, require trade-offs between stability and market discipline.

The focus then shifts to banks. Policy issues related to universal banking with equity ownership by banks in emerging market economies are reviewed and discussed in a paper by J. Kimball Dietrich, Kelvin Pan and Clas Wihlborg (Chapter 8). A theoretical model is developed in which the return to bank monitoring is enhanced by equity-lending. The role of competition in universal banking systems is discussed especially in the situation of the transition economies. The bank-industry groups often associated with universal banking are interpreted as internalized markets for managers.

The analysis then moves to stock markets. In Chapter 9, Richard J. Sweeney presents a study of emerging stock markets in view of the lessons that could be learned from the history of industrialised countries. It is noted that historically, industrialized country stock markets developed more or less in step with the countries' economies, without drastic government guidance; examples are the U.S. and Sweden. The main argument of the paper is that ill-conceived government policies can retard financial development; for example a one percent turnover tax on stock transactions in Sweden in the 1980s and 1990s had harmful effects. It is found that although many observers find great advantage currently to diversification of industrialized country investors across emerging stock markets; international diversification for the period 1914-1924 shows that diversification can sometimes be harmful from disastrous events that can be highly correlated.

The financial sector and the macroeconomy

In the first paper (Chapter 10) in this part of the volume, Niels Hermes and Robert Lensink study the role of business conglomerates in financing investment during macroeconomic adjustment in Chile in 1983-1992. Specifically, the paper investigates how regulatory changes in Chile have had an impact on the decisions of banks with respect to the allocation of resources over different groups of firms. The analysis focuses on the impact of regulations that aimed at reducing the possibilities of firms having close relationships with banks within business conglomerates on the pattern of allocation of finance. To this end, it has been tested whether investments of firms related to a conglomerate are less dependent on internal sources when financing its investment compared to firms without such relations. The outcomes suggest that the regulations have reduced the differences in the access to capital markets of Grupo versus non-Grupo firms.

Formal modelling of the financial sector and the macroeconomy is addressed by Christopher J. Green and Victor Murinde in a paper (Chapter 11) on flow-of-funds and the macroeconomic policy framework for financial restructuring in transition economies. The paper proposes a small macro model suitable for policy analysis during financial restructuring in transition economies. Rather than involving the uncritical application of conventional macrotheory, or departing altogether from orthodoxy, the specification of the model modifies the conventional framework. The model is explicit about the flow-of-funds among various sectors of a representative transition economy and thus has a complete stock-flow accounting structure; it allows for the co-existence of official and informal (curb) financial markets; it also includes curb market effects on both the demand and supply sides; and it treats money as endogenous. The structure of the model is reduced to three equations: aggregate demand, aggregate supply and the exchange rate (foreign balance) schedule; these are used directly to derive policy multipliers. The model is also innovative enough to encompass competing hypotheses from the neo-classical and new-structuralist paradigms on financial sector reforms, and the three-equation format is particularly convenient for simulations and policy experiments in transition economies with finite data.

Privatization and foreign investment

The first paper in this final part of the volume focuses on privatisation. In the paper (Chapter 12) Michael A. Goldstein and N. Bulent Gultekin examine the main issues relating to privatization on post-communist economies. A review is undertaken of the many schemes for privatization programs that have been proposed to speed the privatization process in post-Communist countries. It is noted that most schemes rely on financial markets to solve the privatization problem, using capital markets to provide signals, information, and changes in control. The paper reduces these proposals to three stylized privatization schemes and analyzes the results predicted by finance theory. It is found that none perform as promised: brokerage and control costs hinder the free distribution of shares, efficiency and auction problems result from voucher schemes, and large mutual funds cause economy wide inefficiencies. Overall, it is suggested that different privatization methods should be used for different needs, with the appropriate bundling of securities as a primary concern.

Finally, in Chapter 13, Gunnar Eliasson proposes and analyses an insurance mechanism that should both increase the flow of investments into emerging market economies and provide incentives for governments in these economies to reduce political risk associated with investments. Thus, the proposal is designed to alleviate the moral hazard problem of insurance of investments in politically risky environments. Specifically, it is proposed that an insurance system known as the East-West Insurance Corporation

(EWIC) should be sponsored by western nations, to reduce political uncertainty in the formerly planned economies and to make these economies attractive for normal long term indigenous and foreign investors. It is argued that one of the benefits of the system is to discourage foreign investors and host country politicians from colluding to extract rents from opportunistic behaviour; in addition host country politicians may get concerned about getting their market institutions in order. It is also suggested that the management of EWIC should be freed of all political influence, so that they strive to excel in the competence needed to minimize political uncertainty in the transition economies.

References

Dewatripont, M. and G. Roland, 1995, The design of reform packages under uncertainty, American Economic Review, 85, 5, pp. 1207-1223.

Portes, R., 1994, Transformation traps, Economic Journal, 104, September, pp. 1178-1189.

Rybczynski, T., 1991, The sequencing of financial reform, Oxford Review of Economic Policy, 7, 4, pp. 26-34.

Part One

Micro-studies of the Financial Sector

Financial Sector Reform and
Privatization in Transition Economies
J. Doukas, V. Murinde and C. Wihlborg (Editors)
© 1998 Elsevier Science Publishers B.V. All rights reserved

21 – 33

Chapter 2

BANKING SECTOR RESTRUCTURING
IN TRANSITION ECONOMIES

G-21

G-28

P34   P21

Andy Mullineux
Department of Economics, The University of Birmingham, Edgbaston, Birmingham,
B15 2TT, UK

(E. Eurn)

2.1 Introduction

It has become increasingly evident that the restructuring of the banking
sector should be given a very high priority in the stabilisation and
restructuring of formerly centrally planned economies (CPEs).[1] The
increasing amount of funding allocated by development banks, such as the
World Bank (IBRD) and the European Bank for Reconstruction and
Development (EBRD), for the purpose of recapitalising and privatising
banks, resolving bank debt problems and sponsoring the transfer of banking
"know-how", bears witness to this, as does the prominence given to banking
sector reform in more recent International Monetary Fund (IMF)
programmes.

At the outset of the transition, the ex-CPEs had extremely rudimentary
financial systems which (unlike other transforming economies in Africa and
Asia) had only recently been transformed, from the Soviet "mono-banking"
model, to a "two-tier" banking system.[2] They had only just begun to
develop a third tier of cooperative and private sector banks, which were
often joint ventures with "western" banks. Apart from such banks the
financial sector was virtually non-existent. There were no capital markets
and wholesale money or interbank markets of any significance and no non-
bank financial intermediaries, such as insurance companies and pension
funds, managing portfolios of shares in private companies and holding
government debt (bonds). This was because, at the beginning of the
transition and before the launch of privatisation programmes, the industrial
and retailing sectors were state-owned and the service sector was
underdeveloped.

The remainder of the paper is organised as follows. Section 2.2 deals with financial sector reform in general; Section 2.3 examines the problem of stabilisation, debt consolidation and bank restrucuturing; Section 2.4 considers implications for monetary and exchange rate policy; Section 2.5 highlights the importance of SME financing issues in the privatisation process; and, finally, Section 2.6 makes policy recommendations.

2.2 Financial sector reform

The move away from mono-banking was initiated in China in 1984. China vested the central banking functions of the national bank in the Peoples Bank of China and created separate state-owned "commercial" banks, thereby forming a two-tier banking system. In the second half of the 1980s, first Hungary, then Bulgaria and then other CPEs followed suit as they tried to find a "third-way" by introducing market forces into a central planning framework. Hungary went further by granting licences to joint ventures between the newly created commercial banks and foreign banks. This move was followed in some other CPEs, including the then Soviet Union, which also began to allow the establishment of numerous cooperative banks, and a third tier of banks was created. The development of this third-tier accelerated with the establishment of numerous domestically-owned private sector commercial banks following the collapse of communism in Central and Eastern Europe in 1989. The state-owned commercial banks, however, continued to dominate the banking systems in the transition economies, and privatisation of the state-owned commercial banks only gathered pace in the mid 1990s. Poland has now privatised a number of major banks with the financial support of the EBRD and Hungary has also made significant progress in this area, also with the EBRD's financial assistance.

It should be noted that the "mono-bank" system was always a misnomer since most ex-CPEs had a number of specialised (for example, investment, agricultural, and trade finance) banks, as well a national bank and also a savings bank, whose degree of independence from the national bank varied. When "two-tier" banking was introduced, not only were new commercial banks created, but the specialised banks were usually also permitted to undertake commercial banking business. The new commercial banks were often regionally based (as in Poland) or allocated SOEs on an industrial sectoral basis (as in Bulgaria), which led to a degree of de facto regional concentration. In Poland, for example, nine regional state-owned banks (SOBs) were established alongside a number of formerly specialised banks.

At the time of their creation, the commercial banks clearly lacked experienced staff with well developed lending (risk appraisal) skills, as well as the facilities to collect deposits from the public and to provide modern money transmission services. The public was used to receiving rudimentary services from the state savings banks; whose key function was to collect savings and channel them, via the national banks, to help fund planned expenditure. Under "monobanking", the national banks' roles included the disbursement of planned budgetary allocations, the collection of taxes, and monitoring the use of the allocated credits (i.e. a governance role). It was thus an arm of the planning agency, the finance ministry, and a central bank rolled into one.

The decision to abandon central planning in favour of "capitalism" requires the introduction of an alternative means of allocating "credits", or "capital". In capitalist countries the banks are by far the most important allocators of "capital" through the advancement of loans (debt contracts) to enterprises and households. In some capitalist economies "capital markets" (stock exchanges) also play an important, but normally sub-servient, role in the allocation of capital.[3] These markets allocate debt and equity capital directly to enterprises, who issue securities such as bonds and "shares", without the use of an intermediary such as a bank. The proportion of capital allocated this way has grown significantly over the last two decades as a result of "securitisation" involving "disintermediation". We need not enter here into the reasons for this development, but can note that it is only in the US that the future role of banks has, prematurely and due to special factors prevailing in the late 1980s and early 1990s (in our view), been seriously called into question by some commentators.[4]

It seems likely that, due to information asymmetry, banks will remain the main source of finance for small and medium sized enterprises (SMEs) for the foreseeable future (even in the US). We will return to this point later in this paper when we discuss the problem of SME finance in more detail. It is sufficient to note at this stage that it is only in countries at a very advanced stage of development that capital markets, rather than banks, play significant role in allocating capital and that these markets satisfy the debt and equity needs of only the larger enterprises.

The focus of financial sector reform in transforming economies should therefore be to first establish a well functioning banking sector and then, subsequently, to develop capital markets. The latter will anyway begin to develop as a result of the execution of privatisation programmes and the issuance of government securities (treasury bills and bonds). The restructuring of the banking sector does, however, require the development of wholesale money markets, including an interbank market. These markets facilitate increased efficiency in the allocation of capital by banks, which is the prime goal of the reform process. This is because banks with insufficient profitable lending opportunities and a surplus of (retail) deposits should be able to lend to banks in the opposite position. It is also evident that a rapid transfer of know-how (to practitioners and supervisors) concerning lending techniques and risk control, via asset and liability management, in commercial banking is required if a more efficient allocation of capital is to be achieved.

In capitalist economies, the financial sector not only allocates capital but also monitors its use and imposes sanctions on its misuse. This latter corporate governance function is crucial since if capital, once allocated, is not efficiently used, then it should be withdrawn and re-allocated. It is through this process that continuous restructuring and development occurs under capitalism. For the process to work effectively a legal system has to be developed covering property rights, privatisation and restitution, debt and equity contracts, and bankruptcy inter alia.

The transforming economies had to construct such a legal system from scratch and this ensured that the transition progressed at a tortuous pace in the early stages. If the banks are to play a key role in corporate governance, the question of who should monitor the activities of the monitors arises. The need for bank regulation and supervision is widely accepted (although not undisputed)[5] and rests on the existence of a market failure. As with SME finance (discussed below) this is usually attributed to information asymmetry and the resulting moral hazard, adverse selection, and public choice problems.[6] We lack the space to explore these issues here and merely note that international "best practice" and, in many cases, a desire to join the European Union, made it necessary for the ex-CPEs to develop a bank regulatory and supervisory system.[7] Again this had to be done virtually from scratch, although in this case there were internationally agreed (Basle Committee) standards on which to model the legalisation, rather than the bewildering array of legal models available covering the aforementioned spheres.

Given their key importance in the early stages of transition, the corporate governance responsibility will fall primarily on banks. As the capital markets develop, as a result of privatisation, other institutions, such as the investment funds created in connection with voucher-based mass privatisation programmes in Poland and the Czech Republic, will begin to share this role. As major shareholders, the investment funds will have the potential to influence management behaviour and should be given the incentive to do so. In the "West", and particularly in countries where the capital markets are most developed, particularly the UK and the US, institutional shareholders, such as insurance companies and pensions funds, are playing an increasingly important role in corporate governance. In more bank-oriented countries, such as Germany and Japan, the banks are major shareholders and wield influence as both debt and equity holders.[8]

In Poland fifteen investment funds have initially controlled the shares in enterprises privatised under the voucher-based mass privatisation programme. These shares are tradeable at a future date and this allows the emerging institutional investors to have more influence in this sphere. In the mean time, however, the funds are managed by experienced professional fund managers who tendered for the business and have an incentive to ensure that the firms in which they hold shares perform efficiently.

In the Czech Republic investment funds were established spontaneously. Many of the larger ones are being run by banks, which will therefore be able to exert an influence as both debt and equity holders, in line with German Universal banks. There is considerable debate about the strengths and weaknesses of the German and Japanese models of corporate control in relation to the Anglo-Saxon (more capital market oriented) systems.[9] The latter is often criticized for engendering short-termism, but is praised for its flexibility and dynamism, for example. Again, these issues are not explored further here.

2.3 Stabilisation, debt consolidation and bank restructuring

It has been noted that the need to establish a legal, regulatory and supervisory infrastructure, and the lack of know-how, made instant banking sector restructuring impossible, but another important factor hindered the process. This was the SOBs' inheritance, from the previous (central planning) regime, of debt contracts with SOEs.

In the early stages of the transition it soon became apparent that many of the SOEs were uncompetitive and inefficient and that a large proportion of the loans to them were bad, or at best doubtful. The loans had been made under a directed credit regime, rather than in pursuit of profit, but the banks could not simply cut off supplies of finance in the new regime because they would have revealed themselves to be insolvent. Further, bankruptcy laws were not in place and the banks had no legal claims on the property of the borrowers since the practice of taking collateral against loans, and the law on property rights in general, had not been developed.

In an ideal world the new, democratically elected, governments would have acknowledged the state's responsibility for the debts inherited from the previous regime, taken on the debt (as national debt by swapping it for government bonds) and then recapitalised the banks. The SOBs would then have started with a "clean slate" and been able to develop genuinely commercial relationship with SOEs and private sector borrowers. Already severe budgetary problems would, however, have been aggravated. These problems were becoming worse as demands for state expenditure (to put in place a social safety-net for example) were increasing and state revenues (from the "profits" of struggling SOEs) were falling. Belatedly, the case for external assistance in the funding of the recapitalisation of banks was recognised.

The cost of postponing comprehensive bank restructuring was an accumulation of bad debts in banks. More and more doubtful debts went bad as the "transition recessions" worsened. It should be noted, however, that there was a severe transition (Phillips-curve) trade off between inflation and unemployment. If the banks had been freed of their debt burden and bankruptcy law had been rapidly introduced, then many more SOEs would have been closed (rather than commercialised and restructured) and unemployment would have risen even more rapidly, possibly engendering political instability. By postponing the resolution of the bank bad debt problem, however, capital was missallocated because it continued to be lent to inefficient firms and was not released for lending to new, and potentially more efficient, enterprises. The restructuring of the economy was therefore slowed down and mass privatisation of SOEs (as well as the privatisation of SOBs) was also hindered because the SOEs had inherited debts to banks from the previous regime and they also needed financial restructuring prior to privatisation. The resolution of the bank bad debt problem and the possibility of launching of an early and successful mass privatisation programme were therefore inter-related.

Failure to deal with the bank bad debt problem at an early stage also had implications for the (macro/monetary) stabilization programme. The Russian and Ukrainian experiences have made clear the interplay between the control of the money supply and financial control at the enterprise (micro) level. As the central planning era came to a close, SOEs had come to expect an elastic supply of credit with few sanctions. They faced "soft budget constraints". As long as the SOBs remained unrestructured, SOE managements continued to expect SOBs to supply credit on demand and, when necessary, use their political influence to ensure that the supply was unrestricted by warning of the consequences for unemployment levels and political stability. To the extent that the state controls the central bank and the SOBs have access to central bank refinancing, the result is effectively central bank financing of government subsidies to SOEs. In other words there is a "soft budget constraint" at the macro level and high (or possibly hyper-) inflation persists. The lack of financial discipline at the micro and macro levels leads to capital outflows (flight) and sooner or later foreign exchange reserves become insufficient to cover trade deficits and indebtedness to foreign banks. The currency depreciates as a result. This adds a twist to the inflationary spiral as import prices rise.

The situation is worsened in countries, such as Poland and the former Yugoslavia, that had granted widespread worker control over enterprises whilst seeking a "third way", since bank credits are then sought to cover mounting wage bills. When the international indebtedness mounts to a level which is unserviceable, the assistance of the IMF has to be sought and international debt rescheduling can begin, subject to IMF conditionally. As a result perhaps of their size, some countries, such as Brazil and Russia, have been able to negotiate special conditions from the IMF, but generally the IMF requires the budget deficit to be reduced to facilitate a reduction in domestic credit expansion (DCE).

The reduction in the budget deficit (often bolstered by an incomes policy) reduces pressure for central bank refinancing; to further reduce DCE, measures to curb the growth in bank lending are also required. These may include lending growth ceilings (loan rationing), but suitably positive real interest rates are a preferable means of achieving this through the reduction in the demand for credit. This is because the credit is likely to be allocated more efficiently and internally generated savings will be higher.[10] The beneficial effect on the efficiency of credit allocation is, however, only likely to occur following the restructuring of SOB and SOE debts. This is because the SOBs may feel that, in order to maintain their own (perceived) solvency, they must continue to lend to large SOE debtors, whose debt will probably continue to grow as a result of positive real interest rates.

It should be noted that in the countries which experienced hyper-inflation (e.g. Poland and Russia) the bad debt problem was initially resolved by the wiping out of the real value of old loans. This had temporary benefits in the early phase of the banking sector reform.

However, the aforementioned inexperience in lending, and the fact that, without substantial restructuring, the SOBs remain tied to SOEs, soon led to a re-emergence of bank bad-debt problems.

2.4 Implications for monetary and exchange rate policy

In the light of the foregoing discussion, central bank independence might seem to be an attractive option in transforming economies. However, genuine independence can only be achieved once the budget deficit is under control and the government has established an alternative (to the central bank) source of finance through bond issuance. For the public to be willing buyers of bonds, the government must first achieve credibility for its economic programme. It clearly takes time for governments in fledgling democracies to establish a reputation and bond markets have been slow to develop as a result.

Central bank independence also requires that the government must either adopt a freely floating exchange rate policy or allow the central bank to set foreign exchange policy as well as monetary policy. Otherwise conflicts can arise between the interest rate necessary to maintain an exchange rate target set by the government (finance ministry) and the interest rate required to achieve domestic monetary policy goals. This leads into the much debated issue of the appropriate choice of exchange rate policy and level of convertibility for transforming economies. Again this is too broad an issue to be dealt with here, but we note that, in order to establish a credibly convertible currency, most transforming ex-CPEs have adopted some form of exchange rate target at the outset. This restricts freedom to use interest rates in pursuit of internal monetary policy goals, and may necessitate the use of credit ceilings and variable reserve requirements to control bank credit creation. It may thus limit the scope of central bank independence. Even if a relatively independent central bank could be established, it too would take time to build a reputation and achieve credibility for its anti-inflationary stance. The establishment of an independent central banks is no panacea, therefore, and is unlikely to lead to an immediate reversal of capital flight. The achievement of political stability, in the sense of public acceptance of the stabilisation programme, currency convertibility, and resolution of internal and external debt problems seem to have a more immediate positive impact on net capital inflows.[11] The successful launch of the privatisation programme will also have a positive impact on capital inflows.

It should also be noted that an abrupt tightening of monetary policy, leading to restricted bank lending, may simply change the nature of the internal debt problem and choke off the supply of credit to the SMEs; created as part of the small privatisation programme and through business start-ups, which will also be inhibited. Faced with a restricted supply of, and increasingly costly, bank credits, SOEs initially responded by building up inter-enterprise debts through late or non-payment of suppliers. In many countries attempting stabilisation, the build up of enterprise debt has been very rapid and beyond levels that would be sustainable in western countries. The debt problem therefore continues to worsen and may only unwind once SOEs become susceptible to bankruptcy. The resolution of the bank bad debt problem will thus ultimately lead to a reduction in the inter-enterprise debt problem, but in the mean time the cost of the financial restructuring of SOEs mounts. Inter-enterprise debt also rises in recession in western countries. It has adverse consequences for SMEs, whose insolvency rate rises due to the deleterious effects of late payments on their cash flow. The introduction of a tight monetary policy in ex-CPEs before the resolution of the bank debt problem and the introduction of bankruptcy laws is therefore likely to exacerbate the transition recession and make it very difficult for SMEs to thrive. To contain the growth of inter-enterprise debt, late-payment penalties, in the form of interest on overdue payments, might usefully be introduced. Such measures are being adopted by an increasing number of OECD countries.

2.5 Privatisation and SME financing

The transformation of ex-CPEs into capitalist (or in reality mixed) economies essentially requires privatisation of the industrial and a large part of the rudimentary service sectors of these economies. This can be achieved in part by privatising SOEs (including banks), but will also require the development of new private sector enterprises, especially in the under developed service sector. In other words, an environment must be created in which SMEs can thrive, create new jobs and absorb workers laid off by the SOEs that must be made "leaner and fitter" to compete in the new world order. To facilitate this, capital must be released from inefficient uses in SOEs and redistributed to SMEs. Can the banks and the nascent capital markets in the ex-CPEs be expected to perform this vital task rapidly and efficiently? It should be noted that the private sector in Poland already accounted for over half of national output and exports by 1995, but its growth had been inhibited by lack of suitably priced finance given that unemployment remained at 16 percent after the first year of tentative recovery from the transition recession.

It is widely acknowledged that there is a market failure in the provision of SME finance in Western economies.[12] Its source is again information asymmetry, which leads banks to ration the supply of credit to SMEs and to seek collateral to limit their exposure to losses. For small firms and potential start-ups, the inability to supply sufficient suitable collateral acts as an additional constraint on their ability to raise external finance to develop their enterprises.

The importance of a thriving and innovative SME sector to a country's welfare is increasingly acknowledged. It has long been recognised in Japan and Germany, where the SME sector remains the largest employer despite the presence of numerous industrial giants which have become household names worldwide. It is now accepted much more widely. This is because international competition amongst multinational companies has progressed to the stage where retrenchment of staff in their countries of origin has become more likely the job creation. Increasingly SMEs are looked to as the source of job creation to absorb workers laid off in this process and help resolve the wider unemployment problem.

The ex-CPEs essentially face the same problem, but on a much greater scale. The established enterprises are restructuring at an increasingly rapid rate and new jobs need to be created. This is occurring in an environment where the recession has been much deeper and economic prospects are more uncertain than in the Western industrialised economies in the 1990s.

In Japan and Germany (long-term) "relationship banking" has been the norm. This helps to reduce the information deficiency and allows banks to assist many more SMEs through the difficulties they face in recessions. Nevertheless, post-war reconstruction led the state in each of these countries to intervene to overcome the aforementioned market failure by actively stimulating the revitalisation of the SME sector. This was done through the disbursement of state-subsidised credits using commercial banks and specialised reconstruction or development banks. Despite the subsequent success of their economies, the subsidies and specialist agencies have continued to be used. The German reconstruction bank (KfW) found renewed demand for its services following the unification of East and West Germany in 1990. Germany also has a network of loan-guarantee banks and this has been extended to cover the new Eastern Länder.[13]

Other Western countries have also intervened to overcome the market failure in SME financing by providing state-funded loan guarantees and funds for disbursement through state-owned development and commercial banks. One response by the European Union to its unemployment problem in the early 1990s was to increase the funds made available to the European Investment Bank for disbursement to support subsidised SME financing in member states.

Parallels with reconstruction in post-war Japan and Germany and recognition that, even in industrial countries with seemingly well functioning financial systems, there is a market failure in the supply of finance to SMEs, points to the need for government intervention in ex-CPEs. This is particularly acute whilst the SOBs remain encumbered with their bad debt problems and even the new private sector banks are deterred from lending due to the information asymmetries and the general high level of uncertainty about economic prospects. The lack of suitable collateral is an additional problem due to the low levels of private wealth and home ownership and the additional uncertainty created by restitution claims.

2.6 What should be done?

To induce banks to lend more freely, it is necessary to provide a supply of subsidised credit to the SME sector and state-backed loan guarantees. A state funded reconstruction/investment bank could usefully disburse the loans and provide the guarantees, and the degree of subsidy should be progressively reduced. Over time the guarantee scheme could also usefully replace fixed fees (premia) with risk-related premia, with a view to rewarding banks who manage guaranteed SME loan portfolios efficiently.

Governments could also assist in the establishment of wholesale money and capital markets: through the issuance of benchmark securities, such as treasury bills and bonds; and by overseeing the development of an efficient payments system. The latter is an infrastuctural requirement for an efficient commercial sector and could be developed alongside a modern networked telecommunications and information processing and sharing system; thereby skipping the costly paper-based cheque clearing stage which the western banks are trying to extricate themselves from. Finally, a well managed privatisation process will facilitate the development of capital markets and so too will moves towards private sector provision of pensions.

Notes

The support of the EC(ACE) programme, under contract number ACE-94-0772-R, is gratefully acknowledged.

1. The same holds true for developing countries in Asia and Africa, especially where state ownership of the banking sector has been significant.
2. The main difference between ex-CPEs and the African and Asian developing countries lies in the scale and scope of the restructuring required.
3. See the contribution by John Doukas, Victor Murinde and Clas Wihlborg in this volume (Chapter 1)
4. See Heffernan (1996, Chapter 2) for further discussion.
5. See, for example, Dowd (1992).
6. See Mishkin (1995, Chapter 9) for an introductory discussion.
7. See the contribution by Anthony Santomero in this volume (Chapter 7).
8. The trend towards private pension provision is spreading throughout Europe in response to ageing populations. This will lead to a marked increase in the importance of (non-bank) institutional investors in countries where ageing is particularly rapid, including Germany (and Japan).
9. See the contribution by Ingo Walter in this volume (Chapter 6).
10. See Murinde (1996, Chapter 5) for further discussion on financial repression issues.
11. See Dickinson and Mullineux (1997) for further discussion.
12. See, for example, Stiglitz and Weiss (1981).
13. See Mullineux (1994) for further discussion.

References

Dickinson, D.G. and A.W. Mullineux, 1997, Convertibility, policy credibility and capital flight; in: R. Sweeney and C. Reis, eds., Capital Account Issues for Liberalizing Economies (Westview Press, Boulder, Colorado).

Dowd, K., 1992 Models of banking instability: a partial review, Journal of Economic Surveys, 6, 2, pp. 107-133.

Heffernan, S., 1996, Modern Banking in Theory and Practice (Wiley, London).

Mishkin, F.S., 1995, The Economics of Money, Banking and Financial Markets (Harper Collins, New York).

Mullineux, A.W., 1994, Small and Medium-Sized Enterprise (SME) Financing in the UK: Lessons from Germany (Anglo German Foundation Report, London).

Murinde, V., 1996, Development Banking and Finance (Avebury, Aldershot).

Stiglitz, J. and A. Weiss, 1981, Credit rationing in markets with imperfect information, American Economic Review, 71, 3, pp. 393-410.

Financial Sector Reform and
Privatization in Transition Economies
J. Doukas, V. Murinde and C. Wihlborg (Editors)
© 1998 Elsevier Science Publishers B.V. All rights reserved

35 — 6 7

Chapter 3

M 13   P 34

P 3 1

FINANCIAL CONSTRAINTS ON ENTREPRENEURSHIP IN ESTONIA

G 3 2

Vello Vensel
Department of Economics, Tallinn Technical University,
101 Kopli Str, EE-0102 Tallinn, Estonia

Clas Wihlborg
Department of Economics, School of Economics and Commercial Law, Göteborg
University, Vasagatan 1, S-411 80, Göteborg, Sweden

1.   Introduction

Most empirical research on the emerging market economies in Eastern
Europe is based on survey data. The emergence of these countries as market
economies is still too recent for time-series analyses. Where time-series of
data can be obtained, any tests of theoretical propositions must account for
ongoing structural changes in the transition process.

The existing survey based research covers a wide range of issues
including financial sector reform. Most of the research refer to the central
European countries, mainly the Czech Republic, Hungary and Poland, while
little is done on the former Soviet Union and other countries lagging in the
transition.

Most of the early research on the financial sector in emerging market
economies focused on the restructuring of banks with large amounts of bad
debt and distorted incentives that prevented banks from performing their
role as monitors and enforcers of budget constraints of firms. Griffith-Jones
and Drabek (1994) analyzed the progress of banking reform in the Czech
Republic, Hungary and Poland. Begg and Portes (1993) provided an early
overview of the bad debt problem in Central and Eastern Europe and warned
that successful transition would be in jeopardy in many countries unless
banks were restructured urgently.

The relatively successful emerging market economies in Central Europe have made substantial progress in recapitalization and privatization of banks. The same can be said about Estonia as will be argued below. Perhaps as a result of this progress economic research has shifted towards enterprise development and the restructuring of the manufacturing sector. Survey based research of private investment activity has been conducted by, for example, Genco, Taurello, and Viezzoli (1993). Funck, Kowalski, and Zienkowski surveyed the development of small and medium sized enterprises in Poland. Webster and Charap (1993) surveyed business and financial conditions for private manufacturers in St Petersburg, Russia. Scheinberg and Lundberg (1994) conducted a field study of financial flows to firms in Russia and Estonia.

Another strand of research is concerned with institutional developments such as the development of bankruptcy law and corporate governance structures, that to a large extent depend on regulatory and legal constraints on various financial activities. Eliasson, Rybczynski, and Wihlborg (1993) discuss the role of legal developments in the transition. Portes (1994) notes that formally stated bankruptcy law and procedures may actually worsen the enforcement of financial contracts with firms in distress when the legal capacity to enforce the laws is lacking, as often is the case in the emerging market economies. Regarding corporate governance, Phelps, Frydman, Rapuczynski, and Shleifer (1993) emphasize that functioning structures require regulatory and legal reform. Jaffee and Renaud discuss in this volume institutional reform that would enable mortgage markets to develop (see Paper 4, in this volume).

In this paper we analyze investments, financing, and institutions in Estonia's manufacturing sector based on a relatively detailed survey of firms' relations with suppliers, employees, and lenders. We focus on relations with lenders in order to analyze sources of financing for new and ongoing projects. Our objective is to discover whether financial markets, or the lack thereof, hinder investments and enterprise development in Estonia. If so, the issue is whether hindrances depend on deficient institutions. We ask also whether informal financing and trade credits substitute for formal loans when firms are unable to obtain loans in banks. Estonia is an interesting target for a detailed study because of its history as a part of the former Soviet Union. Estonia lacked the most basic market oriented institutions at the time it started to liberate itself from the Soviet Union soon before independence in 1991.

We proceed in Section 3.2 by describing the relatively fast transition process in Estonia. In Section 3.3 the survey is described. Then, in Section 3.4, the financial structure and the financing of investments of manufacturing firms are discussed with a focus on firm-size as a determinant of access to various sources of financing. Thereafter, in Section 3.5, managers' perceptions of regulatory and legal constraints on investments are presented. In Section 3.6 we analyze whether access to financing can be explained by those firm characteristics that could proxy for riskiness and information availability. We summarize and draw conclusions in Section 3.7.

3.2 Estonian reform and the banking system

Estonia can probably be characterized as the most successful of the former republics of the Soviet Union. In 1996 GDP grew by about 4 percent according to official figures. Unofficial estimates are significantly higher. After independence in 1991 consensus about rapid market oriented reform has been overwhelming and it has remained intact. This consensus may be explained by the small size of the country (1.5 million inhabitants) or by the common anti-Soviet or anti-communist attitudes among the 900,000 ethnically Estonian inhabitants.[1]   The relative openness of Estonia to Western media from Finland during the Soviet years may also have contributed to a mental preparedness for reform.

Table 3.1 shows the timing and characteristics of some important reforms through mid 1996. The liberalization of prices and foreign trade was completed in 1992. By this time, a two-tier banking system was in place and the monetary reform in June 1992 established the Estonian Kroon (EEK) as the currency issued by a politically independent central bank. It is working as a currency board with a fixed exchange rate of EEK 8 per DEM. This exchange rate has remained fixed and credible, while inflation has come down to a level below 15 percent in the first half of 1997. The central bank is also the supervisory agency for the banking system.

Privatization of large enterprises begun in 1992. At that time small enterprises had already been privatized to a large extent. While the privatization of small enterprises occurred rapidly, large enterprises were sold or auctioned off at a slower pace. By mid 1996, the process was near completion.

The one aspect of the transition that has proven difficult to implement is the clarification of property rights to land. Individual claims to land that was nationalized after the communists took control of the country in 1941 must be checked carefully before land is returned to an owner or compensation is paid. As noted below and in Paper 4 by Jaffee and Renault in this volume the lack of clarity about property rights to land hinders both the ability of private individuals to put up property as collateral for loans, and the development of a functioning market for mortgages.

TABLE 3.1
Reforms in Estonia

Reforms	Timing and characteristics
1. Political:	
a) free parliamentary elections	September 1992, March 1995
b) nation-wide referendum	June 1992
c) presidential elections	September 1992; October 1996
d) local government elections	October 1993; October 1996
2. Clarification of property rights:	
a) restitution	return of property or compensation for it to former owners in process; complicated
b) voucher process	started in 1994; in process
c) ownership of land	land reform in process; complicated
d) protection of foreign investors	bilateral agreements, tax allowances
3. Corporatization of state-owned enterprises, privatization:	
a) petty privatization	completed during 1991-1993
b) large privatization	gradually since 1992, mostly completed
c) supervising government agency	Estonian Privatization Agency
d) stock market	embryonic, operating through Estonian Central Depository for Securities, Tallinn Stock Exchange opened in May 1996
4. Changes in price system:	
a) retail prices	liberalized during 1991-1992
b) wholesale prices	liberalized during 1991-1992

TABLE 3.1 concluded

5. *Overhaul of the social safety net:*
a) social insurance system	payroll tax, 13 % of total labor costs
b) health insurance system	payroll tax, 20 % of total labor costs
c) unemployment benefits	about 60 % of minimum wage
d) minimum wages	special agreements; diversity

6. *Overhaul of the fiscal system:*
a) VAT	18 %
b) income tax, personal and corporate	26 %
c) property tax	land tax
d) expenditure reform	balanced budget since fiscal year 1993

7. *Overhaul of the banking system:*
a) two-tier banking system	since 1991
b) independent central bank	since 1992
c) monetary reform	June 1992, Estonian kroons (EEK)

8. *Foreign trade arrangements:*
a) liberalization of trading rights	fully liberalized, no selective tariffs or quotas, bilateral agreements
b) unified exchange rate	since June 1992, peg to DEM (1 DEM=EEK 8)
c) convertibility	both current and capital account transactions are fully convertible

9. *Co-operation with multilateral/international organizations:*
a) EC	free trade agreement, associated member since January 1995
b) IMF/IBRD	member since May 1992
c) EBRD	member since December 1991
d) WTO	under negotiations
e) IFC	member since August 1993

Turning to the banking system the inheritance from the Soviet economy has been eradicated. The rouble inflation that affected Estonia before the monetary reform in 1992 contributed to the shrinking of the banks. A substantial part of the subsequent expansion of the financial system took place through the establishment of new small private banks. The number of banks reached a peak above 40 in 1993 before consolidation began, partly because of the announcement of minimum equity capital regulation that would be enforced beginning in January 1996. The minimum was to be raised to EEK 50 millions in January 1996, and thereafter gradually to EEK 75 millions (ECU 5 millions) in January 1998. After consolidation, the number of banks has fallen to 13 domestically owned banks by early 1997. A bank must have at least 10 shareholders and the shares of one owner must not exceed 33 percent of the total share capital and/or voting rights.[2]

The three largest banks hold more than 60 percent of the total assets of the banking system. The government is still a part-owner in some of the larger banks but it seems that the "commercialization" of these banks has been successful. One reason is that ownership in some cases is mixed. In September 1996 the government's share in bank-ownership was down to 11.2 percent.[3] Another reason is that the currency board arrangement prevents the central bank from acting as a lender of last resort, and the government from borrowing from the central bank. The commercialization gained credibility during the banking crises that erupted in November 1992. Three large banks failed for various reasons. The central bank's demonstration of its willingness to let banks fail and even to let depositors bear losses has speeded up the development of a system, wherein the banks enforce hard budget constraints on borrowers, and where depositors must consider the quality of banks' credit-policies. The reduced government ownership of banks has had the consequence that the entire banking system works without state guarantees.

Ambitions to join the EU has created incentives to harmonize regulation with the EU. There is a draft law that deposits will be insured up to an amount of 10,000 Kroons per deposit. This amount will grow to 20,000 ECUs over a 15 year period but a minimum of 10 percent of each deposit account will remain uninsured.

One interesting question is whether the Estonian banking policy has been effective from an economic growth perspective. The imposition of hard budget constraints is likely to speed up the structural adjustment by the closing of inefficient enterprises. Inevitably in a transition economy, banks have to suffer credit losses in the relatively rapid structural adjustment. On the other hand, the lack of protection of depositors could cause an unwillingness to deposit in banks and thereby hinder the mobilization of financial resources. If banks have responded to the lack of protection by becoming demonstrably more efficient evaluators of credit risk, then the negative effect on savings should have been small.

Table 3.1, which shows reforms in Estonia,,reveals that an organized stock-market has not played an important role as of mid 1996. As privatization of large enterprises nears completion the rapid development of a more active stock-market is to be expected.

Table 3.2 shows how managers of firms perceive the quality of banking services. The answers have been obtained form an interview study of nearly 50 managers. This study will be presented below. Here it suffices to say that the quality of services seems to have been increasing across the board from 1994 to 1996. The improvement is particularly noticeable on credits indicating that fewer firms perceive themselves as rationed in 1996. Managers rate payment services and foreign exchange services particularly high. Judging from these responses, Estonia seems to have developed a functioning banking system.

TABLE 3.2
Average assessment of the quality of banking services
(5 = excellent quality; 1 = bad quality)

Banking service	Year 1994	Year 1995	Year 1996
Arrangement of domestic payments	4.4	4.4	4.5
Arrangement of foreign exchange	3.8	4.4	4.0
Speed of banking operations	4.1	4.2	4.2
Arrangement of foreign payments	3.6	4.1	4.0
Financial consulting	3.8	3.7	3.7
Loans for working capital	2.9	3.0	3.6
Loans for investments	1.9	2.7	3.0
Budgeting assistance	2.0	2.6	2.4

3.3 The interview study

Quantitative and qualitative data on manufacturing firms' contractual relations, operations, and the regulatory environment have been collected by means of direct interviews with top management. While the focus is on financial relations, the interviews also cover investment activity, infrastructure, conflict resolution, regulations, marketing channels, labor relations, and ownership structure. Thus, firms can be characterized in several dimension when studying their financing choices. A pilot study with 20 firms was conducted in 1993. In 1994, 50 firms were approached by mail; 39 firms responded positively and these firms were visited by an interview team for completion of the questionnaire. The same 50 firms and some additional firms were approached in 1995 and 1996 with the ambition to obtain answers from 50 firms. In 1995 the number of respondents were 47 and in 1996 there were 48 respondents. Answers are incomplete in some cases, however.

It would have been desirable with a sample of several hundred firms in order to obtain a sufficient number of observations for multivariate econometric analyses. The costs in terms of time and money would have become too large, however. Instead, an effort was made to have all important industries, and different ownership structures represented. An effort was also made to obtain a reasonably representative size distribution but ultimately the sample depends on firms' willingness to answer the relatively elaborate questionnaire. This aspect is particularly important in the formerly communist countries where openness with information is not a tradition.

Another reason why the sample of firms may be biased is that many businesses in transition economies seem to be involved in quasi-legal or illegal activities. Such firms and those evading unenforceable tax rules are not likely to participate in the study. Thus, the sample is likely to be biased in such a way that many informal arrangements are not captured. We hope to detect the existence of informal financial arrangements, however, even if their importance could be underestimated.

The sample of firms is described in Tables 3.3-3.7, showing the distribution of firms by sector (3.3), geographical location (3.4), legal status (3.5), ownership structure (3.6), and start-up year (3.7). Answers are missing when the total number of firms does not add up to 39 in 1994, 47 in 1995, and 48 in 1996.

The relatively large industries in Estonia are light manufacturing and food production. The same industries were important during the Soviet era. Table 3.4 shows that half of the sample firms are located in Tallinn. The sample is representative in this respect.

The extent of privatization is revealed in Table 3.5 showing that corporate entities have been created from state-owned enterprises. The decline in state ownership shows up in Table 3.6 as well, where it is shown that domestic private owners have taken over. Foreign private owners appear in the 1996 study.

Table 3.7 reveals that most firms have been established after or during the year of independence (1991). Only ten of the firms in the sample were established before 1991.

The size distribution of the firms is shown in Table 3.8. We divide the firms into three groups for the analysis of investment and financing decisions in the sections that follow. Small firms have 10 employees or less, medium firms have at least 11 and at most 200 employees, while large firms have at least 201 employees. These groups have been subdivided further in Table 3.8. The table shows that the size distribution has changed somewhat. It seems that a number of small firms in 1995 became medium sized firms in 1996. Most firms that were added to the sample in 1995 were small while those added in 1996 were medium sized.

TABLE 3.3
Distribution of sample firms by sector
Number of firms (percent of respondents)

Industries	1994	1995	1996
Light industry	7 (18)	5 (10.9)	5 (11.4)
Food industry	7 (18)	4 (8.7)	7 (15.9)
Construction industry	-	4 (8.7)	5 (11.4)
Transportation	-	7 (15)	2 (4.5)
Wood-proceeding industry	3 (7.7)	3 (6.5)	3 (6.8)
Metal-proceeding industry	4 (10.3)	1 (2.2)	4 (9.1)
Other industries	18 (46)	22 (47.9)	18 (40.9)
	39	46	44

TABLE 3.4
Distribution of firms by production location
Number of firms (percent of respondents)

Production location	1994	1995	1996
Tallinn (the capital)	15 (38.5)	24 (57.1)	24 (51.0)
North Estonia	16 (41)	11 (26.2)	10 (21.3)
South-Estonia	6 (15.4)	5 (11.9)	10 (21.3)
Other regions	2 (5.1)	2 (4.8)	4 (6.4)
	39	42	47

TABLE 3.5
Distribution of sample firms by legal status
Number of firms (percent of respondents)

Legal status	1994	1995	1996
Corporate	25 (65.8)	36 (80)	40 (83.3)
State-owned enterprise	7 (18.4)	3 (6.7)	1 (2.1)
Limited liability enterprise	3 (7.9)	3 (6.7)	3 (6.3)
Partnership	1 (2.6)	2 (4.4)	1 (2.1)
Sole proprietorship	1 (2.6)	2 (4.4)	1 (2.1)
Subsidiary of a corporation	2 (5.3)	0	2 (4.1)
	39	47	48

TABLE 3.6
Distribution of firms by ownership structure
Number of firms (percent of respondents)

Ownership forms	1994	1995	1996
Domestic private owners	23 (59)	32 (72.7)	42 (87.4)
Domestic and foreign private owners	6 (15.1)	8 (18.3)	2 (4.2)
State ownership	7 (18)	2 (4.5)	0
State, domestic and foreign joint private owners	1 (2.5)	2 (4.5)	1 (2.1)
Foreign private owners	0	0	2 (4.2)
State and domestic private owners	2 (5.1)	2	1 (2.1)
	39	46	48

3.4. Investment and financing by size group

In this section we present investment and financing data form the interview study emphasizing access to bank loans, the extent of informal borrowing and trade credits substituting for bank-loans. Differences among size groups and changes in the access to financing of these groups from 1995 to 1996 are discussed. The data on financing are of three kinds. First, answers to questions on start-up financing are presented. Thereafter, we turn to the various forms of financing in firms' capital structures. Finally, the financing of the latest investment is presented.

TABLE 3.7
Distribution of sample firms by the start-up year
Number of firms (percent of respondents)

Start-up year	1994	1995	1996
Started before 1980	7 (18)	5 (10.6)	7 (15.2)
Started 1981-1990	3 (7.7)	3 (6.4)	3 (6.5)
Started 1991	13 (33.3)	10 (21.3)	11 (23.9)
Started 1992	8 (20.5)	12 (25.5)	8 (17.4)
Started 1993	8 (20.5)	11 (23.4)	9 (19.6)
Started 1994	-	6 (12.8)	7 (15.2)
Started 1995	-	-	1 (2.2)
	39	47	46

TABLE 3.8
Size distribution of firms

Size-distribution	1994	1995	1996
Small 1-20	7	16	15
1-5	3	7	5
6-10	2	5	6
11-20	2	4	4
Medium 21-200	19	17	23
21-50	8	7	9
51-100	6	6	6
101-200	5	4	8
Large 201-	8	9	8
201-500	6	7	6
501-	2	2	2
Total	34	42	46

Investment activity is described in Table 3.9, to begin with. Each year the firms were asked which year they last invested in buildings and equipment. The table shows the number of firms and the percent of respondents that invested during the year before the interview took place. The share increased from 48 percent to 58 percent.

TABLE 3.9
Firms investing in buildings and equipment
during the year before interview

Characteristics	1994	1995	1996
Number of firms	11	19	23
Percent of respondents	47.9	52.8	57.5

Start-up financing

Turning to sources of financing, Table 3.10 shows how the firms responded to the question of how start-up financing was obtained. We expect consistency across the years, since firms have been added to the sample while most firms are the same from year to year. There are some inconsistencies, however.

Own savings dominate as a source of start-up financing. Two thirds of all firms started up with owner's financing as full or partial financing. Relatives and friends complemented own resources in a few cases. Few firms (7 in 1996) obtained bank-loans for starting-up.

Only three managers answered in 1996 that start-up financing came from money-lenders. This source represents informal financing from unrelated individuals or institutions. It is possible, however, that the large number of "other sources" in 1996 represent informal borrowing. The number of firms using "other sources" increased from two to sixteen between 1995 and 1996, although most of the firms responding are the same. It seems, therefore, that many firms have neglected to mention "other sources" in 1994 and 1995. It is possible that small firms in particular have classified informal sources as "other". Few of these firms would have access to loans from parents or foreign partners.

TABLE 3.10
Sources of firms' start-up financing
Number of answers (more than one per firm)

Sources	1994	1995	1996
Own savings	22	28	33
Loan from domestic commercial bank	4	5	7
Borrowing from relatives and friends	3	4	4
Loan from foreign bank or donor agency	1	3	1
Loan from money-lender	4	2	3
Other sources (restitution, parent firm, foreign partner, etc.)	4	2	16
	38	44	64

Sources of financing in the financial structures

The financial structures of firms of different size are presented in Tables 3.11 and 3.12. These tables are constructed from answers to questions about each one of the various sources of finance. Informal loans appear in Table 3.11a among the liabilities of 26 (17) percent of the firms in 1995 (1996), but these loans represent a very small share of total liabilities (0.2 percent in 1995; 0.7 percent in 1996) as shown by Table 3.12a. As expected, a relatively large share (35.4 percent in 1996) of the small firms have loans from informal sources including relatives and friends, but these loans finance only 0.8 percent of total assets. The informal lending to employees in particular actually exceeds the amount borrowed informally.

The share of firms with formal loans from banks in particular has increased five percentage points to 47.9 in 1996. The increase is particularly large for small firms increasing from 31.2 to 42.1 percent. As expected the share of small firms with bank loans is much lower than the shares of medium and large firms. The disadvantage of small firms in the market for formal loans is even more obvious in Table 3.12a where the share of formal loans in the financing of small firms is only 5.2 percent in 1996 (up from 2.3

percent in 1995). The corresponding share for large firms is 28.6 in 1996, up from 13.5 percent in 1995. There is a substantial increase from 1995 to 1996 in the share of formal loan financing for all firms (from 11.2 to 24.6 percent). Thus, bank loan financing has gained in importance both in the sense that more firms have access to formal loans and in the sense that these loans are a larger share of individual firms' financing. This increase in formal loan financing has its correspondence in the reduced share of retained earnings in the financing of firms (Table 3.12a). Among all firms this share has fallen by nearly eight percentage points. This decline is primarily explained by large firms.

Next, we ask if trade credits and advance payments substitutes for formal loans for small firms. Table 3.11a shows that the share of firms obtaining trade credits lies between 80 and 90 percent for all groups of firms both years. The share of firms giving trade credits in Table 3.11b has increased, however, but this increase has occurred across all size groups. Looking at advance payments as an asset in Table 3.11b, a slight decline in the share of small firms paying in advance has occurred while the share has increased for large firms. At the same time, a larger share of small firms obtain payments in advance (Table 3.11a) while fewer large firms receive advance payments. These shifts seem to indicate a slight decline in the financial burden of small firms.

Tables 3.12a and 3.12b indicate that the shifts above have had relatively small quantitative effects. In Table 3.12a the share of trade credits in financing has declined very little for small firms. The share has increased a little for medium firms but declined substantially for large firms. The share of trade credits among assets has declined for all firms, however (Table 3.12b). Thus, the one substantial change in the use of trade credits between 1995 and 1996 seems to be that large firms have been able to substitute formal loans for trade credits in particular as a source of financing.

The figures for advance payments in Table 3.12a confirm that large firms receive substantially less advance payments in 1996 than in 1995. The same change can be observed for small and medium firms. The latter groups also pay in advance (Table 3.12b) to a lesser extent in 1996 than in 1995, while larger firms have increased their advance payments from 12.4 to 14.2 percent of all assets.

TABLE 3.11

Liabilities and assets 1995-1996

Percent of firms in size group with particular type of liability (asset)

a) Liabilities

Size group Number of firms in 1995		Small n = 16	Medium n = 17	Large n = 9	Average n = 42
Advance payments	95	43.8	47.0	66.7	30.0
	96	50.7	51.1	58.6	56.3
Trade credits	95	81.3	82.4	87.0	81.0
	96	80.7	84.4	86.1	83.1
Formal loans	95	31.2	41.1	66.7	42.9
	96	42.1	50.8	67.4	47.9
Informal loans	95	37.5	17.6	22.2	26.2
	96	35.4	16.4	12.3	16.7
Retained earnings	95	100.0	100.0	100.0	100.0
	96	100.0	100.0	100.0	100.0

b) Assets

Size group Number of firms in 1995		Small n = 16	Medium n = 17	Large n = 9	Average n = 42
Advance payments	95	25.0	41.0	33.3	33.3
	96	23.7	37.6	36.4	38.7
Trade credits	95	62.5	88.0	66.6	73.8
	96	70.5	91.2	81.4	86.4
Informal lending	95	31.3	29.4	33.3	31.0
	96	27.4	37.8	31.2	31.6
Real assets	95	100.0	100.0	100.0	100.0
	96	100.0	100.0	100.0	100.0

The overall impression concerning the role of trade credits and advance payments is that small firms have slightly more favorable financial conditions in 1996 than in 1995, in particular because they have decreased their lending through trade credits and advance payments. On the other hand, large firms that have increased their access to formal loans, borrow much less as trade credits and advance payments while they lend more.

Medium sized firms, like small firms, provide less trade credits for other firms in 1996, while they borrow slightly more than in 1995. Thus, the improved access to bank loans for large firms seems to have spilled over to other firms to some extent.

TABLE 3.12

Liabilities 1995-1996

Percent of total assets in each size group

a) Liabilities Size group Number of firms		Small n = 16	Medium n = 17	Large n = 9	Average n = 42
Advance payments	95	2.5	4.4	5.6	4.8
	96	1.3	3.6	2.2	1.2
Trade credits	95	17.3	16.0	11.7	15.0
	96	16.6	17.6	8.0	12.4
Formal loans	95	2.3	10.6	13.5	11.2
	96	5.2	17.4	28.6	24.6
Informal loans	95	0.3	0.1	2.3	0.2
	96	0.8	0.8	0.3	0.7
Retained earnings	95	77.6	68.9	66.9	68.8
	96	76.1	60.6	60.9	61.1
b) Assets					
Size group Number of firms		Small n = 16	Medium n =17	Large n = 9	Average n = 42
Advance payments	95	2.0	0.7	0.2	0.6
	96	1.7	1.4	0.8	1.4
Trade credits	95	18.0	21.3	12.4	17.1
	96	14.6	17.7	14.2	14.9
Informal lending	95	0.4	0.3	0.4	0.3
	96	1.1	0.5	0.2	0.3
Real assets	95	79.6	77.6	87.0	82.0
	96	82.6	80.4	84.8	83.4

An important determinant of access to bank-loans is the ability of individuals and firms to put up collateral. In Section 3.2 it was mentioned that delays in the process of establishing property rights to real property would reduce the access to bank-loans for many individuals.

The value of collateral put up by firms relative to the size of formal loans is shown in Table 3.13. The table shows that this ratio on the average has increased substantially between 1995 and 1996 and that this increase has affected medium and large firms but not small firms. On the other hand, the ratio was much higher for small firms than for others in 1995 (1.77 for small firms versus 0.68 and 0.52 for medium and large firms). These figures indicate that small firms are at a disadvantage in terms of access to bank-loans.

The average ratio of collateral relative to bank loans is not abnormally large by the standards of western industrialized countries. The high ratio for small firms in Estonia may indicate uncertainty about enforcement of loan contracts in case of bankruptcy, however. Although laws exist, the enforcement of contracts in courts is still weak.

TABLE 3.13
Value of collateral relative to formal loans by firm size, 1995-96

	Small	Medium	Large	Average
1995	1.77	0.68	0.52	0.73
1996	1.65	1.26	1.11	1.38

Financing the latest investment

To shed further light on the various forms of financing firms were also asked how they financed their latest investment. Tables 3.14 and 3.15 show the responses. As opposed to the data about investments in Table 3.9, inventory and working capital investments are included in Tables 3.14 and 3.15. Therefore, the share of firms that have invested recently is higher (89.5 percent) in these tables than in Table 3.9.

In comparison with Tables 3.11 and 3.12, the tables do not include advance payments and trade credits as sources of financing for a specific investment. Credits from suppliers appear as a category and a distinction is made between retained earnings and own savings as sources. Table 3.14 showing the percent of firms in a size group using a particular source indicates that the share of small firms relying on retained earnings and own saving as opposed to money lenders and "other sources", is higher in 1996 than in 1995.

TABLE 3.14

Percent of firms in each size group using particular source
of financing for investments (including working capital investments)
during previous year, 1995-96

Size group Number of firms		Small n = 16	Medium n = 17	Large n = 9	Average n = 42
Retained earnings	95	43.8	73.3	75.0	63.2
	96	80.0	63.6	25.0	60.4
Personal savings	95	20.0	20.0	0	15.8
	96	30.0	0	0	10.4
Bank loans	95	13.3	26.5	12.5	18.5
	96	10.0	22.7	43.7	27.1
Supplier credits	95	6.7	0	0	2.6
	96	10.0	4.5	6.2	6.3
Money lender	95	6.7	0	0	2.6
	96	0	0	0	0
Other sources	95	40.0	6.7	25.0	38.0
	96	10.0	13.6	18.8	12.5
Share of firms investment during the last year	95	93.8	88.2	88.9	89.5
	96	100.0	100.0	87.5	95.8

Table 3.15 reveals that the shares of different sources have changed in
a similar way for small firms from 1995 to 1996. The share of retained
earnings dominates in 1996 (83.3 percent) while money lenders, "other
sources" and supplier credits are unimportant this year. The decline in "other
sources" is especially striking. It is likely that both this category and money
lenders include informal sources of finance for small firms.

TABLE 3.15
Share of different sources in the financing of investments
(including working capital investments)
during previous year by size group, 1995-1996

Size group Number of firms		Small n = 16	Medium n = 17	Large n = 9	Average n = 42
Retained earnings	95	38.5	36.6	42.1	39.7
	96	83.3	41.0	55.5	52.7
Personal savings	95	8.4	8.6	0	5.8
	96	4.4	0	0	1.5
Bank loans	95	15.3	46.4	34.7	36.6
	96	3.8	39.6	36.4	38.4
Supplier credits	95	8.1	0	0	0.5
	96	2.1	8.3	1.8	1.7
Money lender	95	1.2	0	0	0.1
	96	0	0	0	0
Other sources	95	28.5	8.4	23.2	17.3
	96	6.4	11.1	6.3	5.7

Bank loans financed small firms' investments only for a small share of the firms in 1995 (13.3 percent) as well as 1996 (10 percent). The share of the investments financed by bank loans fell from 15.3 percent in 1995 to 3.8 percent in 1996. This low figure is of the same order of magnitude as the share of bank loans in the capital structure of small firms in Table 3.12. The access to bank loans for financing of investments seems to increase sharply for firms with more than 20 employees. Although only 20-23 percent of the firms obtained bank loans for financing (Table 3.14), around 40 percent of the investments were financed this way both years (Table 3.15). The figure for large firms was slightly lower - around 35 percent - both years. Supplier credits and "other sources" were important for medium firms in 1996 and for large firms in 1995. It is likely that "other sources" for these firms include parent firms and foreign partners, as shown in Table 3.10, rather than unspecified informal loans.

The picture in Tables 3.14 and 3.15 confirm the conclusions drawn above: Small firms have very little access to bank loans for their financing. These firm must rely on personal savings by the owner, retained earnings and informal sources, including relatives and friends, as well as money lenders. The figures indicate that informal sources may be utilized by a large number of firms but the share of financing obtained through these sources is small and most likely below ten percent.

Tables 3.16 and 3.17 contain more information about informal lending and borrowing by firms. Table 3.16 shows that lending to employees dominates but there is also some lending to other firms. This lending appears most likely as supplier credits in Tables 3.14 and 3.15.

TABLE 3.16

Informal lending by firms to different types of recipients in percent of all firms lending informally during a year and number of firms lending informally

Loan recipient	1994	1995	1996
Relatives and friends	14.8	27.8	5.3
Suppliers domestic commercial bank	0	0	0
Clients	14.8	0	0
Employees	48.2	55.6	73.7
Other firms	22.2	16.6	21.0
Number of firms	12	13	13

TABLE 3.17

Primary reasons for informal borrowing
Number of firms (percent of firms borrowing informally)

Reasons	1994	1995	1996
More favorable interest rate	2 (33)	5(46)	1 (12.5)
More flexible repayment schedule	1 (17)	3 (28)	2 (25)
Member of own family as lender	2 (33)	0	0
Collateral is not needed	0	2 (18)	2 (25)
Did not reveal reason	1 (17)	2 (18)	1 (12.5)
Number of firms	6	12	6

Managers' stated reasons for informal borrowing are given in Table 3.17. The number of firms responding is small, unfortunately. Nevertheless, the answers indicate that the firms that received informal loans chose these loans because of an inability to put up collateral, or because of an unwillingness or inability to meet the conditions of bank-loans. The responses "more favorable interest rates" and "more flexible repayment schedule" could very well indicate an inability to obtain bank-loans with normal conditions.

3.5 Assessment of regulatory constraints

The overview of the transition process in Section 3.2 indicated that most of the necessary institutional change has been completed. Table 3.18 confirms this view. This table reveals the responses when managers were asked to assess the relevance of various types of remaining regulation. Regulations of no relevance are given the figure one while those of very high relevance are given the figure five. All categories of regulation in Table 3.18 were felt to be of no or little relevance already in 1994. Thereafter the relevance of regulation has declined even further. Only capital requirements were felt to be of more relevance in 1996 than in 1994. These requirements refer either to a minimum equity investment in a limited liability firm or to restrictions on ownership in the privatization process.

Perceived restrictions on business activity are shown in Table 3.19. The listed restrictions are in many cases described in a more general way than by a specific type of regulation. The assessment scale is the same as in Table 3.18 with a one for "no relevance" and a five for "very high relevance".

The restrictions mentioned in Table 3.19 are perceived to be more serious than the regulations in Table 3.18. In particular "obtainability of credits" was perceived to be relevant or very relevant each of the three years. Among restrictions related to financial markets "ownership regulations" were felt to be of some - but little - relevance. More relevant were "taxes", "getting investment facilities", and "lack of demand for output".

"Obtainability of credits" was the most relevant restriction in 1995 but its relevance declined substantially in 1996. These perceptions are consistent with the data for sources of financing presented above. Formal loans financed on the average only 11.2 percent of total assets in 1995. This figure increased to 24.6 percent in 1996.

TABLE 3.18
Average assessment of relevance of various regulations
5 = very high relevance; 1 = no relevance

Regulations/Restrictions	1994	1995	1996
Domestic finance restrictions	2.2	1.7	1.6
Earnings repatriation restrictions	2.0	1.5	1.2
Restrictions on main activities	1.7	1.5	1.5
Capital requirements	1.7	1.5	1.9
Exchange restrictions on business travels	1.7	1.3	1.2
Foreign loan restrictions	1.7	1.9	1.5
Restrictions on technology licenses and royalties	1.6	1.2	1.3
Joint venture restrictions	1.3	1.0	1.0
Restrictions on payment of salaries to non-residents	1.2	1.6	1.4

It is not very surprising to find that taxes and lack of demand are considered relevant restrictions for many firms. More serious is the finding that "getting investment facilities" is considered a hindrance. This response indicates that firms face problems buying or renting locations and buildings for business activity. Such problems may be caused by imperfections in the market for real property caused by the still unsettled property rights to land.

The list of suggested restrictions in the interviews includes labor regulation, price controls, and license requirements. These restrictions were found to be nearly irrelevant, as they should after a successful liberalization process.

TABLE 3.19
Average assessment of relevance of regulations
affecting firms' expansion decisions
5 = very high relevance; 1 = no relevance

Regulations/Restrictions	1994	1995	1996
Obtainability of credits	3.5	4.2	3.1
Taxes	3.0	4.1	3.5
Getting investment facilities	3.7	3.4	3.7
Prices of public services	2.2	2.5	2.3
Lack of demand for output	3.1	2.4	2.9
Infrastructure and location problems	1.4	2.2	2.1
Ownership regulations	2.2	2.1	1.8
Competition with imports	2.9	2.0	2.4
Lack of business support services	2.6	1.9	1.8
Labor regulations	1.7	1.5	1.6
Price controls	1.6	1.5	1.14
Getting licenses	1.5	1.5	1.5
Restrictions on main activities	1.3	1.3	1.3
Exchange controls	1.3	1.1	1.05

3.6 Firm characteristics, investments and financing

In order to analyze determinants of access to different sources of financing, and financial constraints on investment activity two kinds of more formal tests were performed. First, probit analysis of firms being investors, borrowers in banks, receivers of trade credits, and lenders by advance payments could shed light on factors that determine access to financing. Second, regression analysis of the investments to asset ratio, the share of formal loans in the financing, and the trade credits to asset ratio is employed to explain the variation in investments among firms that invested during the previous year, and the importance of different sources of financing given access to these sources.

TABLE 3.20

Probit analysis of firms being investor, being a borrower in a bank, obtaining trade credits, and paying in advance

a) Investor

	1995		1996
Debt/Total assets	0.560 (1.93)	Exporter	0.248 (1.93)
Labor regulations	-0.445 (-3.20)	License problems	-0.342 (-1.89)
Number of disputes	-0.0008 (-2.53)	License time	0.0071 (1.68)
Managing director shares	-0.0033 (-1.64)	Financial assets	0.354 (2.42)
$R^2 = 0.392$, F = 5.29		$R^2 = 0.476$, F = 6.78	

b) Borrower in a bank

	1995		1996
Debt/Total assets	0.340 (2.0)	Debt/Total assets	0.717 (2.61)
Collateral/Total assets	0.815 (1.56)	Collateral/Total assets	0.746 (3.12)
License problems	-0.427 (-2.37)	Bankruptcy problems	0.226 (1.86)
Financial assets	0.221 (1.84)	Number of disputes	0.0017 (1.71)
Business support services	0.324 (2.16)		
$R^2 = 0.332$, F = 4.07		$R^2 = 0.524$, F = 8.01	

TABLE 3.20 (concluded)

c) Obtaining trade credits

	1995		1996
Exporter	0.350 (2.05)		
Financial assets	-0.291 (-1.21)	Capital/Total assets	0.386 (1.68)
Number of disputes	-0.00065 (-2.16)	Business support services	0.460 (2.51)
$R^2 = 0.278$, F = 2.15			$R^2 = 0.392$, F = 5.15

d) Paying in advance

	1995		1996
Product diversification	-0.205 (-1.83)	Inventories/Total assets	0.764 (2.01)
Labor regulation	0.195 (1.39)	Bankruptcy problems	0.198 (1.76)
Business support services	0.173 (1.23)		
$R^2 = 0.238$, F = 2.09			$R^2 = 0.311$, F = 4.08

V. Vensel and C. Wihlborg

TABLE 3.21

Explaining investments, formal loans, and trade credits in regression analysis:
Observations include firms that have obtained particular type of financing
or invested in the previous year.

a) Investments/Total assets

1995		1996	
Capital/Total assets	0.234 (2.92)	Profits/Total assets	0.297 (1.8)
Well-educated staff	0.384 (1.74)	Financial assets	0.101 (2.1)
Number of disputes	-0.00012 (-.50)	Managing director shares	-0.00107 (-1.7)
$R^2 = 0.347$, F = 4.10		$R^2 = 0.337$, F = 4.16	

b) Formal loans/Total assets

1995		1996	
Profits/Total assets	-0.208 (-1.89)	No sign level < 10 %	
Debt/Total assets	0.270 (2.25)		
Foreign owner	0.076 (1.52)		
$R^2 = 0.387$, F = 4.21			

TABLE 3.21 (concluded)

c) Trade Credits/Total assets

1995		1996	
Demand problems	-0.086 (-2.15)	Demand Problems	-0.126 (-1.8)
Capital/Total assets	-0.170 (-2.12)	Capital/Total Assets	-0.402 (-2.0)
Joint Stock Co	0.072 (1.44)	Business Support Services	0.177 (1.9)
Foreign owner	0.089 (1.68)		
$R^2 = 0.319$, F = 3.74		$R^2 = 0.321$, F = 4.07	

Tables 3.20 and 3.21 show the results of the two types of tests with a restricted set of variables. The variables are chosen because each was significantly correlated with one of the mentioned dependent variables.

A major constraint on the use of formal tests is the number of firms in the sample. The number of observations falls in the regressions, because only firms that actually invest, borrow in a bank, etc. are included. Nevertheless, we proceed to present the results in Tables 3.20 and 3.21.

The independent variables capture or proxy for aspects of riskiness of the firms and information availability.[4] Many variables qualifying for inclusion may be related to the dependent variables by balance sheet identities or for reasons unrelated to financial considerations. This must be born in mind when results are interpreted.

Our fears that results may be difficult to interpret proved to have some foundation. The results presented in Tables 3.20 and 3.21 shed only marginal insight on the issue. We focus below on a few interesting results in the two tables.

Financial assets

A firm with financial assets on the balance sheet was more likely to be a borrower in a bank (Table 3.20, panel b) and less likely to be a receiver of trade credits in 1995 (Table 3.20, panel c). In 1996 the firms with financial assets were more likely to have invested (Table 3.20, panel a) and this contributes in explaining the size of investments (Table 3.21, panel a).

The firm with financial assets may be seen as a relatively less risky and less financially constrained firm. The positive relation with bank-borrowing and the negative relation with trade credits is the only result indicating a degree of substitutability between these forms of financing. The positive relation with investments in 1996 may indicate that financial constraints affect investments.

Foreign owner, exporter, limited liability company

The variables listed are likely to be characteristics of relatively well-known and established firms. One of these variables have a positive relation with being a receiver of trade credits (Table 3.20, panel c), the ratio of formal loans to assets (Table 3.21, panel b), and the ratio of trade credits to total assets (Table 3.21, panel c) in 1995. Being an exporter also contributes to the probability of investments in 1996 (Table 3.20, panel a).

Managing director shares

It would be expected that managers' incentives would be better aligned with shareholders' objectives, when managers own shares in the firm. It is therefore surprising to find that increasing shareholdings of managers (as percent of total equity) are associated with a lower probability of being an investor in 1995, and with less investments relative to assets in 1996. It is possible that the shareholdings have contributed to managerial risk-aversion.

Regulatory and legal variables

We include labor regulation, license problems, license time, and bankruptcy problems among variables indicating regulatory or legal hindrances for business activity.[5]One of these variables are negatively related to being an investor in 1995 and 1996 (Table 3.20, panel a), being a borrower in a bank in 1995 (Table 3.20, panel b), and positively related to being an advance payer in 1995 and 1996 (Table 3.20, panel c). The impression that regulatory and legal hindrances affect investments and financing negatively is somewhat weakened by the license time - and the bankruptcy variables (Table 3.20, panels a and b). The positive coefficients for these variables are smaller than the negative coefficients for another regulatory variable in the same panel, however.

The variable "Business support services" is one for firms that have received such support. This variable appears positively in a number of panels both years including the one for firms paying in advance. Thus, the services seem to have had a positive impact on both investments and the relaxation of financial constraints.

The variable "Number of disputes", showing that a firm has had disputes about receiving payments, may also be considered a legal variable, because many firms have indicated that the court system is weak in helping with enforcement. A high number of disputes is negatively related to being an investor in 1995 (Table 3.20, panel a), being a receiver of trade credits in 1995 (Table 3.20, panel c), and the ratio of investments to assets in 1995 (Table 3.21, panel a). The variable is positively related to being a borrower in a bank in 1996, however (Table 3.20, panel b).

The overall impression of this group of variables is that managers' perceptions about regulation and imperfections in the legal system have had a negative effect on both investments, and access to sources of financing. Thus, it seems that regulatory and legal constraints on business activity remains in spite of the fast progress of the liberalization process described in Table 3.1.

The results for regulatory and legal variables do not generally indicate a substitutability among different kinds of financing. On the contrary, this group of variables appears as having a negative impact on both investment activity and access to financing.

3.7 Summary and conclusions

Managers responding that lack of finance is a constraint on firms' activities do not prove that a country's financial system is inefficient. It is to be expected that many managers consider their projects worthwile and that they seek financing for negative value projects at the market rate. The low level of debt in the capital structure of firms in Estonia does not prove that banks lend too little. It is very likely that the average investment project in an emerging market economy like Estonia has a greater probability of failure than the average project in an industrialized, western economy.

There are indications that the financial system is undersupplying financial resources to firms. One such indication is that firms holding financial assets showed a higher likelihood of being an investor and a borrower in a bank. More financial assets were also associated with larger investments in 1996. The undersupply need not imply that the Estonian banks perform worse than western banks, but it could be the result of an undeveloped legal system. The court system's ability to enforce contractual promises of payments seems to be weak, and bankruptcy procedures in law cannot be enforced within a reasonable time-period. The high value of collateral relative to loan size for small firms could be an indication of weak enforcement. The financing of entrepreneurs is also made difficult by the yet unsettled private claims on former state property. As a result only about five percent of the small firms' assets were financed by formal loans in 1996. This debt was held by about one half of the small firms in the sample indicating that formal loans to small firms were quite small relative to firms' assets. Our results with respect to bank loans and collateral are consistent with those presented in Scheinberg and Lundberg (1994) who conducted a more informal survey of financing in Estonia.

It was noted that informal loans from other sources rather than relatives and friends are likely to be understated. Nevertheless, almost one third of the firms seemed to have had some form of informal start-up financing, and in 1995 informal loans financed investments to a non-negligible extent. The order of magnitude was around 10 percent in 1995 and substantially smaller in 1996. The general impression is that many firms have borrowed informally but that the share of these loans in total financing is quite small.

The supply of bank loans seemed to improve during our sample period. The number of firms borrowing in banks and the share of formal loans in the financial structure increased from 1995 to 1996. Large firms in particular increased their formal loans. This increase had a spill-over effect on smaller firms in two ways. First, large firms reduced their trade credit financing. Second, they reduced their receipts of payments in advance. Thus, although it does not seem as if trade credits and advance payments to small firms from larger firms substitute for bank-loans, greater access to loans for large firms can relax the financial burden of small firms having to provide trade credits and to pay in advance.

A final observation is that Estonia does not seem to differ much from most countries, including western industrialized countries, with respect to financing of entrepreneurship. Own savings is the primary source of an entrepreneur's start-up financing with some help from family and friends. Swanson and Webster (1992) have noted this for western countries and the data here, as well as the data in Scheinberg and Lundberg (1994), confirm it for Estonia. Webster and Charap (1993) found that loans from suppliers was a frequent source of financing in Russia but not in Poland, Hungary and the Czech Republic. In Estonia we found that suppliers' financing of investments was important in 1995 but less so in 1996.

Notes

This research has been supported by the European Commission's Phare/ACE Programme 1994 under contract number 94-0685R entitled "Coping with Financial Reforms in EMEs: Analytical Tools, Policy Implications, and Case Studies of Estonia and Poland". Support from the Royal Swedish Academy of Sciences, as well as Göteborg University the Estonian Science Foundation, is also gratefully acknowledged. We want to thank Aita Tammeraid and Asta Teearu for their active and invaluable participation in conducting and interpreting the responses to interviews.

1. Few of the 600,000 ethnic Russians seem to be in opposition to the reforms.
2. This description is based on Vensel (1996).

3. See Eesti Pank (1997) pp 44 and 66.
4. See Vensel and Wihlborg (1995).
5. Labor regulation =1 for firms indicating that such regulation has strong or very strong relevance. License problems = 1 for firms indicating that license requirements have strong or very strong relevance. License time = no of days it takes to obtain relevant licenses. Bankruptcy problems = 1 for firms indicating that there are significant regulations on bankruptcy procedures or on selling the firm.

References

Begg, D. and Portes, R., 1993, Enterprise debt and economic transformation: financial restructuring in Central and eastern Europe in: Mayer, C. and X. Vives (eds), Capital Markets and Financial Intermediation, (Cambridge University Press, Cambridge).

Calvo, G. A. and F. Coricelli, 1993, Output Collapse in Eastern Europe: The Role of Credit, IMF Staff Papers, 40, 1, pp. 32-51.

Eesti, Pank (1997), Annual Report 1996 (The Bank of Estonia, Tallinn).

Eliasson, G., T. Rybczynski, and C. Wihlborg, 1993, The Necessary Institutional Framework to Transform Formerly Planned Economies (IUI Industrial Institute for Economic Research, Stockholm).

Funck, R., T. Kowalski, and L. Zienkowski, 1995, The Role of Small and Medium Enterprises in the Restructuring of the Polish Regions (Nomos Verlag, Baden-Baden).

Genco, P., S. Taurello, and C. Viezzoli, 1993, Private investments in Central and Eastern Europe: Survey results, The European Bank for Reconstruction and Development, Working Paper No 7, London.

Griffith-Jones, S. and Z. Drabek, 1994, Financial Sector Reform in Central and Eastern Europe, (MacMillan Publishers, London).

Hillman, A.L., 1994, The transition from socialism: an overview from a political economy perspective, European Journal of Political Economy, 10, pp. 191-225.

Phelps, E., R. Frydman, G. Rapuczynski, and A. Shleifer, 1993, Needed mechanisms of corporate governance and finance in Eastern Europe, The European Bank for Reconstruction and Development, Working Paper No 1, London.

Portes, R., 1994, Transformation traps, Economic Journal 104, September pp. 1178-1189.

Rojec, M. and P. Artisien, 1995, Foreign Investment in Slovenia (MacMillan Publishers, London).

Scheinberg, S. and H. Lundberg, 1994, The role and flow of capital in Estonian and Russian companies, Working Paper No 2, Center for Russian and East European Studies, Göteborg University, Göteborg.

Swanson, G. and L. Webster, 1992, Private sector manufacturing in Czech and Slovak Federal Republic: A survey of firms, The World Bank, Industry and Energy Department, Industry Series Working Paper No 67, Washington DC.

Tammeraid, A., A. Teearu, and V. Vensel, 1996, Results of firms interview study about the development of financial relationships, Tallinn Technical University Working Paper in Economics, TTUWPE (BFE) No. 96/8, Tallinn.

Webster, L. and J. Charap, 1993, A survey of private manufacturers in St Petersburg, The European Bank for Reconstruction and Development, Working Paper No. 5, London.

Vensel, V. 1996, Results of Estonian banks performance analysis, Tallinn Technical University Working Paper in Economics, TTUWPE (BFE), No. 96/9.

Vensel, V. and C. Wihlborg, 1995, Financial contractual relations in Estonia, presented at conference on Microlevel Studies of Transition in the Baltic States, mimeo, Stockholm School of Economics, Riga.

Financial Sector Reform and
Privatization in Transition Economies
J. Doukas, V. Murinde and C. Wihlborg (Editors)
© 1997 Elsevier Science Publishers B.V. All rights reserved

Chapter 4 /ξ, ξ∪ ∿ぇ |

STRATEGIES TO DEVELOP MORTGAGE MARKETS IN TRANSITION ECONOMIES

Dwight M. Jaffee
Haas School of Business, University of California,
Berkeley, CA 94720-1900, USA

Bertrand Renaud
The World Bank, 1818 H Street, N.W.,
Washington DC, 20433, USA

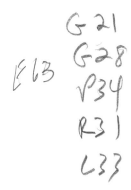

4.1 Introduction

The transformation of the planned economies of central and eastern Europe to market economies has focused on three key processes:
1) economic stabilization and liberalization,
2) privatization,
3) financial sector development.

The housing sector and its financial dimension, the mortgage market, have been a factor in each of these processes, although, sad to say, not always a positive one.

The housing sector has not contributed to *economic stabilization*, since new housing construction in most transition economies has plummeted since 1988, as shown in Figure 4.1. Even if we take into account the statistical under-reporting problems for private investment activities in housing rehabilitation, it is undeniable that the withdrawal of the state from direct housing production has led to a precipitous fall in annual output. The housing sector has also lagged in terms of *economic liberalization*, since house rents continue to be among the most regulated prices in the transition economies, although some rent controls appear in many economies.[1]

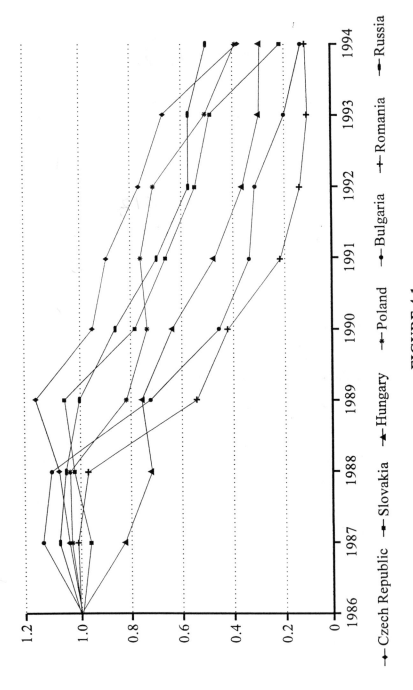

FIGURE 4.1
Collapsing output of completed dwellings

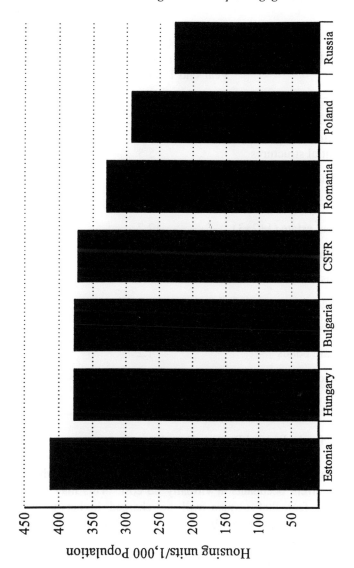

FIGURE 4.2
Housing stock in transition countries, 1991

Source: UN-ECE, Annual Bulletin of Housing and Building Statistics, November 1994

TABLE 4.1
U.S. tangible capital assets and debt instruments,
Year-end 1993

		$ Trillion	Percent
	Tangible capital assets		
1	Residential structures	5.5	29
2	Non-residential structures	3.0	16
3	Land	4.2	23
4	Total real estate (1+2+3)	12.7	68
5	Total tangible capital	18.7	100
	Debt instruments		
6	Mortgages	4.2	34
7	U.S. Government	3.4	27
8	Corporate bonds	1.2	10
9	State and local government	1.2	10
10	Total debt	12.4	100

Source: Flow of funds, Federal Reserve Board

Housing *privatization* has also been painfully slow, even when it is available to the current occupants at virtually no cost. This may reflect, at least in part, the fear that owners will be charged higher utility and maintenance costs than are renters. In any case, this slows down the overall process of privatization since housing generally represents a large part of any country's tangible capital. In the United States, for example, residential structures (excluding land) represent almost 30 percent of all tangible capital, and all real estate (including land) represents almost 70 percent of all tangible capital (see Table 4.1). These ratios may be somewhat lower for the transition economies, but not by a large margin. This is illustrated in Figures 4.2 and 4.3, which show the number of housing structures per 1000 population for groups of transition and developed economies respectively.

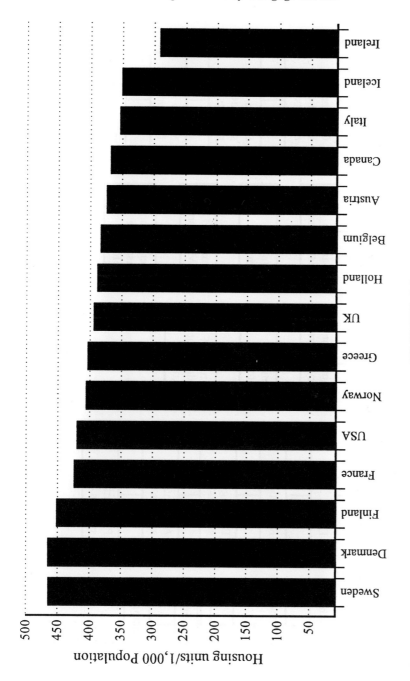

FIGURE 4.3

Housing stock in developed countries, 1990

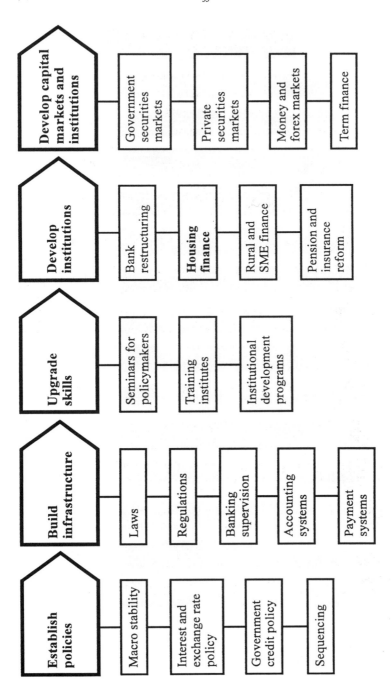

FIGURE 4.4

A framework for sustainable financial development

In terms of *financial sector development,* housing finance has remained in a primitive state compared to the rapid development of banking. This is particularly striking because, in most developed countries, the *mortgage market* (meaning the market for financing real estate assets) is among the largest components of the capital markets. In the United States, for example, mortgage debt is the largest component of the domestic debt markets (see Table 4.1).

Mortgage market development is likely to be a key factor in overall financial market development. In particular, an efficient mortgage market will act as a positive externality for the other capital markets, creating pressure for higher efficiency in these markets. On the other hand, a poorly functioning mortgage market is likely to "pollute" other financial markets with its inefficiency. For example, governments are likely to "support" inefficient mortgage markets with subsidies and regulations, which then act as implicit taxes and constraints on the rest of the capital markets. In fact, controlling the proliferation of quasi-fiscal subsidies is a generic problem of transition economies.

Our primary goal in this paper is to analyze the problems that are inhibiting the development of viable housing finance systems in transition economies and to draw relevant policy conclusions. Figure 4.4 shows graphically that housing finance is just one part of a much larger program for developing sustainable financial sectors in the transition economies. We shall refer to other components of the financial system in our discussion of housing finance.

The rapid development of the banking sector in most transition economies raises an immediate question, namely why the banks in the transition economies have failed to take the lead in developing a housing finance system. We deal with this question in Section 4.2, focusing on a series of risks (credit, interest rate, and liquidity) that have constrained the ability of transition economy banks to develop housing finance systems

The slow development of mortgage markets in transition economies indicates the need to create a coherent housing finance strategy. In Section 4.3, we first approach this topic by evaluating the housing finance systems used in the developed economies. We contrast the two primary systems that are observed: depository institutions acting as portfolio lenders and secondary market systems. We further analyze the alternative versions of secondary market systems.

In Section 4.4, we evaluate the likely efficacy for the transition economies of the alternative systems used in developed economies. Our conclusions favor secondary mortgage markets as the key instrument to eliminate the constraints that have slowed the development of housing finance systems. Secondary markets confer two main benefits. First, banks can shed the risks associated with holding mortgage loans by selling the loans to other investors through the secondary market. Second, secondary markets create standards for credit evaluation and collateral procedures that directly increase the efficiency of the primary markets for new mortgage originations. Although this paper focuses on the development of secondary mortgage markets, fundamental changes are also required to develop the primary mortgage markets in the transition economies (see World Bank (1995) for a discussion of primary mortgage markets in Russia).

In Section 4.5, we summarize our conclusions.

4.2   Banking and housing finance in transition economies

We have seen that the rate of new housing construction in most transition economies has plummeted since 1988. This could suggest that the failure to develop housing finance systems has been the result of little demand for mortgage loans to finance new construction. The same transition economies, however, have a pent-up demand to exchange existing residential structures, either to match housing locations with job locations or for family life-cycle reasons. Such trading of existing structures generally creates a large demand for housing finance. Furthermore, the low levels of new housing construction and the value of a housing asset as an inflation hedge have raised the excess demand for housing (housing shortages), thereby creating an excess demand for housing finance. In short, there is ample demand for housing finance in the transition economies. Therefore, the source of the failure to develop housing finance systems can be reasonably associated with supply side lenders, primarily the commercial banks.

We now consider a series of risks that are directly tied to the reluctance of banks to make housing finance loans. In all economies, long-term housing loans create significant credit, interest rate, and liquidity risks for bank management. In the transition economies, volatile inflation and the political pressures to control interest rates have expanded these risks even further. The financial instruments and markets that are used to manage these risks in the developed economies are just now beginning to function properly in the group of advanced reformers. The lack of credit evaluation skills and inadequate capital are other constraints to mortgage lending that are only slowly being resolved. We now look at these factors individually.

Credit risk

In developed mortgage markets, credit risk (that is, the risk of default) on a real estate loan is usually measured by two ratios, with a lower value of either ratio indicating less credit risk:

- The loan to value ratio is the ratio of the loan amount to the property value.
- The payment to income ratio is the ratio of the annual mortgage payment (including payments for insurance, property taxes, and the like) to the borrower's annual income.

Loan to value ratios

The loan to value ratio is generally considered the more basic determinant of credit risk because, as long as the loan amount is less than the property value, the lender can always recover the loan principal by taking over the property and selling it. In transition economies, however, this is unlikely to be the case for two reasons. First, the property rights and foreclosure procedures that are needed for real estate to function as loan collateral are not well established in the legal and institutional structures of the transition economies. Second, accurate methods for estimating property values in transition economies are just now being developed, and this is made even more difficult by the inflationary conditions in many of these countries.

Real estate property rights

In most transition economies, property laws had to be rewritten to recreate the concept of real estate. Privately managing the bundle of land and building rights that constitute real estate property in a market economy is still a new way of operating. The requirements of residential and business real estate development often remain poorly understood or accepted by central and city administrations. In Russia, in particular, it is proving politically very difficult to develop the concept of private land ownership and to accept the trading of land and the emergence of land markets.[2] The privatization of the housing stock is also incomplete. Apartments units can be privatized, but in the absence of condominium laws and the creation of

condominium associations, the financing and maintenance by residents of
the public space and the networks within the buildings is inadequate.
Another frequent problem was, and still is, that land property boundaries
were not drawn up and recorded at the time of construction under the state
system. They now need to be defined and accepted by parties often
suspicious of each other.

Secured lending and real estate

In all transition economies, the weak environment for secured lending
affects all types of loans, including loans to small and medium sized
enterprises. Loans secured by real estate lending suffer especially from the
legacy of poor land titling. Even in countries with a tradition of high quality
registration, like east Germany, "land books" were no longer properly
maintained during the socialist era. Stable and sound land use systems are
emerging in a painfully slow way from the legacy of the state urban
planning. Old urban plans and old urban cadres constrain the entire property
sector and therefore all forms of physical investment. Incomplete and
untested collateral and foreclosures laws create large credit risks for lenders.
Alternative forms of collateral lending that differ from the usual Western
foreclosure practices may therefore be useful.

Payment to income ratios

In the absence of real estate as a source of dependable collateral, payment
to income ratios become a more critical determinant of credit risk. In the
transition economies, however, the payment to income ratio is also unlikely
to provide lenders with dependable protection against loan default. The
primary problem is that average income to property value ratios tend to be
an order of magnitude lower in the transition economies. Specifically, in
most developed economies, the average income to property value ratio
ranges from about 1/4 to 1/3, while in most transition economies the same
ratio tends to be 1/10 or lower. Although this is likely to be temporary,
since it is primarily the result of highly depressed income levels in the
transition economies, it makes housing loans in the transition economies
extremely risky in the early years of reform. Furthermore, the difficulty of
verifying income--due to significant underground economic activity and the
absence of credit bureaus--increases credit risks and leads to credit rationing
on the part of the banks that cannot properly address that particular

information asymmetry.

Interest rate risk

In developed economies, housing finance lenders are sometimes short funded, meaning that the maturity (or duration) of their mortgage assets exceeds the maturity of their funding sources (such as bank deposits). This occurs because mortgage borrowers generally wish to match their durable housing assets with long-term mortgage loans, while depositors prefer the liquidity of short-term investments. The short funding creates an interest rate risk for the lenders, since an increase in market interest rates raises the cost of deposits without immediately raising the return on the mortgage assets. The interest rate risk can be hedged using capital market instruments, but they have a high cost, approximately equal to the difference between short-term and long- term interest rates. Alternatively, the interest rate risk can be controlled by using adjustable-rate or floating-rate mortgages, but these instruments only displace the interest rate risk to the borrower.

In the transition economies, capital market instruments are unlikely to be available to hedge the interest rate risk, so floating-rate mortgages will be the norm. This means that borrowers face the interest rate risk, which increases their likelihood of loan default. In other words, floating-rate mortgages tend to transform the banks' interest rate risk into credit risk, not necessarily a significant improvement. Furthermore, real interest rates (nominal interest rates minus the expected inflation rates) have been high (often in excess of 15 percent) and volatile in the transition economies, further raising the credit risk on adjustable-rate mortgages.

In fact, price-level indexed mortgages, which contractually set a fixed real interest rate for the mortgage, offer a potentially better solution for controlling both interest rate and credit risk in the transition economies. There are also hybrid instruments, such as the dual interest rate mortgage (DIM) used in Mexico, which create variable, real-rate, mortgages. However, these mortgages remain relatively complex instruments, and therefore are likely to be difficult to introduce in an otherwise under-developed housing finance system.

Liquidity risk

The depositors in transition economies are likely to value liquidity--meaning the ability to convert deposits rapidly to cash--reflecting the high risks associated with the macroeconomy, individual banks, and the consumer's individual needs for funds. The banks must therefore anticipate large and unexpected deposit outflows, which require that assets be rapidly sold to finance the deposit outflows. Government securities are good assets for this purpose, since they trade in active and liquid markets and their prices are accurately determined. Business loans are more difficult to sell, but their short-term maturities make them essentially self-liquidating. Mortgages do not have short-term maturities and they do not easily trade in secondary markets (because buyers find it costly to verify the credit quality of each mortgage offered for sale). Taking these factors together, mortgages create significant liquidity risks for lenders.

4.3   Efficient mortgage markets in developed economies

Efficient mortgage markets require that the lending risks--credit, interest-rate, and liquidity--be allocated to the long-term investors who are best able to handle them.   Many alternative systems have been used, reflecting different economic conditions and attitudes toward risk. For example, the late 19th century saw the development of what we call the mortgage credit institute (MCI), created throughout Europe and most common in Northern Europe.[3] The structure of these banks reflected the tradeoff between credit risk on one hand and interest rate and liquidity risk on the other hand. Its German version (the Hypothenken Bank), for example, minimized credit risk by making mortgage loans with loan to value ratios below 60 percent. Although this reduced the credit risk faced by the bank, it forced the borrowers to delay their first home purchase until they had accumulated the substantial equity required for the downpayment.

In the United States and England, until recently, most home loans have been made by depository institutions, including commercial banks, Savings and Loan Associations in the United States, and Building Societies in England. How the various risks are shared between the lender and borrower then depends on the particular form of the mortgage instrument.   For example, in the United States during the Great Depression of the 1930s, many borrowers suffered the unexpected loss of their homes when lenders suddenly stopped renewing short-term mortgage loans. On the other hand, in the United States during the early 1980s, the Savings and Loan Associations (S&Ls) suffered massive losses and many of the institutions ultimately failed when interest rates rose unexpectedly while the institutions were following a short funding strategy using fixed-rate mortgages.

A key advantage of the depository institution system is that three distinct mortgage market functions can be vertically integrated within the depository institution:

- *Mortgage origination* is the process through which mortgage debt is created, comparable to the underwriting function for other capital market securities.[4]

- *Mortgage holding* refers to the activity of institutions and other investors who own or hold mortgage debt. When the mortgage originator and the mortgage holder differ, it is necessary to transfer mortgage ownership. The high risk, high information costs, and small size of individual mortgages complicate the mortgage transfer process.

- *Mortgage servicing* refers to a series of activities, including (1) collecting the monthly payments from the borrowers and transmitting the funds to the holders, (2) confirming that the borrower maintains property insurance and pays property taxes, and (3) carrying out the foreclosure process in cases of default.

The last 30 years, however, have seen a trend toward separating or unbundling these mortgage market functions. The new developments can be described as secondary market systems, in which mortgages are originated by one agent (a depository institution or specialized mortgage originator), but are then transferred to a capital market institution or other investor who serves as the final holder. In many European countries, the final holder is a mortgage credit institution, which issues its own debt. In the United States, there are two government sponsored agencies--Federal National Mortgage Association (FNMA, or Fannie Mae) and Federal Home Loan Mortgage Corporation (FHLMC, or Freddie Mac)--which purchase mortgages directly from originators. Another government agency, the Federal Home Loan Banks, lends funds to mortgage originators.

Criteria for evaluating efficient mortgage market systems

The most basic indicator for evaluating alternative structures is the borrower's "all-in" cost. The all-in borrowing cost incorporates both the direct interest rate and the costs associated with the non-price terms of the mortgage instrument such as maturity, floating interest rates, downpayment requirements, and credit availability.   In principle, each of the three mortgage functions--origination, holding, and servicing--can have an independent impact on the borrowing cost.   In practice, however, the holding function is the primary economic factor, since the mortgage holder can then choose the most efficient institutions for administering the mortgage origination and servicing activities.

The all-in borrowing cost also includes the government's cost of guaranteeing or otherwise administering the housing finance system. For example, under the depository institution system, some of the government's costs associated with safeguarding deposits should be included in the all-in costs of the housing finance system. Under a secondary market system, the same is true for the government's cost of providing credit guarantees on mortgage instruments and/or the liabilities of the mortgage holding institutions. The government may try, of course, to deny responsibility for the housing finance system's credit risks, but this is rarely successful.

We now apply the all-in borrowing cost criteria to alternative mortgage systems.[5]

Depository "portfolio lenders"

Depository institutions acting as portfolio lenders have three key advantages as the central source of funds for mortgage lending. First, the interest rates on deposits tend to be among the lowest in an economy, reflecting the "retail" nature of this source of funds.   Second, by integrating all the mortgage functions--origination, holding, and servicing--in a single institution, the depository system avoids the costs of transferring mortgages to other holders, an efficiency of vertical integration.   Third, retail lenders may have informational advantages in extending credit to households who are also customers for other banking services.

Factors raising the all-in costs of depository lenders A closer examination of these advantages of the depository system reveals, however, that they may be more apparent than real. First, the all-in cost of retail deposits must include the costs of hedging the interest rate risks that result from a short funding strategy.[6] The all-in cost of retail deposits should also include the institutions' costs of satisfying required capital ratios and other supervisory standards, and the government's cost of insuring retail deposits.

Second, the economies of scale in mortgage origination and servicing created by recent technological innovations in computers, communications, and information retrieval appear now to dominate the economies of vertical integration that underlie the depository system. This change is evident in the innovative unbundling of mortgage functions and activities occurring in many developed countries.

Third, depository lenders often find it more profitable to apply their credit evaluation expertise to business and consumer loans than to mortgage loans. This occurs because the more complex nature of the credit risk on business and consumer loans allows the institutions to create greater value added. In addition, the maturity of most business and consumer loans is quite short-term, so these loans do not entail the maturity mismatch discussed above for mortgages.

Specialized depository lenders The high all-in costs of mortgage lending by depository intermediaries often makes the activity unprofitable, which is the basic reason why banks often do not participate in housing finance. To deal with this, governments were often tempted to create a specialized depository group dedicated to mortgage lending. The Savings and Loan Associations (S&Ls) in the United States and the Building Societies in England are examples of this approach. To maintain their special status, these institutions were required to maintain the greater part of their assets in home mortgages. In exchange, they received tax benefits and lower capital requirements. They were also allowed to follow a short funding strategy.

Specialized lenders, however, often create as many problems as they solve. In particular, since they are not well diversified across asset categories and are likely to follow a short funding strategy, they tend to be fragile with respect to changes in the economic environment. Specialized institutions also tend to avoid competition and to lag in introducing new technologies. In the United States, for example, the sharp increase in interest rates during the early 1980s created large losses for these S&Ls, resulting in large-scale failures. Currently, regulations are being developed to transform the remaining S&Ls into commercial banks, thereby eliminating this class of specialized lenders. Comparable changes are now occurring in the British Building Societies.

Conclusions regarding commercial banks as housing finance lenders The private commercial banks in transition economies are a natural starting point to initiate a housing finance system, based on their low-cost deposits, expertise in lending, and access to retail customers.[7] In practice, however, there has been very little mortgage lending by transition economy banks, because the activity is not profitable once the all-in costs are considered. Governments could revert to a subsidized set of specialized depository lenders, but the experience in developed economies suggests this is likely to be expensive and inefficient.

Secondary mortgage market (SMM) systems

We have seen that the mortgage holding function is the strategic focus for dealing with the risks of mortgage lending. We now consider secondary mortgage markets (SMMs) as a solution for handling risk in the housing finance system. The basic principle of a SMM is to tap capital market investors as the long-term funding source for the mortgage market, thus mitigating interest rate and credit risk. Mortgages are first originated by depository institutions or other mortgage bankers[8] who are expected to have expertise in risk evaluation and underwriting new mortgage loans. The mortgages are then sold to the final investors who hold the mortgages. There are various forms for SMM systems, based on differences in the instruments used for the mortgage sale and in the type of investors or institutions who buy the mortgages.

The problems of selling existing mortgages The SMM buyer of existing mortgages faces asymmetric information in that the mortgage seller is likely to have much better information regarding the credit risk of the underlying mortgages than does the buyer. This creates the moral hazard risk that the seller may claim that the mortgages are of high quality, whereas in fact they are of low quality. Furthermore, the low quality of the mortgages may not be revealed until several years later when higher than expected default rates begin to occur. At that time, it may also be difficult to determine whether the high default rates result from low quality mortgages or simply bad luck (high default rates on high quality mortgages)[9]. As a result, most buyers of mortgages impose conditions or otherwise take actions to control these effects of asymmetric information.

One solution, for example, is for the buyer to evaluate the quality of the mortgages with the same level of diligence carried out by the mortgage originator (i.e. the mortgage seller), thereby eliminating the informational asymmetry.[10] This process, however, is cumbersome and costly, since individual mortgages are of small size relative to investor portfolios and each mortgage must be evaluated. As a result, mortgage sales are rarely based on a re-evaluation of the individual mortgages. Instead, asymmetric information is controlled through a number of devices, including underwriting standards, reputation of the seller, and credit guarantees. These are now briefly described.

Underwriting standards The SMM buyer can specify that the mortgages meet certain underwriting standards, such as maximum values for the loan to value ratio or income to payment ratio. Of course, reporting problems still make underwriting standards an imperfect solution to the asymmetric information problem. Nevertheless, in the case of unexpectedly high default rates, the buyer may be able to claim restitution by documenting a violation of the agreed upon standards.

Reputation In practice, most SMM buyers "prequalify" mortgage originators from whom they expect to purchase mortgages. If a SMM seller anticipates many transactions with a buyer, then the seller may not take advantage of his superior information in order to protect his reputation. The reliance on reputation is most effective for buyers with a dominant market position, since the sellers will anticipate future transactions and attempt to maintain a high reputation.

Credit guarantees The buyer may require that there be guarantees on the mortgages sold. When the SMM seller has a high credit rating, it can provide the credit guarantee directly. Often, however, the credit rating of the SMM seller will not be that high, and it will have to rely on external guarantees from third-parties, including the government. Such third party guarantees may apply either to the selling institution or to the individual mortgages.

Purchases by mortgage credit institutions In many developed countries, the SMM is dominated by large institutions which specialize in either purchasing mortgages or in lending funds to the institutions that hold the mortgages. Examples include the Federal National Mortgage Association (FNMA) in the United States and the Stadshypothek in Sweden. Bond issues in the capital markets are the principal funding source for the institutions. The large size of these institutions allows them to set underwriting standards and to rely on the sellers' reputations. The large scale of their bond issues and their continuing presence in the capital markets also provides liquidity benefits that result in lower interest rates. The interest rates paid by these institutions are generally very close to the rates on government securities of the same maturity, reflecting little or no risk premium, either because the MCI has successfully insulated itself from mortgage credit risks that remain with primary lenders and provides good credit enhancements, or more often because investors treat the bonds as if they had an implicit government guarantee. The basis for this belief is either that the government would not allow a primary component of the mortgage market to fail and/or that the institution is too large a component of the overall financial markets to be allowed to fail.

The FNMA institution of the United States provides a useful case study for how such institutions are created and the role they play in the mortgage market. FNMA was started as a government agency to create a secondary mortgage market, meaning that it was to provide liquidity by standing ready to buy and sell mortgages. In practice, FNMA primarily bought mortgages, accumulating a large and profitable portfolio (given its low cost of borrowing). At a later date, FNMA was reorganized as a stockholder-owned corporation, although the government retained some control. Most recently, FNMA has served, in addition, as a conduit for securitized mortgages (see discussion below). Another secondary market institution, the Federal Home Loan Mortgage Corporation (commonly called Freddie Mac), operates in a very similar fashion. The government imposes capital ratios on both institutions, although the requirements are approximately one-half those imposed on commercial banks. The two institutions dominate those parts of the mortgage market in which they are allowed to operate.

A recent paper by Hermalin and Jaffee (1996) evaluates the implicit U.S. government guarantee of FNMA and Freddie Mac (F&F) debt and carries out a welfare analysis of the effects of removing the guarantee. The evidence suggests that the implicit government guarantee creates an interest cost saving on the order of 50 basis points, which appears to be shared between F&F shareholders and the country's mortgage borrowers. The country's taxpayers, however, bear the cost of the F&F subsidy, in the form of incrementally higher government borrowing costs and the potential costs of a F&F bailout. Overall, Hermalin and Jaffee conclude that a removal of the implicit government guarantee would be welfare enhancing, although it remains an open question whether the government could credibly shed its implicit guarantee given the importance of F&F in both the mortgage market and the overall capital markets.[11]

Loans by mortgage credit institutions (MCIs) MCIs can also support the mortgage market by lending funds to depository institutions who then hold the mortgages. The Federal Home Loan Banks (FHLBs) in the United States and the Caisse de Refinancement Hypothécaire (CRH) in France operate in exactly this manner. Under this system, the MCI bears the risk of bankruptcy of the institution to which it makes the loans, but bears no direct risk with regard to the mortgages held by the institution. In practice, however, the MCI will generally hold mortgages of the borrowing institution as collateral to back its loans, so that the MCI will suffer losses only as a result of the default risk on the mortgages held as collateral. The overall effect on the mortgage market are likely to be very similar whether the MCIs buy the mortgages or advances loans to another institution to hold the mortgages, although the precise form of the risk borne by the MCI is potentially different.

Mortgage securitization Mortgage securitization, a third form for the SMM, has developed very rapidly in the United States and is used occasionally in Europe. The process begins with the MCI purchasing mortgages from an originator in the same manner described above. The purchased mortgages are then combined to form a mortgage pool and prorated shares in the cash flow of the mortgage pool are sold to investors as mortgage securities. The mortgage pool and the mortgage securities are thus directly linked, and neither appears on the balance sheet of the MCI.

In the traditional mortgage purchase model described above, in contrast, the purchased mortgages and the issued bonds both appear on the MCI's balance sheet. This difference is less important than it may appear, however, since under the securitization system the MCI continues to guarantee the mortgage securities against losses created by defaults on the underlying mortgages. A more important difference is that unexpected timing variations in the cash flow from the mortgage pool, created by early repayments on the mortgages, are passed through to the mortgage security investors, whereas they are not when the MCI issues regular bonds. A more detailed discussion of mortgage securitization is provided in Jaffee and Renaud (1995). We shall not discuss mortgage securitization further in this paper, because the refinements offered by mortgage securitization are unlikely to be relevant in the context of the transition economies.

4.4   Secondary mortgage markets in transition economies

SMMs can aid the development of a housing finance system in a transition economy by removing the risks of holding mortgages from the commercial banks or others who originate the mortgages. In this section, we discuss the principles that should be applied in organizing the SMM and the issues that are likely to arise in the process. We take as the basic format a single MCI that will purchase mortgages from the institutions originating the mortgages, although we also discuss alternative frameworks. The funding source of the MCI would be bonds of various maturities issued in the capital markets.

The essential role for government in organizing a secondary mortgage market

The question can be asked, if a SMM helps create an efficient housing finance system, then why do the private commercial banks not create the MCI themselves. The short answer is that the MCI must have a high enough credit rating to issue bonds in the capital markets, and B rated commercial banks basically cannot create A rated MCIs. Furthermore, the MCI requires stature and size to set standards for the entire mortgage market, and it is difficult for private market institutions to cooperate in order to cover the large initial costs required to set up such an institution. In particular, a fully private MCI would likely be initially too small to achieve the liquidity benefits that arise from issuing large amounts of securities on a continuing basis.

A well functioning mortgage market, however, provides enormous external benefits to the economy, including capital market development, increased labor market mobility, construction sector employment, and the efficient allocation of real estate assets. Initial government support of the SMM is therefore likely to be both essential and beneficial, which is why governments have always helped to create the MCIs in the developed economies. At the same time, the experience gained in creating SMMs in the developed economies can be usefully applied by the new transition economies.

The form of government support for a secondary mortgage market

We now analyze some specific principles that can help guide a government toward providing efficient support of the SMM. We assume that the SMM takes the form of a MCI which issues debt in the capital markets and uses its funds to purchase mortgages from the private market institutions that originate them. In the initial stages, the government should share ownership with private market participants, with each side contributing to the MCI's equity capital. International organizations, such as the International Finance Corporation (the private sector arm of the World Bank Group) might also contribute equity capital to the MCI. This has the further advantage that such international organizations would also contribute expertise and management experience .

Government guarantees of MCI debt The government's primary role in the secondary mortgage market is to guarantee the bonds issued by the MCI. This guarantee should be explicit. It is inefficient to use implicit guarantees because the government remains obligated, but the MCI does not receive the full benefit.[12] Furthermore, the government should charge the MCI a user fee, to defray the cost of the guarantee. This makes the amount of the subsidy transparent, and also provides an incentive for the MCI to eliminate the guarantee at a later date when it can generate a high credit rating based on its own assets and management skills. At the same time, if the government chooses to introduce other direct subsidies for housing construction or home purchase, these should be handled within the government budget or with special donor programs, not through the SMM.

Level playing field for all lenders and borrowers The goal is to create an effective housing finance system, not to support any specific class of lenders or borrowers.[12] Therefore, access to the SMM should be available to all lenders and borrowers who are able to offer properly underwritten mortgage instruments for sale. In this way, those private sector institutions that are most efficient in making mortgage loans and using the SMM would be encouraged to do so, without the need for any central agency to prejudge which specific institutions will participate. This criterion seems particularly important given that most transition economies are adopting universal (or rather full service) banking systems, in which competition and efficiency will determine which individual banks choose to specialize in each form of lending.

Government regulation, but not government management In the transition economies, as in the developed economies, government is unlikely to manage financial institutions efficiently. Therefore, even if the ownership of the MCI is shared between the government and private banks, the banks should be the managers.[14]

The government, of course, should maintain an important supervisory role, reflecting its stake in the guarantees it provides on mortgages and the institutions operating in the SMM. In particular, it should set regulations specifying the type of mortgage assets purchased and bond liabilities issued by the MCI. Furthermore, it should specify required capital ratios and related supervisory standards for the MCI on a basis comparable to its commercial bank requirements.[15]

Competition, privatization, and sunset provisions   As the housing finance system develops, the MCI is likely, sooner or later, to become quite profitable. It is therefore worthwhile to anticipate, even from the beginning, how the system should evolve. For one thing, as soon as it becomes practical, charters should be provided for the entry of additional and competitive MCIs. Otherwise, a single MCI will use its monopoly power to maximize profits, to the detriment of the housing finance system. For another thing, procedures should be established to allow the private owners of the MCI to purchase the government's share, leading eventually to a fully privatized institution. This principle was used in the United States, for example, to organize the Federal Home Loan Bank System. To remove any ambiguity whether privatization will occur, it can be useful to set a sunset date, by which the government's participation must be fully eliminated. As an example, the French government provided guarantees on the MCI securities for only four years when it created a privately owned SMM institution.

Public policy in support of primary lenders   Although our discussion has focused on secondary mortgage markets as a mechanism to allocate the risks of mortgage holding, a well functioning mortgage market also requires an efficient system for mortgage originations in the primary market. The institutions to carry out the primary mortgage functions are likely to arise naturally once the secondary market is established. However, the government must first take on the responsibility to create the legal and financial infrastructure-- real estate property rights, foreclosure procedures, and secured lending laws--that are the necessary first step for the development of any meaningful mortgage market activity.

4.5   Conclusions

A housing finance system is an essential component of the development of an efficient financial system in a transition economy. Given the importance of real estate's share of all the tangible capital in a country, and the potential for real estate collateral to secure large mounts of secured debt, the housing finance system should become an engine of innovation for the rest of the financial sector. On the other hand, if the housing finance system is stunted, then other non-market devices will develop for financing and subsidizing the housing sector, creating negative externalities for the rest of the financial system.

A housing finance system, however, is unlikely to spring up without government support, whatever one's faith in the dexterity of Adam Smith's invisible hand. Government support was required in the developed economies, and it is required now in the transition economies. In fact, the transition economies face the additional major hurdle that they must first create an economic and legal infrastructure that can support the long-term and complex market relationships and contracts that constitute a housing financial system.

We have seen in Figure 4.4 that the creation of a housing finance system is an integral component of the overall development of the financial sector. We also noted in the introduction that the transformation of the previously planned economies should focus on three key processes: (1) economic stabilization and liberalization, (2) privatization, and (3) financial sector development. The development of a housing finance system should reflect this sequencing, since a mortgage market can be included as a core component in step (3) only after meaningful progress has first occurred in steps (1) and (2).

Notes

The authors would like to thank participants at the Poznan conference on Financial Markets in Emerging Market Economies (Poland, 20 January 1996) and the European Financial Management Association annual meetings at Innsbruck (Austria, 27 June 1996) and especially Victor Murinde for comments on early versions of the paper.

1. They take on an extreme form in most transition economies as a legacy of central planning.
2. See Bertaud and Renaud (1994).
3. See European Mortgage Federation (1990) for further background. The MCIs made mortgage loans to various borrowers including households, commercial enterprises, and local governments.
4. Strictly speaking, real estate loans generally consist of two documents: the *bond* (or note) which documents the terms of loan repayment; and

the *mortgage* which provides the collateral. We will follow common usage, however, in using the term "mortgage" to refer to both sets of loan documents.

5. For further discussion see Diamond and Lea (1992a; 1992b).
6. Alternatively, institutions may try to profit from a short funding strategy, but they then bear the risk of an occasional disaster.
7. Most transition economies have also inherited a set of savings banks from their socialist era. These banks dealt exclusively with the household sector, and developed little skill in credit evaluation.
8. The term *mortgage banker* is used here to refer to institutions which specialize in originating new mortgages. It should not be confused with *mortgage credit banks*, which specialize in holding mortgages purchased from mortgage bankers.
9. The fact that "seasoned" (long outstanding) mortgages have a lower default rate is observed in all existing mortgage systems.
10. This is exactly the method used by many venture capitalists and investment bankers when evaluating investments in new start-up companies.
11. An alternative to removing the government guarantee would be to assess a fee for it. Such a fee would remove market distortions -- provided its rate is correctly assessed which may be an uncertain outcome given the political processes involved.
12. The gap between the benefits of the guarantee to the MCI and its potential cost to the government results from the uncertainty regarding the exact conditions under which this guarantee would actually be exercised.
13. Government on-budget fiscal subsidies should be used if certain social groups are deemed to require special help.
14. In other words, the agency cost of mixing private management with government ownership is likely to be less than the cost of inefficient government management.
15. For this reason, the agency to supervise the MCIs should be the same agency that supervises the commercial banks, which, in most cases, will be the country's central bank.

References

Bertaud, Alain, and Bertrand Renaud, 1994, Cities without land markets, lessons of the failed socialist experiment, World Bank Staff Discussion Paper 227.

Caprio, Gerard, David Folkerts-Landau, and Timothy Lane, 1994, Building Sound Finance in Emerging Market Economies (International Monetary Fund and World Bank, Washington D.C.).

Diamond, Douglas and Michael Lea, 1992a, Housing finance in developed countries: an international comparison of efficiency, Journal of Housing Research, 3,1.

Diamond, Douglas and Michael Lea, 1992b, The decline of special circuits in developed country housing finance, Housing Policy Debate, 3,3.

European Mortgage Federation, 1990, Study of European Mortgage Markets, Brussels.

Jaffee, Dwight and Bertrand Renaud, 1995, Securitization in European mortgage markets, paper presented at the First International Real Estate Conference, Stockholm, July.

Hermalin, Benjamin and Dwight Jaffee, 1996, The Privatization of Fannie Mae and Freddie Mac: implications for mortgage industry structure, U.S. Department of Housing and Urban Development.

International Securitization Report, 1995, IFR Publishing, Aldgate House, 33 Aldgate High Street, London EC31DL

Renaud, Bertrand, 1995, Housing finance in transition economies, the early years in Eastern Europe and the former Soviet Union, Housing Finance International, X, 2, December, pp. 35-46.

Stone, Charles A. and Anne Zissu, 1994, The French secondary mortgage market, Housing Finance International, March, pp. 15-21.

Weiss, Richard, 1991, A primer on French mortgage-backed securities, in Charles A. Stone, Anne Zissu and Jess Lederman, Asset Securitization: Theory and Practice in Europe, (Euromoney, London).

_____, 1995, Titrisation: en attente du démarrage, Paris: Crédit Foncier de France, L' Observateur Immobilier, No.30 February.

World Bank,1995, "Russia Housing Reform and Privatization: Strategy and Transition Issues," Country Report No. 14929-RU, pp. 187.

Financial Sector Reform and
Privatization in Transition Economies
J. Doukas, V. Murinde and C. Wihlborg (Editors)
© 1998 Elsevier Science Publishers B.V. All rights reserved

120

Chapter 5

DIVIDENDS AND CONFLICTS BETWEEN EQUITYHOLDERS AND DEBTHOLDERS WITH WEAK MONITORING: THE CASE OF INDIA

51 6

435 G32 L60

Shubhashis Gangopadhyay
Indian Statistical Institute, Delhi Centre, 7 SJS Sansanwal Marg, New Delhi 11006,
India

John D. Knopf
Pace University, 1 Pace Plaza, New York, NY 10038, USA

5.1   Introduction

In a well-functioning economy, firms that have positive cash flows, but lack profitable investment opportunities, should pay dividends so that capital can be put to its best use. However, there is an important distinction between a firm that has more capital than it can invest profitably, but is still profitable, and a firm that is unprofitable and faces a significant likelihood of financial distress. For firms that face financial distress, if the equityholders are properly monitored by debtholders, the equityholders will be required to pay down debt rather than pay out dividends at the expense of debtholders. In this paper we present evidence that Indian firms with impending financial distress are likely to pay out dividends in the interest of equityholders and at the expense of debtholders. We argue that this is a result of a strong alignment of interests between managers and shareholders, and a lack of effective monitoring by debtholders.

Banks have been the major suppliers of debt to Indian firms. Around 90 percent of all banking assets are with nationalized commercial and investment banks. The Indian banking sector is thus beset with all the problems of state run banks. Bank management was never subjected to worker incentives associated with market driven banking activities. Promotions and bonuses were determined on the basis of seniority and adherence to guidelines set up by the Reserve Bank of India, the central bank. Guidelines involved whom to lend and whom not to, based on industrial sectors, size of the firm, whether the loan was for agriculture, or not, etc. Bank managers, consequently, had no incentives to exercise judgement before making a loan. Also, since managers, were rewarded for achieving targets, the emphasis was more on quantity rather than quality of the loans made.

In the US, in the 1980s and even more so in the 1990s, firms have come under increased pressure to improve their performance. Consequently, poor performance or financial distress is no longer a prerequisite to the restructuring of a firm. As a matter of fact, more and more firms (for example AT&T) are making pre-emptive strikes by cutting costs through employee layoffs and other means even during periods of positive earnings. Firms that are unprofitable are under even greater pressure to restructure compared to the marginally profitable firms. John, Lang and Netter (1992) looked at a sample 46 US firms that performed poorly and later recovered. They found that firms cut costs by asset sales, employee layoffs, R & D fund cuts and debt reduction.

Jensen (1989) argues that large amounts of debt induce managers to react more forcefully and quickly to declines in performance. This is because smaller declines in performance are more likely to result in default. Ofek (1993) finds evidence directly supporting this hypothesis. He shows that there is a positive correlation between predistress leverage and operational changes such as asset restructuring, employee layoffs, and dividend cuts. In India this is not the case. For political reasons discussed in the next section, unprofitable firms are not shutdown and unproductive workers are not laid off. Furthermore, we find that for firms that suffer substantial declines in performance, those with higher levels of debt are more likely to pay dividends, which is the opposite of Ofek's findings for US firms.

Another important consideration, the interests of managers, places an added layer of complexity of the agency problem among stakeholders of a corporation. Managers receive pecuniary rewards such as salary and equity and non-pecuniary incentives such as status and power. An additional complication for managers is how their actions within the firm affect their future job prospects inside and outside of the firm. For example, by taking on risky investments their stock and option holdings may increase in value, while their present jobs may become less secure and their chances of future employment outside of the firm may decrease.[1]

Indian firms have large insider (manager) holdings of equity, which contributes to the alignment of the interests of managers and shareholders. This reduces the agency costs between the manager and shareholders as in Schooley and Barney (1994). Indian companies are characterized by family holdings. A manager, often called a promoter, may have only 10-20 percent of equity holdings. However, he or she, is supported by friends and relatives who together own a majority share. The manager, in turn, reciprocates a similar factor that contributes to the alignment of managers' and shareholders' interests in India. Because of government policy, insolvent firms are almost always restructured with managers keeping their jobs. This is in sharp contrast to evidence provided by Gibson (1989), where over 50 percent of top managers lose their jobs if a firm goes bankrupt.

If managers' and shareholders' interests are aligned so that they are willing to increase leverage at the expense of debtholders, the debtholders would be expected to closely monitor the actions of the firm and prevent excessive levels of debt. Firms can increase their leverage by (i) increasing debt through borrowing, and/or (ii) decreasing equity by paying dividends. A study by Anant, Gangopadhyay and Goswami (1992) of financially troubled firms in India shows that banks were willing to grant additional credit to firms that showed clear signs of approaching financial distress. This paper, on the other hand, shows that Indian creditors fail to adequately monitor dividend payments. Similar to evidence by DeAngelo and DeAngelo (1990, 1992) for US firms, Indian firms are reluctant to omit dividends, unless they suffer a loss. A substantial portion of firms that display signs of impending sickness continue to pay dividends. Furthermore, for dividend paying firms, dividend payout ratios (dividend/profits) are inversely related to profitability while being positively related to interest payments. The findings in this paper are, therefore, different from that in Long, Malitz and Sefcik (1994) who had been unable to find any significant evidence of wealth transfer from debtholders to equityholders through various dividend policies. Our sample is comprised of engineering and textile firms in India. We find that debtholders monitor dividend payments by engineering firms less closely than those by textile firms.

Conventional literature suggests that paying out dividends is one method of signalling low agency cost. Here we are arguing that dividend payouts in Indian firms can often be associated with resources being taken away from debtholders in favour of equityholders. Obviously, this depends on weak monitoring of firms. In general, firm management in India does not face too much scrutiny. This is for a number of reasons. First, the stock market in India is very thin. There are very few shares held by non-residents. Second, after the managers and their relatives, the largest shareholders are government controlled financial institutions who also are not good at monitoring firm performance. Third, banks and financial institutions have always provided capital in times of need. This became necessary as the stock markets were heavily regulated (during the time for which data are used in this study) in terms of the maximum price of a new issue, making the capital market a very costly way of raising funds. Consequently, the argument in Hansen, Kumar and Shome (1994) cannot be applied here.

These results provide evidence of a lack of monitoring by Indian debtholders. If firms actually continue to receive additional credit and pay dividends during periods of imminent financial distress, this would be a clear indicator of ineffective monitoring by banks. One, would, therefore, expect increased leverage in firms approaching distress. If creditors monitor firms effectively, dividend payments for firms with substantial debt burdens and a high probability of distress should be positively related to profits and negatively related to interest payments.

In the next section we outline important elements of industrial policy in India and the role it plays in allowing equityholders to transfer resources to themselves at the expense of debtholders. Section 5.3 discusses the data used for the study. Section 5.4 is the main body of the paper describing the methodology and results obtained. Section 5.5 concludes the paper.

5.2   Industrial regulation in India

To understand the process by which shareholders gain at the expense of debtholders, one has to look at the legal and institutional environment in which the firms operate. There are two parts to this: the laws that impose barriers to exit and, the capital structure of firms.

Industrial regulation in India prevents the easy exit for financially distressed firms. Labor laws impose strict conditions regarding the firing of labor. These are contained in Section 25(N) of the Indian Industrial Disputes Act. Retrenchment is distinguished from simple firing of labor. Retrenchment occurs when a laborer's employment is terminated for reasons other than punishment for indiscipline or criminal offence. In other words, all economic reasons for firing labor, during economic crises, must be obtained from the local government. The local government is usually the state government, and their decision is binding on all parties. The state governments, more often than not, refuse to grant permission to retrench labor (J.L. Bajaj Committee's Report of the Inter-Ministerial Working Group on Industrial Restructuring, March 1992). A major reason is that industrial units are concentrated in regions and the recessionary pressures affect all units in the region. Consequently, the absolute size of retrenched labor typically tend to be large. The local government, for political reasons, refuse to generate a large mass of unemployed labor among its voters. Another reason is that only a part of the cost, of supporting units in financial crises, is borne by the state government; the bulk of such costs are borne by the nationalized financial institutions and, therefore, taxpayers from all over the country.

However, the law does not disallow units from being 'locked out'. In such a situation, labor need not be paid and the local government need not be consulted because labor has not been retrenched. This, of course, means a greater burden on the laborers than the original purpose of the law. It was felt that, given the unwillingness of state governments to allow closures, it was better for ailing units to be restructured quickly and efficiently. The Central government, therefore, came up the Sick Industrial Companies (Special Provisions) Act (SICA) of 1985. According to this law, any company that has been registered for at least 7 years, has a negative net worth, and has incurred cash losses in the current and the immediately preceding year, will be deemed 'sick' and must apply to the Board for Industrial Financial Reconstruction (BIFR). This Board was supposed to provide a single point reference and, therefore, streamline and quicken the restructuring process without going through lengthy legal proceedings during which units remain locked out.

On paper, this is a powerful provision for closing down non-performing units. According to the SICA provisions, and the powers vested in the BIFR, the decisions taken by the Board override all other laws excepting those concerning foreign exchange regulations (governed by federal legislation) and the urban land ceiling laws (of the local governments). In practice, however, the present structure is ineffective and time consuming. There are two major reasons. First, the BIFR has shied away from ordering closures and continued with sick firms by forcing nationalized financial institutions to pump in more money. The escape clause allowing such deals is the one regarding 'public interest'. Under this clause, even if the unit is unviable economically, it can be allowed to exist if it is in the general 'social' interest. Second, there is a serious overlap and hence, conflict in the laws governing closure. While the BIFR is empowered to sell off the assets of a company it wants closed down, the proceeds of the sale must be given to the corresponding (state) high courts for distribution among creditors. The law governing distribution of such proceeds does not make a distinction between closures being ordered by BIFR and others. The latter is a time consuming process and contradicts the principle of SICA. Consequently, the BIFR has been reluctant to order closures knowing that it will not lead to a speedy resolution.

In addition, the BIFR has no expertise in selling off assets or, liquidating an industrial concern. Furthermore, decision making is through consensus among all parties; labor, management and creditors. Since the largest creditors are *nationalized* banks and financial institutions, the BIFR has a tendency to force them to accept rehabilitation packages which a rational, profit seeking, lending organisation would never accept. In other words, a firm is prevented from being bankrupt.

A manager, if rational, should be able to figure out this whole process. She knows that, in case of impending bankruptcy, the BIFR and financial institutions will work out a deal that involves the unit in a greater inflow of funds at highly subsidized rates. The unit will not be allowed to close down and the consequent losses from closure are non-existent. These losses could be of types: a deadweight loss during closure proceedings and the manager's reputational loss. Most of the economic cost of continuing with a bad firm is borne by the nationalized institutions. The loss in the manager's reputation is avoided because she continues in her job after the unit is restructured.

The financial structure of Indian firms is important in this regard. As stated in the last section, the conflict between shareholders and equityholders is minimal, if not non-existent. Consequently, knowing that subsidized credit is available for distressed firms, it pays managers (and, therefore, shareholders) to 'strip' down the equity through dividend payouts, regardless of the cashflow situation in the unit. Thus the general public has been subsidizing inefficient units through nationalized financial institutions while promoter/managers have been avoided much of their costs.

5.3   Data

The data for this study are drawn from the profit-and-loss statements and balance sheets of firms in the Indian textile and engineering industries.

They are published in the Bombay Stock Exchange Directories and are in the public domain. We study 73 firms, comprising 35 textile and 38 engineering firms. The main reason for choosing this sample is that these firms had data going back all the way to 1970. The period covered in this study is from 1970 and 1990. All these firms are medium to large enterprises in terms of either sales or gross fixed assets. Nevertheless, wherever necessary, the variables we have used have been normalized to correct for any size difference among these firms.

The textile sample consists of large and medium composite mills. This industry is relatively homogeneous in its product mix and operates in a competitive market. It is also regionally concentrated in the states of Gujarat and Maharashtra, two of the most commercialized regions in India. One would, therefore, expect them to face similar economic environments. The engineering units are more heterogeneous but most of the non-performing ones are in the state of West Bengal. This state has a long history of Trade Union movements and the local government has remained in leftist hands since 1977. The political climate in West Bengal is more strongly opposed to employment cuts, or reorganisations, than in the states of Gujarat and Maharashtra. This would mean that the probability (however small) of closure would be even less in West Bengal than in the other two states. Institutional lenders, therefore, would have even less power to withhold credit and bring about changes in poor management bodies. As we will demonstrate, our hypothesis of equityholders gaining at the expense of debtholders is stronger for the engineering units when compared to the textile industry.

The variables we use in this study which are calculated for every firm in every year are:

ZWAGSALE	Wages and salaries divided by sales
ZINTSALE	Interest costs divided by sales
ZPRFSALE	Profits divided by sales
1-ZPRFDIV	1 - Profits divided by dividends
ZPBIDINT	(Profits before interest and taxes) divided by (interest)
DUMMYDIV	A dummy variable taking on the value one if the company paid a dividend that year and zero otherwise
SICADUMMY	A dummy variable taking on the value one if the firm is classified as sick (BIFR) by the Sick Industrial Companies Act (SICA) and zero otherwise

It should be noted that, though these are firms listed in the stock exchange, we have used any stock market variable for these firms. This is because during the period of study, the stock market was highly controlled and the major purpose for having them listed was to achieve limited liability and other benefits. This aspect is highlighted by the fact that stocks of the sample of firms in our list were often not traded more than once or twice during the year. Some of them were not traded at all.

The use of the 1-ZPRFDIV variable deserves special clarification. Firms sometimes pay dividends when they have zero profit or loss. Using the payout ratio dividend by profit would not yield a continuous function (the function is discontinuous around zero). Although we compute the variable for every firm in every year, we only use the variable 1-ZPRFDIV for firms in years that they actually pay positive dividends. 1-ZPRFDIV, therefore, yields a continuous function that, *ceteris paribus*, increases as dividend paid out increases. It is also useful to mention that the variable 1-ZPRFDIV would be positive only if a firm pays out a dividend when it suffers a loss the same year. Otherwise, since profit is usually no less than the dividend, it should be negative.

One last explanation is needed before we analyze the data. The sick firms are as defined by SICA. These applied to BIFR and are referred to here as BIFR firms. Since the BIFR came into operation in 1987, BIFR firms came to be known as such after 1987. Thus, when we follow a BIFR firm from 1970, we mean a firm that came under the BIFR post 1987. In the seventies, it could have been a perfectly healthy firm. Indeed, our whole emphasis is to be able to identify problem firms *before* they become bankrupt. Firms that are financially viable in 1990 are non-BIFR firms.

A particular advantage of the data is that we have reasonably large samples from two different industries. We can therefore make comparisons among firms without having to adjust the data for industry specific variations as well as make inter-industry comparisons.

5.4   Methodology and results

Under perfect markets, a firm unable to meet its obligations to creditors, would be forced to restructure with the equityholders being the residual claimants. For bankrupt firms, this would usually mean zero value to equity. Equityholders in inherently unprofitable firms would, therefore, try to withdraw resources before the creditors can close in. This is essentially due to the limited liability of equity. One way the equity base can be reduced, or 'stripped' is by paying out large dividends from accumulated reserves even when the firm's current financial situation does not warrant such payouts. In publicly held companies, this tendency may be somewhat diluted by agency problems between managers and equityholders. Managers lose during bankruptcy, mostly through a loss in reputation. In India, as argued before, the agency problems between managers and equityholders are minimal. Indian companies are run by promoter/managers who, along with their friends and relatives, own major shares in them. This trend towards taking out equity value, when the firm is financially troubled, but before the firm becomes insolvent, is therefore, to be expected if creditors do not effectively monitor the firms.

The Indian environment, and most importantly its labor laws, have set up barriers to exit. In other words, a financially unviable firm is not necessarily liquidated. Nationalized lending agencies are forced to offer cheap credit to financially distressed firms. The process of restructuring often leaves the erstwhile management in place. There is, thus, no loss of management jobs and subsidized credit is made available to poor performers. This has an obvious incentive effect of rewarding bad managers; healthy companies have to borrow money at 25 percent while sick ones can get it for as low as 10 percent (Anant, Gangopadhyay and Goswami, 1992). Furthermore, it has another effect. The promoters of inherently unprofitable firms would like to take out their equity before creditors can close in. There is no cost to reducing accumulated reserves since the cost to promoters in case of interest default is negligible, if at all. In this section we will argue that this is exactly what happened in Indian industries. If firms actually continue to receive additional credit and pay dividends during periods of imminent financial distress, this would be a clear indicator of ineffective monitoring by banks.

The basic premise in our argument is that the managers, or promoters, have better knowledge of the economic position of the firm than banks, financial institutions and other creditors (or worse, creditors do not act on their information). Consequently, they have prior information about the firm's impending financial crisis before it is observed by the creditors. Given the limited liability of equity, it pays the promoters to take out their equity before the creditors can step in to liquidate the assets of a bankrupt firm. This is accentuated by the ineffectiveness of creditors to take any steps against bad management unless firms become chronic defaulters on interest payments. In principle, if the creditors are alert, they should be able to identify such tendencies by firms. However, given the aversion to granting closures or liquidation, by both state and central governments, monitoring by banks and financial institutions cannot be very effective. The 'equity stripping' by promoters and subsequent erosion of networth would not, therefore, be surprising.

5.4.1 Dividend policy

Consider two sets of firms: strong and weak. Both groups have large debt burdens and have shown a profit in the current year. The strong firms have many investment opportunities, which in the long-run are expected to be profitable. The weak firms, on the other hand, have a single investment which is unprofitable in the long-run and no other profitable investment opportunities. In an efficient capital market, dividend payments for the Strong firms (because they have so many profitable ways to invest their excess cash) would be negatively related to long-run profitability and, furthermore, given the stability of the strong firms' cash flows, dividends may even be positively related to interest expense. If creditors monitor firms effectively, the weak firms (substantial debt burdens and a high likelihood of distress) should not pay any dividends at all, and if they pay dividends, they should be negatively related to interest expense and positively related to long-term profits. In other words, firms with a high likelihood of financial distress should not pay dividends which drain the cash of firms at the expense of debtholders.

However, if debtholders don't monitor firms closely, and therefore are unable to distinguish strong firms form weak firms, the latter will take advantage of debtholders. An inherently healthy firm suffering a temporary setback will endeavour to maintain its dividend to signal to its shareholders that it is a profitable venture. An inherently unprofitable firm, on the other hand, given the conflict of interest between promoter/managers and debtholders, would pay out as much dividend as possible, and whenever it can. Such a firm would be unlikely to keep accumulated reserves and will make dividend payments when it makes profits; it will also cut dividend payments (due to lack of cash) when it does not make profits. Given that managers have better information about the future potential of a firm, one would, therefore, expect financially distressed firms (i) to pay out large dividends before it actually becomes, sick and (ii) to pay dividends whenever it makes profit, not to keep any reserves and, thus, not be able to maintain dividends when it does not earn enough profit. *Inherently profitable firms should have a more stable dividend policy.*

First, we will establish that for firms that pay dividends, dividends paid out for less profitable firms are higher and become even higher as the debt burden increases, whether or not they are financially viable. Second, we will demonstrate that firms are unlikely to cut dividends unless they suffer a loss. Third, for firms that have suffered a loss (a strong signal of possible financial distress) the more financially troubled firms are more likely to omit dividend payments, however, we show that this is too little, too late: the dividends are not cut sufficiently given their financial troubles. These problems are more pronounced among non-performing engineering firms that are, as pointed out before, more concentrated in a leftist dominated state. Here, social justice is often equated with job security for unionized labor; firm closure, or layoffs, are discouraged. Firms under financial distress are bailed out through increased inflow of funds from government banks. The left bias makes these companies less liable to early restructuring and/or closure and consequently, the financial institutions have even less effective monitoring than in the textile industry. Of course, the laws governing restructuring takes the bite out of any meaningful monitoring in the first place. Finally, for engineering firms, we provide evidence of a positive relationship between financial distress (BIFR) and dividend payout.

For all of the tests performed in this paper we report separate results for both the engineering and textile industries, along with results for the two industries combined. This allows us to determine whether our hypotheses concerning dividend payments are more or less strongly supported for a particular industry and whether or not our hypotheses are supported for Indian firms in general. We also often subdivide these groups into BIFR and non-BIFR firms to check if dividend policy is related to whether firms eventually become insolvent.

5.4.2   Firm dividend policy for all firms that pay dividends

Now we examine the financial health of all firms in our sample in the years that they paid dividends. This is important in light of the prior information that promoters have about the future health of their firms. Specifically, we look at how a firm's profitability, interest expense and wage expense affect dividend payments. If our hypothesis that more financially troubled firms pay higher dividends is correct, then, we would expect BIFR firms to pay higher dividends than non-BIFR firms whenever they can. Table 5.1 compares BIFR and non-BIFR firms in terms of their ZINTSALE,

ZWAGSALE, ZPRFSALE, 1-ZPRFDIV, and ZPBIDINT across those years for which firms pay dividends. Not surprisingly, in all the three panels the BIFR firms have significantly lower profits (ZPRFSALE) and interest coverage ratios (ZPBIDINT), using a parametric (t-) or a non-parametric (Wilcox-) test. However, for engineering firms, the dividend payout ratio (1-ZPRFDIV) is significantly higher for BIFR firms than non-BIFR firms, while they are not significantly different for textile firms or the sample as a whole. If debtholders monitored the firms closely, BIFR firms, which have significantly less profitability and interest coverage ratios, should have lower dividend payout ratios. This indicates that both textile and engineering firms pay dividends at the expense of debtholders and that the problem is more severe for engineering firms.

TABLE 5.1

Preliminary test results

Panel A: Textile fims						
			T-test		Wilcox test	
Variable	Mean BIFR N=166	Mean non-BIFR N=303	t-value	p-value	z-value	p-value
ZINTSALE	0.04	0.04	-0.71	0.48	0.39	0.76
ZWAGSALE	0.17	0.12	9.26	0.00	8.7	0.00
ZPFRSALE	0.06	0.08	-2.96	0.00	-3.58	0.00
1-ZPRFDIV	-5.51	-4.89	-1.59	0.11	-1.04	0.30
ZPBIDINT	3.30	4.08	-2.16	0.03	-3.15	0.00

Panel B: Engineering fims

			T-test		Wilcox test	
Variable	Mean BIFR N=94	Mean non-BIFR N=378	t-value	p-value	z-value	p-value
ZINTSALE	0.04	0.03	7.84	0.00	7.66	0.00
ZWAGSALE	0.14	0.11	4.20	0.00	5.00	0.00
ZPFRSALE	0.04	0.05	-2.11	0.04	-3.03	0.00
1-ZPRFDIV	-0.60	-3.38	4.04	0.00	3.97	0.00
ZPBIDINT	3.37	5.97	-3.24	0.00	-5.37	0.00

Panel C: All fims

Variable	Mean BIFR N=260	Mean non- BIFR N=681	T-test t-value	p-value	Wilcox test z-value	p-value
ZINTSALE	0.04	0.03	5.17	0.00	6.30	0.00
ZWAGSALE	0.16	0.12	10.67	0.00	10.45	0.00
ZPFRSALE	0.05	0.06	-2.52	0.01	-3.46	0.00
1-ZPRFDIV	-3.73	-4.05	0.82	0.41	0.33	0.74
ZPBIDINT	3.33	5.13	-4.38	0.00	-6.50	0.00

Note: For years that firms pay dividends, comparisons between the BIFR and non-BIFR firms of ZINTSALE, ZWAGSALE, ZPRFSALE, 1-ZPRFDIV, and ZPBIDINT is made using parametric (t-) and non-parametric (Wilcox) tests. Separate tests are performed for textile firms (Panel A), engineering firms (Panel B) and for all firms (Panel C). N is the total number of observations for each group.

More evidence from regression analysis is provided in Table 5.2. The estimation and testing technique is explained in the note at the bottom of the table. The dependent variable is 1-ZPRFDIV. The independent variables are ZPRFSALE, ZINTSALE, and ZWAGSALE. The 1-ZPRFDIV variable is negatively and significantly related to ZPRFSALE: less profitable firms pay out higher dividends. In and of itself this result is not surprising. One would expect less profitable firms to pay higher dividends to allow shareholders to invest the money in more profitable firms. However, when the negative relationship between ZPRFSALE and 1-ZPRFDIV is coupled with the highly significant positive relationship between ZINTSALE and 1-ZPRFDIV, there is evidence of a lack of monitoring by debtholders (and agency problem between shareholders and debtholders). Not only are less profitable firms draining equity that protects debtholders, but the greater the cost of debt the more they drain the equity through dividend payments. This effect is much stronger for engineering firms (the R-square and significance levels for the variables are higher for engineering firms than textile firms).[2]

TABLE 5.2
Regression results

Panel A: Textile firms (sample size = 469)			
	Coefficient	Standard error of coefficient	t-statistic	p-value
Intercept	-1.92	0.55	-3.52	0.00
ZPFRSALE	-41.82	2.64	-15.86	0.00
ZINTSALE	14.77	7.60	1.94	0.05
ZWAGSALE	-2.16	1.96	-1.10	0.27

Note: Multiple R-square = 0.41, model p-value < 0.0001 (the significance level that the F-statistic rejects the hypothesis that all the coefficients in the regression are zero).

Panel B: Engineering firms (sample size = 472)			
	Coefficient	Standard error of coefficient	t-statistic	p-value
Intercept	-2.05	0.30	-6.77	0.00
ZPFRSALE	-54.66	2.16	-25.31	0.00
ZINTSALE	19.64	2.16	3`.74	0.00
ZWAGSALE	10.85	1.47	7.38	0.00

Note: Multiple R-square = 0.71, model p-value < 0.0001 (the significance level that the F-statistic rejects the hypothesis that all the coefficients in the regression are zero).

Panel C: All firms (sample size = 941)			
	Coefficient	Standard error of coefficient	t-statistic	p-value
Intercept	-1.67	0.27	-6.09	0.00
ZPFRSALE	-49.59	1.63	-30.38	0.00
ZINTSALE	19.31	4.41	4.38	0.00
ZWAGSALE	2.34	1.18	1.98	0.05

TABLE 5.2 (concluded)₁

Notes: Multiple R-square = 0.57, model p-value < 0.0001 (the significance level that the F-statistic rejects the hypothesis that all the coefficients in the regression are zero). The regressions were corrected for heterscedasticity by using the converged Huber estimate followed by two iterations of Bisquare (a robust iteratively reweighted least square method). Multiple regression results using profitability (ZPRFSALE), interest expense (ZINTSALE), and wage expense (ZWAGSALE) are used to predict a firm's dividend payout ratio(1-ZPRFDIV), given that it pays a dividend. Separate regressions are performed for textile firms (panel A), engineering firms (panel B) and for all firms (panel C).

In our final set of tests in this section, we examine whether dividend payments can predict the possibility of classifying a firm as BIFR. In Table 5.3 we report results of a logit regression of SICADUMMY on 1-ZPRFDIV. It shows that for engineering firms there is a positive and highly significant relationship between dividend payout and financial distress. This is direct evidence of the costs to debtholders of the lack of monitoring of dividend payments by engineering firms. In the textile industry, dividend payments are not correlated with financial distress.

TABLE 5.3
Logit results

Panel A: Textile firms (sample size = 469)				
	Coefficient	Standard error of coefficient	z-value	p-value
Intercept	-0.80	0.16	-5.05	0.00
1-ZPRFDIV	-0.04	0.02	-1.58	0.11

Note: Model p-value < 0.11 (the significance that the likelihood ratio rejects the hypothesis that all the coefficients in the regression are zero).

Table 5.3 (concluded) .

Panel B: Engineering firms (sample size = 472)			
	Coefficient	Standard error of coefficient	z-value	p-value
Intercept	-1.23	0.13	-9.80	0.00
1-ZPRFDIV	0.07	0.02	3.39	0.00

Note: Model p-value < 0.00 (the significance that the likelihood ratio rejects the hypothesis that all the coefficients in the regression are zero).

Panel C: All firms (sample size = 941)

	Coefficient	Standard error of coefficient	z-value	p-value
Intercept	-0.92	0.09	-10.28	0.00
1-ZPRFDIV	0.01	0.01	0.82	0.41

Notes: Model p-value < 0.41 (the significance that the likelihood ratio rejects the hypothesis that all the coefficients in the regression are zero).
Logit results using dividend payout (1-ZPRFDIV) to predict whether a firm eventually meets the SICA norm of financial distress (SICADUMMY), given that it pays a dividend in that year. Separate regressions are performed for textile firms (panel A) engineering firms (panel B) and for all firms (panel C).

5.4.3   Firm dividend policy after a loss

When a firm suffers a loss, we would expect debtholders to pay particular attention to the firm's financial condition. In the year that a firm suffers a loss, the equityholders should be able to clearly show that the firm is financially strong before debtholders allow dividend payments. In Tables 5.4, 5.5 and 5.6 we present results for various tests of how firms react to losses and why firms cut or omit dividend payments. First, we examine the relationship between profitability and the decision to omit or or cut dividends, given that a firm paid a dividend the previous year. Table 5.4, which reports the frequencies of profits and losses for firms that eliminate dividends, provides support for the claim that firms are reluctant to eliminate dividends, unless they suffer very poor performance. Panel C indicates that 85 percent of all firms suffered a loss in the year in which they omitted dividends. For the remaining 15 percent of the firms that did not suffer a loss, their profits averaged 58 percent of the previous year's profits.

These results imply that low profitability is typically *not sufficient* for firms to eliminate dividends, but rather firms must *actually suffer a loss*. However, the decision to omit dividends does not appear to be related to which industry the firm is in: 83 percent of textile firms had a loss in the years they omitted dividends as shown in Panel A, compared to 88 percent of engineering firms as presented in Panel B. Nor, in this set of tests, does eliminating dividends appear to be related to whether it eventually becomes a BIFR firm: 87 percent of all BIFR firms and 82 percent of all non-BIFR firms suffered a loss in the years that they omitted dividends, as shown in Panel C.

Table 5.5 looks at the same question from a slightly different angle. Panel C shows how all firms that paid a dividend in the previous year react to losses. Approximately 52 percent of firms that suffer losses omit dividends in the same year. Table 5.2 also provides some informative inter-industry comparisons. We argued above that for political reasons engineering firms were not as closely monitored as textile firms. Therefore, engineering firms would be expected to pay out larger dividends, around (periods of) losses, at the expense of the debtholders. Comparisons of panels A and B in Table 5.2 support this hypothesis. When suffering a loss, engineering firms were less likely to cut dividends - 44 percent of engineering firms compared to 66 percent of textile firms - and the average dividend as a percentage of the previous dividend was much higher for engineering than textile firms, 62 percent and 25 percent, respectively. *It should also be pointed that the 25 percent payout for textile firms would have been much lower if a single outlier of 600 percent had been deleted!*

Comparing the results from Tables 5.4 and 5.5 implies that although most firms (85 percent) that omit dividends suffer a loss, only about half (52 percent) of the firms that suffer a loss eliminate dividends. In other words although a loss appears to be a necessary condition for omitting dividends it is not a sufficient condition.

Upon further examination of Table 5.5, it is interesting to note that (eventual) BIFR firms reacted more strongly to losses. For 76 percent of BIFR firms dividends were eliminated when they incurred losses compared to 33 percent for non-BIFR firms.

TABLE 5.4
Evidence on why firms eliminate dividend

Panel A: Textile firms

Firm type	Losses		Profits			Total	
	Frequency	Percent frequency	Frequency	Percent frequency	Profit as % of last year profit	Frequency	Percent frequency
BIFR	22	85%	4	15%	41%	26	74%
non-BIFR	7	78%	2	22%	22%	9	26%
Total	29	83%	6	17%	35%	35	100%

Panel B: Engineering firms

Firm type	Losses		Profits			Total	
	Frequency	Percent frequency	Total Frequency	Percent frequency	Profit as % of last year profit	Frequency	Percent frequency
BIFR	19	90%	2	10%	107%	21	53%
non-BIFR	16	84%	3	16%	71%	19	47%
Total	35	88%	5	12%	85%	40	100%

TABLE 5.4 (Concluded)

Panel C: All firms

Firm type	Losses Frequency	Profits Percent frequency	Total Frequency	Percent frequency	Profit as % of last year profit	Frequency	Percent frequency
BIFR	41	87%	6	13%	63%	47	63%
non-BIFR	23	82%	5	18%	51%	28	37%
Total	64	85%	11	15%	68%	75	100%

In this table we examine why firms eliminate dividends. We only consider those years that firms eliminated dividend payments after at least one year of dividends. For the years that firms eliminated dividends, we compare the frequencies of losses and profits.

TABLE 5.5
Evidence on how dividend paying firms react to losses

Panel A: Textile firms

Firm type	Omit		Cut		Maintain		Total	
	Frequency (%)	Dividend as % of last year dividend	Frequency %	Frequnecy as % of last year dividend	Frequency %	Dividend as % of last year dividend	Frequncy %	Dividend as % of last year dividend
BIFR	20(95 %)	0 %	0	0 %	1(5 %)	100 %	21(53 %)	5 %
non-BIFR	7(37 %)	0 %	7(37 %)	43 %	5(26 %)	120 %	19(47 %)	47 %
Total	27(68 %)	0 %	7(17 %)	43 %	6(15 %)	117 %	40(100 %)	25 %

Panel B: Engineering firms

Firm type	Omit		Cut		Maintain		Total	
	Frequency (%)	Dividend as % of last year dividend	Frequency %	Frequnecy as % of last year dividend	Frequency %	Dividend as % of last year dividend	Frequncy %	Dividend as % of last year dividend
BIFR	19(63 %)	0 %	6(20 %)	49 %	5(17 %)	283 %	30(44 %)	57 %
non-BIFR	16(32 %)	0 %	15(30 %)	65 %	19(38 %)	122 %	50(56 %)	66 %
Total	35(44 %)	0 %	21(26 %)	60 %	24(30 %)	156 %	80(100 %)	62 %

TABLE 5.5 (Concluded)

Panel C: All firms

Firm type	Omit		Cut		Maintain		Total	
	Frequency (%)	Dividend as % of last year dividend	Frequency %	Frequency as % of last year dividend	Frequency %	Dividend as % of last year dividend	Frequncy %	Dividend as % of last year dividend
BIFR	39(76 %)	0 %	6(12 %)	49 %	6(12 %)	252 %	51(43 %)	36 %
non-BIFR	23(33 %)	0 %	22(32 %)	58 %	24(34 %)	122 %	69(57 %)	61 %
Total	62(52 %)	0 %	28(23 %)	56 %	30(25 %)	148 %	120(100 %)	50 %

In this table we examine how firms, that are currently paying dividends, react to losses. We only consider those years that firms suffered losses after paying dividends for at least one year. For the years that the firms suffered a loss, we compare the frequencies of cutting, omitting, or maintaining dividends.

TABLE 5.6

Further empirical evidence

Panel A: Textile firms (sample size = 40)			
	Coefficient	Standard error of coefficient	z-value	p-value
Intercept	-0.04	0.70	-0.05	0.96
DUMMYDIV	-2.75	1.19	-2.31	0.03
ZPFRSALE	-24.44	15.39	-1.59	0.12

Note: Model p-value < 0.0001 (the significance level that the likelihood ratio rejects the hypothesis that all the coefficients in the regression are zero).

Panel B: Engineering firms (sample size = 80)			
	Coefficient	Standard error of coefficient	z-value	p-value
Intercept	-0.7	0.48	-0.85	0.40
DUMMYDIV	-1.00	0.52	-1.95	0.05
ZPFRSALE	-7.86	4.76	-1.65	0.10

Note: Model p-value < 0.01 (the significance level that the likelihood ratio rejects the hypothesis that all the coefficients in the regression are zero).

Panel C: All firms (sample size = 120)			
	Coefficient	Standard error of coefficient	t-statistic	p-value
Intercept	-0.07	0.37	-0.19	0.85
DUMMYDIV	-1.57	0.44	-3.55	0.00
ZPFRSALE		4.76	-1.65	0.03

Note: Model p-value < 0.0001 (the significance level that the likelihood ratio rejects the hypothesis that all the coefficients in the regression are zero).

Table 5.6 provides similar evidence. The results are from a logit regression, for years that a firm suffers a loss, where the dependent variable is SICADUMMY. For both textile and engineering firms the variable DUMMYDIV is significant which means: *given that a firm suffers a loss, a firm that pays a dividend is less likely to become a BIFR firm, regardless of the extent of its losses (ZPRFSALE is insignificant)*. These results should not be interpreted as more conservative dividend policies by BIFR firms.

Anant, Gangopadhyay and Goswami (1992) demonstrated that BIFR firms were in much more severe financial difficulties when they incurred their first losses. A reasonable interpretation of these results is that creditors do not constrain firms' dividends unless they actually incur a loss, which is often too late to prevent financial distress. This supports the hypothesis that firms which face impending financial distress pay dividends until they are forced to curtail dividends.

5.5   Conclusions

If a firm becomes less profitable (less competitive) it makes sense that it increases its dividend payout in order to allow investors to place their money in alternative more profitable investments. However, if the firm is closely monitored by debtholders it should pay down its debt at the same time. For our sample of Indian firms, this was clearly not the case. As firms became less profitable and borrowed more money, they increased their dividend payouts. A stronger agency problem between debtholders and equityholders was demonstrated for engineering firms than textile firms, which we have argued is due to less restrictive monitoring of engineering firms. We have also argued that this is mainly due to the legal and institutional environment in which Indian firms operate. Labor laws make closures of bankrupt firms impossible. Financial distress is overcome by nationalized financial institutions being forced to lend at subsized rates to insolvent firms. Banks and other financial institutions, therefore, have no recourse to punishing errant firms and this discourages effective monitoring of firms by creditors. The capital structure of firms, on the other hand, is such that the agency conflict between shareholders and managers is minimal, resulting in the equityholders of Indian firms gaining at the expense of debtholders.

There are two important lessons for transitional economies that can be drawn from the Indian experience. First, in the initial stages of a developing capital market, one does not expect outsider, small shareholders to play any role in firm management through the stock market. This period is likely to be characterised by large insider shareholding. This suggests that the agency cost between the shareholders and the managers may be small. Second, much of the capital in private firms may come from financial institutions and banks, as an individual small shareholder may not have adequate amounts of discretionary savings to directly supply the capital market. Moreover, their knowledge and understanding of the capital market is limited. This forces the banks and other financial institutions to be major suppliers of capital. However, in many transitional economies, such institutions are government controlled, or have been so in the immediate past. In the first instance, public sector banks are not good monitors; in the second instance, there is often no experience of monitoring debtors. Monitoring is, therefore, weak at best. One way of correcting the situation is to allow foreign banks and other financial institutions into the domestic economy. In other words, privatization of financial institutions along with foreign entry may be an important way to tackle the issues of corporate governance.

Notes

A first draft of the paper was completed while the authors were visiting the Göteborg University. The paper was first presented at a conference in Tallinn, Estonia. It has benefitted from discussion with the participants at the conference, Bharat Ramaswamy, Victor Murinde and Clas Wihlborg. The authors bear complete responsibility for any of the remaining errors.

1. Numerous studies of US firms have shown that firms may increase their limited liability equity value by increasing the riskiness of their assets (Kraus and Litzenberger, 1973 and Galai and Masulis, 1976). Equity may be regarded as an option on the firm's assets; thus equity will increase as the risk of the underlying asset risk increasees. In effect, due to limited liability, stockholders may benefit from the "gambling" of creditor's claims without fully sharing in the losses. Thus, wealth is transferred directly from creditors to stockholders. This wealth transfer effect is more pronounced in highly leveraged firms. Therefore, one might expect the managerial team with the higher shareholdings to act more on behalf of shareholders and assume higher levels of risk. Knopf and Teall (1996) find evidence that risk levels are related to officer and manager proportions in shareholdings. These results imply that corporations with high proportions of insider shareholdings are more likely to engage in risk-taking activity, corporations with more diverse shareholdings are more likely to be controlled by managers who may value job security and reputation most highly.

2. In order to increase the power of our tests we have pooled time-series data for a cross-section of firms. Although we do not report the results here, it should be pointed out that these results hold for cross-sectional regressions using the averages of these variables for the various firms.

References

Anant, T.C.A., S. Gangopadhyay and O. Goswami, 1992, Industrial Sickness in India: Characteristics, Determinants and History, 1970-1990, Report to the Ministry of Industry, Government of India.

DeAngelo, H., L. DeAngelo and J Skinner, 1992, Dividends and losses, The Journal of Finance, December, pp. 1837-63.

DeAngelo, H., and L. DeAngelo, 1990, Dividend policy and financial distress, The Journal of Finance, December, pp. 1415-31.

Galai, D. and R. Masulis, 1976, The option pricing model and the risk factor of stock, Journal of Financial Economics, 3, pp. 53-81.

Gilson, S.C., 1989, Management turnover and financial distress, Journal of Financial Economics, 25, pp. 241-62.

Hansen, R. S., R Kuman and D.K. Shome, 1994, Dividend policy and corporate monitorig: evidence from the regulated electric utility industry, Financial Management, 23, pp. 16-22.

Jensen, M.C., 1989, Active Investors, LBOs, and the privatization of bankruptcy", Journal of Applied Corporate Finance, 2, pp. 235-44.

Jensen, M.C. and W. H. Meckling, 1976, Theory of the firm: managerial behaviour, agency costs and ownership structure, Journal of Financial Economics, October, pp. 305-60.

John, K., L. Lang and J. Netter, 1992, The voluntary restructuring of large firms in response to performance decline, Journal of Finance, 47, pp. 891-918.

Knopf, J. and J. Teall, 1996, Risk taking behaviour in the US thrift industry: ownership structure and regulatory changes, Journal of Banking and Finance.

Kraus, A. and R.A. Litzenberger, 1973, A state preference model of optimal financial leverage, Journal of Finance, September, pp. 911-22.

Long, M. S., I. B. Malitz and S. E. Sefcik, 1994, An empirical estimation of dividend policy following debt issues, Journal of Financial and Quantitative Analysis, 29, pp. 131-44.

Ofek, E., 1993, Capital structure and firm response to poor performance: an empirical analysis, Journal of Financial Economics, August, pp. 3-30.

Schooley, D.K. and L.D. Barney, Jr., 1994, Using dividend policy and managerial ownership to reduce agency costs, Journal of Financial Research, 17, pp. 363-73.

Part Two

The Financial Sector in the Development of Market Economies

Financial Sector Reform and
Privatization in Transition Economies
J. Doukas, V. Murinde and C. Wihlborg (Editors)
© 1997 Elsevier Science Publishers B.V. All rights reserved

123

Chapter 6

DESIGN OF FINANCIAL SYSTEMS
AND ECONOMIC TRANSFORMATION

Ingo Walter
Leonard N. Stern School of Business, New York University Salomon Center, 100
Trinity Place, New York, NY 10006, USA

6.1   Introduction

Few issues are more important in setting the agenda of economic growth
and development than the structure, conduct and performance of a nation's
financial system. Standing at the center of the transactions and resource
allocation process, high-performance financial systems are increasingly
important as determinants of sustainable economic progress and stability.
This is as true domestically as it is internationally, where global financial
market developments require an efficient "window" on sources and uses of
capital, as well as fast-moving market developments and financial
technologies that change in substance and form at a rapid pace. Few
countries can afford to be de-linked from these developments -- especially
as they develop mature industrial structures and rapidly evolving services
sectors -- or fail to create and maintain domestic financial systems that can
eventually meet world performance standards.

This paper outlines the framework parameters of high-performance
financial systems that can be applied in a transition-economy context. We
begin with an intuitive structural model of financial intermediation, and
discuss the various stages of its evolution in terms of static and dynamic
efficiency characteristics. We continue with an emphasis on the critical role
of regulation as a major factor affecting the performance of the financial
system itself, both in the context of national economic growth and
competitiveness, and as a factor in defining the role of various types of
financial firms. We next consider a critical and controversial dimension in
the design of the financial system, the relationship between the structure of
financial institutions, and the linkages to ownership and the control process

in industry. How countries deal with this issue can have dramatic effects on both the financial system and the fundamentals of economic performance.

In the case of the transition economies of Eastern Europe and Asia, a choice has had to be made as to the type of financial system that is likely to deliver the best economic performance over the long term, while at the same time being adequately capable of dealing with the kinds of crises and market inefficiencies that are characteristic of the transition process.

6.2   Stylized process of financial intermediation

The central component of any model of the modern financial system is the nature of the conduits through which the financial assets of the ultimate savers flow-through to the liabilities of the ultimate users of finance, both within and between national economies. This involves alternative and competing modes of financial intermediation, or "contracting" between counterparties in financial transactions. A convenient model that can be used to guide thinking on financial contracting and the role of financial institutions and markets is summarized in Exhibit 6.1 -- a generic flow-of-funds diagram that can apply equally at the domestic and global levels.

The diagram depicts the financial process among the different sectors of the national and international economy in terms of: (1) the underlying environmental and regulatory determinants, or drivers; (2) the financial infrastructure services that need to be provided -- market information, financial research and its dissemination, financial rating services and portfolio diagnostics on the one hand, and trading, payments, transactions clearance and settlement, and custody services on the other; as well as (3) the generic information, interpretation and transactions cost advantages or "competencies" needed to add value and profit from the three primary intersectoral linkages, namely:

●   Savings/commercial banking and other traditional forms of intermediated finance.
●   Investment banking and securitized intermediation.
●   Various financial direct-connect mechanisms between borrowers and lenders.

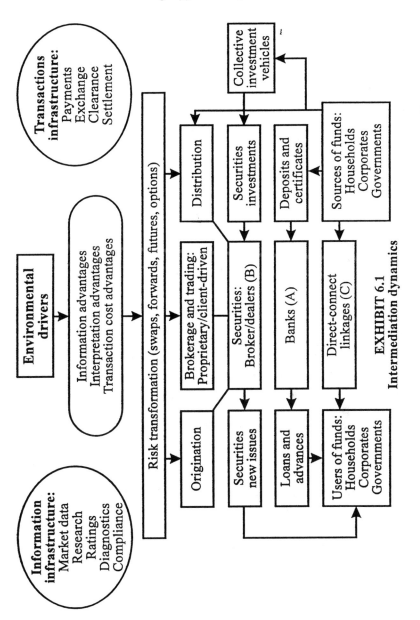

**EXHIBIT 6.1
Intermediation dynamics**

Ultimate sources of surplus funds tapped by financial intermediaries arise in the household sector (deferred consumption or savings), the corporate sector (retained earnings or business savings) and the government sector (budgetary surpluses and external reserve buildups).

- Under the first or "classic" mode of financial intermediation, savings (or funds-sources) are held in the form of deposits or alternative types of claims issued by commercial banks, savings organizations, insurance companies or other forms of financial institutions entitled to finance themselves by placing their liabilities directly with the general public. Financial institutions then use these funds flows (liabilities) to purchase domestic and international assets issued by non-financial institution agents such as firms and governments.

- Under the second mode of funds flows, savings may be allocated directly (or indirectly via so-called collective investment vehicles) to the purchase of securities publicly issued and sold by various governmental and private sector organizations in the domestic and international financial markets.

- Under the third alternative, savings held in collective investment vehicles may be allocated directly to borrowers through various forms of private placement and other (possibly automated) direct-sale mechanisms to distribute their obligations, or they may be internally deployed within the saving entity (e.g., retained earnings of nonfinancial corporations).

Ultimate users of funds comprise the same three segments of the economy -- the household or consumer sector, the business sector and the government sector.

- Consumers may finance purchases by means of personal loans from banks or by loans secured by purchased assets (hire-purchase or instalment loans). These may appear on the asset side of the balance sheets of credit institutions on a revolving basis for the duration of the respective loan contracts, or they may be sold off into the financial market in the form of structured securities backed by various types of receivables.

- Corporations may borrow from banks in the form of unsecured or asset-backed straight or revolving credit facilities and/or they may sell debt obligations (e.g., commercial paper, receivables financing, fixed-income securities of various types) or equities directly into the financial market.

- Governments can likewise borrow from credit institutions (sovereign borrowing) or issue full faith and credit or revenue-backed securities directly into the market.

With the exception of consumers, borrowers such as corporations and governments also have the possibility of privately issuing and placing their obligations with institutional investors, thereby circumventing both credit institutions and the public debt and equity markets, and even consumer debt can be repackaged as structured asset-backed securities and sold to privately investors. And as noted, internal financial flows within economic entities comprising the end-users of the financial system is an ever present alternative to external finance.

Alternative modes of financial contracting

In the first mode of external financial contracting (Mode A in Exhibit 6.1), depositors buy the "secondary" financial claims or liabilities issued by credit institutions, and benefit from liquidity, convenience, and safety through the ability of financial institutions to diversify risk and improve credit quality through professional management and monitoring of their holdings of primary financial claims (debt and equity). Savers can choose among a set of standardized contracts and receive payments/transactions services and interest that may or may nor be subject to varying degrees of government regulation.

In the second mode (Mode B), investors may select their own portfolios of financial assets directly from among the publicly issued debt and equity instruments on offer. This may provide a broader range of options than standardized bank contracts, and permit the larger investors to tailor portfolios more closely to their objectives while still achieving acceptable liquidity through rapid execution of trades -- aided by linkages with banks and other financial institutions that are part of the domestic payments mechanism. Investors may also choose to have their portfolios professionally managed, through various types of collective investment vehicles (mutual funds, pension funds, life insurance companies).

In the third mode (Mode C), institutional investors buy large blocks of privately issued securities. In doing so, they may face a liquidity penalty -- due to the absence or limited availability of a liquid secondary market -- for which they normally are rewarded via a higher yield. On the other hand, directly-placed securities usually involve lower issuing costs and can be specifically "tailored" to more closely match issuer and investor requirements than can publicly-issued securities. Institutional and regulatory developments, especially in the United States, have added to the liquidity and depth of some direct-placement markets in recent years.

Value to ultimate savers and investors, inherent in the financial processes described here, accrues in the form of a three-way combination of yield, safety and liquidity. Value to ultimate users of funds likewise accrues in the form of a combination of financing cost, transactions cost, flexibility and liquidity. This value can be enhanced through credit backstops, guarantees and derivative instruments such as forward rate agreements, caps, collars, futures and options provided by financial institutions acting either as banks or as securities firms.

Finally, the three intermediation channels identified in Exhibit 6.1 can be linked functionally and geographically, both domestically and internationally.

- Functional linkages permit bank receivables, for example, to be repackaged and sold to nonbank securities investors. Or bank credit facilities or insurance company guarantees can support the issuance of securities. Or privately placed securities may eventually be eligible for sale in public markets.
- Geographic linkages make it possible for savers and issuers to access markets in foreign and offshore markets, thereby improving risk, liquidity and yield or reducing transaction costs.

If permitted by financial regulation, various kinds of financial firms emerge to perform one or more of the roles suggested in Exhibit 6.1 -- commercial banks, savings banks, postal savings institutions, savings cooperatives, credit unions, securities firms (full-service firms and various kinds of specialists), mutual funds, insurance companies, finance companies, finance subsidiaries of industrial companies, and others. Members of each strategic group compete with each other, as well as with members of other strategic groups. Assuming it is allowed to do so by the regulators, each firm elects to operate in one or more of the three financial-process modes identified in Exhibit 6.1, according to its own competitive advantages -- i.e., its comparative efficiency in the relevant financial production mode compared to that of other firms.

Static and dynamic efficiency aspects

Issues relating to the static and dynamic efficiency of the three alternative, stylized financial processes depicted in Exhibit 6.1 can be summarized as follows.

Static efficiency is represented as the all-in, weighted average spread (differential) between rates of return provided to ultimate savers and the cost of funds to users. This "gap" depicts the overall cost of using a particular mode or type of financial process, and is reflected in the monetary value of resources used-up in the course of financial intermediation. In particular, it reflects the direct costs of production (operating and administrative costs, cost of capital, net regulatory burdens, etc.). It also reflects losses incurred in the financial process, as well as liquidity premia and any monopoly profits earned. Financial processes that are considered "statically inefficient" are usually characterized by high spreads due to high overhead costs, high losses, high levels of regulation including barriers to market-access, excess intermediation profits and the like.

Dynamic efficiency is characterized by rates of financial product and process innovation through time.

- *Product innovations* usually involve creation of new financial instruments (e.g., caps, futures, options, swaps) along with the ability to replicate certain instruments by bundling existing ones (synthetic securities) or to highlight a new financial attribute by re-bundling existing instruments. New approaches to contract pricing, passive or index-based portfolio investment techniques also fall under this rubric.
- *Process innovations* include contract design (e.g., cash settlement futures contracts), methods of clearance, payments, custody, securities settlement and trading, and techniques for efficient margin calculation.

Successful product and process innovation broadens the menu of financial services available to ultimate issuers, ultimate savers, or other agents along the various financial channels described in Exhibit 6.1. Probably the most powerful catalyst affecting the competitive dynamics of the financial services industry has been technological change. However, there may be costs associated with financial innovation as well. Examples include financial instruments and processes that take substantial resources to develop but that ultimately fail to meet a need in the marketplace, that are misrepresented to end-users, or that are inadequately managed with respect to the various market or credit risks involved.

It is against a background of continuous innovation and pressure for dynamic efficiency that financial markets and institutions have evolved and converged. Global financial markets for foreign exchange, debt instruments and to a lesser extent equity have developed various degrees of "seamlessness". Indeed, it is arguable that the most advanced of the world's financial markets are approaching a theoretical, "complete" optimum where there are sufficient financial instruments and markets to span the whole spectrum of risk and return outcomes.

Both static and dynamic efficiency are obviously important from the standpoint of national and global resource allocation, not only within the financial services industry itself but also as it effects users of financial services. That is, since financial services can be viewed as inputs to the overall real-sector production process, the level of national output and income -- as well as its rate of economic growth -- is directly or indirectly affected by the static and dynamic efficiency attributes of the financial system. A "retarded" financial services sector can represent an important impediment to a nation's overall real economic performance. As such, inefficiencies distort the patterns of allocation of labor as well as capital. One major reason for progressive deregulation in many countries during the 1980s and 1990s has been an attempt to capture, for the countries involved, static and dynamic efficiency gains -- and at the same time to maximize the real value-added generated in the financial services industry itself.

Structural shifts in the intermediation process

As noted, the three alternative channels of financial funds flows identified in Exhibit 6.1 often compete vigorously with each other for transactions volume in the financial intermediation process. The winners and losers among institutions competing in this process tend to be relatively consistent across national and international financial markets. In the case of the most highly developed financial systems, the securities industry (Mode B in Exhibit 6.1) has gained at the expense of the banking industry (Mode A). The reason for this migration of financial flows from one process to another arguably has much to do with changes in the relative static and dynamic efficiency characteristics and costs (or spreads) of intermediation via traditional financial institutions as against more direct securities market processes — and less oppressive regulation (see below).

On the borrower side of Exhibit 6.1, this has been manifested in the increasing use of the commercial paper markets as a substitute for bank credit lines as well and medium-term note programs and domestic and international bond issues for longer-term debt financing. Nonbank lending to business by finance companies and insurance companies, as well as private placements of securities with such institutions, have further eroded the market share of banks in a number of national financial environments. Whereas corporate and institutional access to the securities markets is obvious, even households have greatly increased their access to financing via securities issues in a number of countries via securitized liabilities such as mortgage loans and credit card debt -- i.e., the issuance of traded financial instruments against anticipated cash-flows of interest and principal from various kinds of receivables. Securitization tends to allow increased asset portfolio liquidity and better ability to manage interest-rate risk exposures. Most types of bank loans have become potentially securitizable -- a trend that has not necessarily abated, as governments in various countries change bank and securities regulations to allow the process to spread and as pressure mounts from financial services firms as well as non-financial corporations for access to this technology. Thus, a major integrating factor in world financial markets is likely to come from the direct recycling of bank loans through one of the many available securitization vehicles.

On the investor side of Exhibit 6.1 the same migration from banks to the securities industry is evident in the growing share of investments as a form of savings, particularly through fiduciaries such as pension funds, insurance companies and mutual funds.

The next set of developments in some of the most innovative financial markets is likely to involve replacement of traditional banking and securities forms of financial intermediation by direct financial links between sources and users of funds that have the potential of further cutting-out traditional financial intermediaries -- the direct-connect mechanisms identified as Mode C in Exhibit 6.1. This includes direct intercompany payments clearing such as electronic data interchange (EDI) and automated private placements of securities, for example, as is already done in some European financial markets using automated Dutch auction distribution of government securities. Although they are often closely interrelated, the three intermediation modes in Exhibit 6.1 thus compete with one another in a modern financial system on the basis of static and dynamic efficiency as well as differential regulatory burdens to which they are exposed.

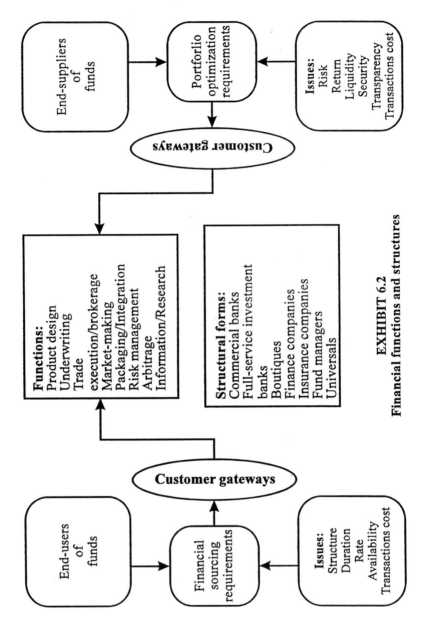

EXHIBIT 6.2
Financial functions and structures

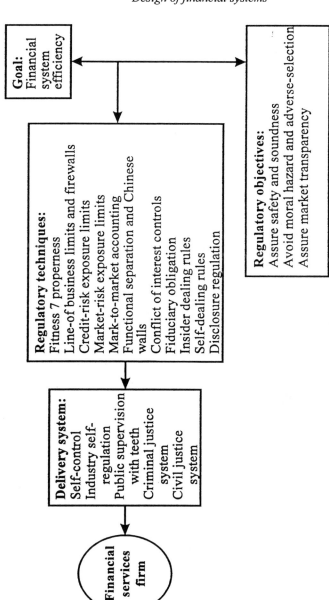

Goal:
Financial system efficiency

Regulatory techniques:
Fitness 7 properness
Line-of business limits and firewalls
Credit-risk exposure limits
Market-risk exposure limits
Mark-to-market accounting
Functional separation and Chinese walls
Conflict of interest controls
Fiduciary obligation
Insider dealing rules
Self-dealing rules
Disclosure regulation

Delivery system:
Self-control
Industry self-regulation
Public supervision with teeth
Criminal justice system
Civil justice system

Financial services firm

Regulatory objectives:
Assure safety and soundness
Avoid moral hazard and adverse-selection
Assure market transparency

EXHIBIT 6.3
Regulatory tradeoffs, techniques and control

As a consequence of these developments, borrowers in many national financial systems today face a range of alternatives for obtaining financing, and even households and small or medium-size companies which are basically limited to bank credit can subsequently have their loans securitized, and benefit from both access to a much broader pool of funding sources as well as conversion of illiquid bank loans into liquid securities forms. The gains from both activities will tend to be partially passed backward to the borrower. Similarly, today's modern financial systems tend to provide a wide range of opportunities and services to investors which allow them to optimize their asset portfolios by taking advantage of the domestic and international portfolio diversification across the range of financial instruments being offered, as well as improvements in the securities market infrastructure services. Again, even the retail investor can access these investment alternatives and process-technology improvements by taking advantage of the broad array of mutual funds, unit trusts and other collective investment vehicles being aggressively marketed to households -- in many cases using imaginative, high-technology non-stationary distribution techniques backed by extensive macroeconomic, financial market and securities research.

Even as intense competition across financial intermediation channels has developed, similar competition has emerged among national financial systems, as well as between them and offshore financial markets. Again, the borrower not only has the choice between bank credits and securities issues in the domestic market, but also has the alternative of borrowing or issuing abroad if foreign or offshore financing alternatives are more attractive. Similarly, savers and their fiduciaries have the option of going abroad to place funds if the returns and portfolio alternatives on offer are superior to those available at home. The general structure of financial intermediation and the alternative organizational forms of financial services firms are depicted in Exhibit 6.2.

6.3   Regulatory determinants of financial structures

The financial flows that are the basis of the preceding discussion of financial intermediation in general are dramatically affected by regulatory factors. Financial services comprise an industry that has usually been, and will continue to be, subject to significant public-authority regulation and supervision due to its fiduciary nature and the possibility of social costs associated with institutional failure (see the contribution by Anthony

Santomero (Paper 7) in this volume). Indeed, small changes in financial regulation can bring about truly massive changes in financial activity. In the process, they can affect the competitive viability and performance or different types of financial institutions spreading their activities across the financial spectrum depicted in Exhibit 6.1.Regulatory tradeoffs

Exhibit 6.3 depicts the policy tradeoffs that invariably confront those charged with designing and implementing a properly structured financial system. On the one hand, they must strive to achieve static and dynamic efficiency, with respect to the financial system as a whole, as well as the competitive viability of financial institutions that are subject to regulation -- characteristics discussed in the first section of this paper. On the other hand, they must safeguard the stability of institutions and the financial markets as a whole, in addition to encouraging what is considered acceptable market conduct, including the politically sensitive implied social contract between financial institutions and small, unsophisticated customers as well as problems of contagion and systemic risk. The problem of safety-net design is beset with difficulties such as moral hazard and adverse selection, and becomes especially problematic when products and activities shade into one-another, when on- and off-balance sheet activities are involved, and with domestic and offshore business is conducted. Regulators constantly face Type-I and Type-II problems -- i.e., inadequate regulation resulting in costly failures versus overregulation resulting in opportunity costs in the form of efficiencies not achieved.

Some of the principal options that regulators have at their disposal are also listed in Exhibit 6.3. These range from "fitness and properness" criteria under which a financial institution may be established, continue to operate or be shut-down -- including jurisdictional issues -- line-of-business regulation as to what specific types of institutions may do, as well as regulations as to liquidity, various types of exposures, capital adequacy, and the like, as well as marking-to-market (or lack thereof) of assets and liabilities. Regulatory initiatives, however, can have their own distortive impact on financial markets, and regulation becomes especially difficult when financial markets evolve rapidly and the regulator can easily get one or two steps behind.

The final element of Exhibit 6.3 involves the control techniques that may be applied, ranging from reliance on self-control on the part of boards and senior managements of financial firms concerned with protecting their franchises, through industry self-regulation, to public oversight by regulators with teeth -- including civil suits and criminal prosecution.

Just as there are tradeoffs implicit in Exhibit 6.3 between financial system performance and stability, so also there are tradeoffs between regulation and supervision, with some regulatory options (e.g., capital adequacy rules) fairly easy to supervise but full of distortive potential due to their broad-gauge nature, and others (e.g., fitness and properness criteria) possibly highly cost-effective but devilishly difficulty to supervise. Finally there are tradeoffs between supervision and performance, with some supervisory techniques far more costly to comply with than others. Regulators must try to optimize across this three-dimensional set of tradeoffs under conditions of rapid market and industry change, blurred institutional and activity demarcations, and international regulatory fault-lines.

It is useful to think of financial regulation and supervision as imposing a set of "taxes" and "subsidies" on the operations of financial firms, whether banks or securities firms, exposed to them. On the one hand, the imposition of reserve requirements, capital adequacy rules, interest/usury ceilings and certain forms of financial disclosure requirements can be viewed as imposing additional implicit "taxes" on a financial firm's activities in the sense that they increase the costs of financial intermediation. On the other hand, regulator-supplied deposit insurance, lender-of-last resort facilities and institutional bailouts serve to stabilize financial markets and reduce the risk of systemic failure, thereby lowering the costs of financial intermediation. They can therefore be viewed as implicit "subsidies" by taxpayers (see Kane, 1987).

The difference between these "tax" and "subsidy" elements of regulation can be viewed as the net regulatory burden (NRB) faced by financial firms in any given jurisdiction. In an individual economy with a single regulatory body, competition will spark a dynamic interplay between demanders and suppliers of financial services. Banks and securities firms will seek to reduce their NRB and increase their profitability. If they can do so at low cost, they will actively seek product innovations and new avenues that avoid cumbersome and costly regulations. This may be facilitated both in the case of multiple and sometimes overlapping domestic regulatory bodies as well as in the global case of multiple and often competing regulatory bodies.

In the international financial system, with many governments and many regulatory authorities, there is fertile ground for banks and securities firms to reduce NRB. National regulatory authorities may compete among each other on the basis of NRB to preserve or reclaim financial activities within their respective regulatory domains, and firms benefit from such international competition, especially if financial innovation and technological change allows them to operate successfully at a distance from their home bases. Users of financial services also benefit to the extent that competition forces financial firms to pass-through to them the lower NRB. This view results in a "regulatory dialectic" -- a dynamic interaction between the regulator and the regulated, in which there is continuous action and reaction by all parties, in which the players may behave aggressively or defensively, and adapt with varying speed and degrees of freedom in line with their "average adaptive efficiencies" as follows (Kane, 1987):

- Less-regulated players move faster and more freely than more tightly regulated players.
- Private players move faster and more freely than governmental players.
- Regulated players move faster and more freely than their regulators.
- International regulatory bodies move more slowly and less freely than all of the other players.

Given this ordering of adaptive efficiencies, we expect that the lag between a regulation and its avoidance is on average shorter than the lag between avoidance and re-regulation. The lag in re-regulation may be shorter for industry-based, self-regulatory groups than for governments. It may be longest when international regulatory efforts are involved.

6.4   Financial system structure and industry linkages

A key question in the design of financial systems that is particularly important in the context of transition economies is the relationship between banks and nonfinancial firms. Should banks own and or control industrial companies? Should industrial companies own or control banks? Several models are available for examination (see Walter, 1993). These are depicted in Exhibit 6.4.

The equity-market system

In this essentially Anglo-American approach, bank functions are split by legislative action between commercial banking and financial market institutions. The former may provide short-term financing for firms, but the major source of external financing for firms is the capital market. In the capital markets, shares of corporations are held by the public, either directly or through institutional vehicles—like funds managed by insurance companies, mutual funds and pension funds—and are actively traded. Corporate restructuring, involving the shrinking of the firm's assets or their shifting to alternative uses or locations—is triggered by exploitation of a control premium between the existing market capitalization of a firm and that which an unaffiliated acquirer (whether an industrial company or an active financial investor) perceives and acts upon by initiating a takeover effort designed to unlock shareholder value through management changes (see Ergas, 1986). There is a high level of transparency and reliance on public information provided by auditors, with systemic surveillance by equity investors and research analysts. Concerns about unwanted takeover efforts prompt management to act in the interests of shareholders, many of whom tend to view their shares as put-options—options to sell. The control structure of this essentially outsider-based system is mainly confined to arm's length financing, including takeovers and internal corporate restructuring, although investment banks may be active in giving strategic and financial advice and sometimes taking equity positions in (and occasionally control of) firms for their own accord (see Rybczynski, 1989).

This model, to operate to maximum effect, assumes that the more powerful stakeholders in the firm (shareholders, managers and customers) regard this process as legitimate. Its central claim to that legitimacy resides in an assertion that, everything else being equal, it is the most efficient to maximizing wealth. Its supporters also argue that free markets are the most compatible of all systems with democracy as a system of limited government. If, for instance, financial markets are free to allocate savings to the most efficient rather than the most politically influential users of capital, then the returns for the savers will be higher than if some of them use their vote to extract rents from less remunerative, but politically-determined investments. Labor market legislation in particular has to be supportive, so that labor forces may be shrunk or shifted in task or location with the minimum of friction. The model also assumes that the government will not prove a light touch for corporate lobbies seeking to avoid restructuring or takeover through access to the public purse, as a less demanding source of funds. Government's major task is to provide the regulatory and legal structure within open capital markets may function, and to supply a safety net for the unemployed, the infirm or the old. Not least, this Anglo-American approach assumes that the two kings of the corporate roost are shareholders and customers—if other types of financial systems in world markets have different priorities, benefitting other interests they will eventually be forced to adapt or to lose market share to rivals focusing firmly on consumer and shareholder interests.

The bank-based system

The bank-based system of corporate control is often associated with Germany, where the rules of the game have traditionally enabled banks to take deposits, extend loans to firms and issue securities on capital markets in a tight relationship to clients. In this system, significant equity stakes in nonfinancial companies are held by banks and by investment companies run by banks, who act as both commercial and investment bankers to their clients. With significant equity as well as debt exposures to their clients, banks exert a vital monitoring role in the management of corporations, including active boardroom participation and guidance with the benefit of non-public (inside) information. Insurance companies may hold significant stakes in banks and nonfinancial companies, which in turn may also hold shares in insurance companies. The public holds shares in both banks and corporations, but these shares tend to be ceded by individual owners for voting by banks on the grounds that the banks have superior information about corporate policy and performances as a result of their expertise and of their privileged access to corporate information. However, markets for corporate equity and debt tend to be poorly developed in bank-based systems, with relatively large investor holdings of public-sector bonds as opposed to corporate bonds or stocks. The investing public in such a system tends to be risk averse, preferring predictability and reliability to lack of transparency and the "surprises" that come with it. This attitude among the public is reciprocated by the management of firms who invite patient investors to hold their shares in return for capital gains and collateral business in the long run as the firm expands, rather than to higher dividends now that could deprive management of the financial resources needed to invest in the firm. Financial disclosure tends to be relatively low as accounts are drawn up essentially to meet tax and reporting obligations rather than to inform a shareholding public. The portion of shares which float freely on the market is small, so that stock markets may be thin and volatile as investors (including foreigners) move in and out of shares.

1. The equity-market system

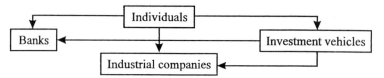

2. The bank-based system

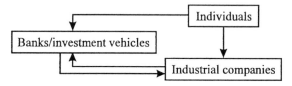

3. The bank-industrial cross-holding system

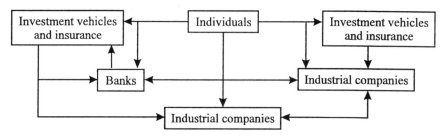

4. The state-centered system

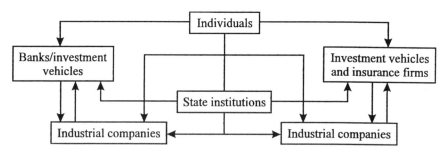

EXHIBIT 6.4
Alternative corporate control structures

The bank-based system is embedded in a regime which buttresses its legitimacy (see Röller, 1990). Regulatory bodies are supported by framework laws, which provide ample discretion for both regulators and the market operators in the relevant sectors of the financial system to adapt to changing circumstances and market processes. The central bank gives priority to maintaining the value of the currency, in order to secure the adherence of depositors and investors. With its related banking and insurance regulators, the central bank polices the financial system, imposing reserve requirements on banks, requiring financial institutions to maintain provisions and capital reserves, and placing limits on exposures to credit risk. As the bank-based system personalizes many of the market functions performed by impersonal capital markets, trust is an essential ingredient of relations among its insider élites. Bankers play a central "coordinating" function through their positions on corporate supervisory boards, their close relations with the central bank, and managing the bond markets, their administration of delegated shares in annual general meetings or their provision of multiple services to clients (see Schonfield, 1965).

This role, however, is shared with other bodies, such as labour unions, local or central government officials, and managers in their capacity as stakeholders in corporations. Bankers are not, therefore, left alone to carry the burden of public acclaim or hostility through fluctuating corporate performances over the business cycle. Above all, they are guardians of a stable, property-holding democracy which has co-opted labour unions through their representatives' acquired positions on works councils and on corporate supervisory boards (see Baums, 1996)

The bank-industry crossholding system

The crossholding system is rooted in close collaboration between government bureaucrats, corporate managers, and party politicians who share a common aim to achieve rapid economic growth. This is achieved initially through a favorable combination of external circumstances and in the abundance of low-cost capital and labour (see Prouse 1990). As corporations develop under this system, they seek stable shareholders who are sufficiently patient to enable managers to recuperate investments in the development of products and processes, and in their stable labour force. Corporations prefer other corporations as shareholders to banks because they share similar concerns, as compared to banks which are suspect of wanting even a modest flow of income from their lending exposures as market processes start to alter the financial system. The best condition for corporations with high fixed costs is to achieve self-financing by building market-share. If bank-industrial crossholdings are pervasive, banks in any event are most comfortable when the corporations in which they hold stakes rely mainly on their own resources. The financial system as a whole must be prepared to deal with the consequences of large trade surpluses, which flow from joint corporate interest in market shares. Domestic inflationary pressures have to be kept down through rapid recycling of funds earned from exports. This entails the building up of portfolio investments in other markets around the world. Revaluations of the currency from exports and investment income abroad may be delayed by further external portfolio investments, as well as by corporate direct investments abroad as domestic production costs continue to rise relative to other locations around the world.

The bank-industry crossholding system is perhaps best embodied in Japan's *keiretsu* (see below), where nonfinancial corporations as well as banks hold significant stakes in each other and hold reciprocal seats on boards of directors. Both linkages may complement close domestically-based supplier-customer relationships, with dependability and cooperation often dominating price as transactions criteria. The central paradox of such a bank-industrial crossholding system is that it seeks to exclude foreign ownership and market access, while requiring open markets for corporate assets in other countries alongside open access for exports—including heavy reliance on export finance.

The state-led financial market system

France is the reference-point for the *state-led financial market* system. The Ministry of Finance is the dominant focus for savers and borrowers as it regulates the capital market directly. Deposit taking institutions with surplus funds place them in the capital markets, and are taken-up by public-sector institutions which lend them to specific industries, such as housing, agriculture, nuclear energy, or regional investments. Both lending and borrowing institutions fall under the tutelage of the Ministry of Finance, which formally draws-up investment priorities through elaborate consultations with trade associations recorded in "The Plan", through negotiations with the Ministry of Industry or in response to requests filtered through the political parties. Public officials in the Finance Ministry enjoy prestige conveyed by their position in the state hierarchy, and because of the value of their contacts across the extensive state sector to those seeking access to it.

As resources of personnel and time are scarce, such a state-centered administrative mechanism at the heart of the financial system promotes a queue. Organizations with close contacts and claims on the loyalties of public officials, such as state-controlled economic enterprises or large private firms, get served first. Small and medium-size firms are squeezed aside, so their representatives join one or another of the political armies contending for privileged access to the state's resources through elections. The regular cycle of local, regional or national elections are thus also contests between competing producer coalitions for a silver key to public finance.

A state-led financial system also features other characteristics as well. Financial resources are not alone in flowing through the hands of public officials. Patronage flows too, in the form of appointments to the management and boards of state enterprises or to large private enterprises in receipt of various state benefits. Public officials enter into competition among themselves, through their own organizations and to a lesser extent through their proclamations of party political fealty. Their legitimacy derives from a claim to act in the public interest. Yet the institutions whose resources they deploy directly or indirectly may expand their stakes in business enterprises, extending further the field open to public patronage in the pursuit of private promotion.

Indeed, a cynic could argue that such a state-led system has a vested interest in nationalizing private enterprise in order to expand the reach of public officials, and then of privatizing the assets in exchange for comfortable positions in the management or on the boards of companies. Ownership of these corporations is less significant than the fact that they remain on the career circuit, and that they stay within the bounds of what is in effect a political market for economic control. Such a political market extends throughout the multiple levels of government, as local mayors become businessmen and bankers for their local communities through resources obtained through the political process. Ultimately, the state can lose its status as acting in the public interest, and merges into the surrounding maze of non-transparent political markets.

(a) Full integration

Universal Bank

Bank activities	Securities activities	Insurance activities	Other

(b) German variant

Universal Bank

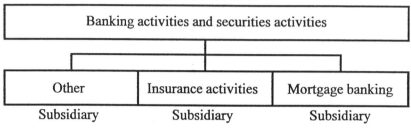

Banking activities and securities activities		

Other	Insurance activities	Mortgage banking
Subsidiary	Subsidiary	Subsidiary

(c) U.K. variant

Universal Bank

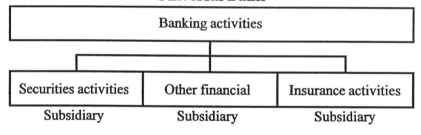

Banking activities		

Securities activities	Other financial	Insurance activities
Subsidiary	Subsidiary	Subsidiary

(c) U.S. variant

Holding Company

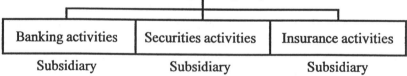

Banking activities	Securities activities	Insurance activities
Subsidiary	Subsidiary	Subsidiary

EXHIBIT 6.5
Universal bank organization structures

Organizational design

A final question related to financial structures in transition economies is the degree of universality that should be incorporated in financial institutions. Universal banking can be defined as the conduct of an array of financial services comprising credit, trading of financial instruments and foreign exchange (and their derivatives), underwriting of new debt and equity issues, brokerage, corporate advisory services (including mergers and acquisitions advice), investment management and insurance. Clearly, the more important are economies of scale and scope, the more competitive should universal financial institutions be as against smaller and more narrowly-focused financial institutions. Universal banking can take the basic forms depicted in Exhibit 6.5.

- The fully-integrated universal bank, capable of supplying the complete range of financial services from one institutional entity.
- The partially-integrated financial conglomerate, capable of supplying substantially the same set of services but with several (such as mortgage banking, leasing and insurance) provided through wholly-owned or partially-owned subsidiaries.
- The bank-subsidiary structure, under which the bank focuses essentially on commercial banking and all others, including investment banking and insurance, are carried out through legally separate subsidiaries of the bank.
- The holding company structure, where a holding company owns both banking and non-banking subsidiaries that are legally separate and individually capitalized, insofar as financial activities other than "banking" are permitted by law. These may be separated by Chinese walls and firewalls if there are internal or regulatory concerns about institutional safety and soundness or conflicts of interest. The holding company may also be allowed to own industrial firms (see below). Or the holding company may itself be an industrial company. Both cases raise the issue of central bank bailouts of industrial companies.
- The separated system, in which banks are not allowed to engage in securities or insurance activities, as has been true in the United States and Japan until relatively recently.

Recent studies have suggested that the separated system, as has existed in the United States and Japan, incorporates a number of competitive disadvantages against various forms of universal banking practices in most of the rest of the world. In particular, the holding company form and the bank-subsidiary form of universal banking appear to offer many of the scale and scope advantages of fully integrated universal banking without necessarily encountering some of the disadvantages that accompany bureaucracy and inflexibility in fast-moving financial markets. This does not suggest that smaller, leaner, faster specialist firms, such as investment banks focusing on corporate finance, will be driven from the market by universals. Problems of potential conflicts of interest, cost structures and agility virtually assure such firms a viable role in the financial system. It does suggest, however, that competitive conditions in the open market should drive the structural forms that financial firms decide to adopt.

6.5   Conclusions

Transition economies have a rare opportunity to configure their financial systems, after scrapping the mono-banks and related financial apparatus of the central planning era, without a great deal of excess baggage in the form of vested interests in the status quo. The installation of high-performance financial systems that combine strong efficiency characteristics with acceptable safety and soundness will arguably be more influential than most other considerations in charting the path of economic growth.

Recent World Bank evidence (Levine, 1996) suggests that the development of local financial markets plays a critical role in the economic growth process:

- Countries that had more-liquid financial markets in 1976 tended to grow much faster over the next 18 years than those which did not.
- High levels of financial liquidity, measured by the turnover ratio (trading volume divided by market capitalization in the case of equities) tends to be associated with more rapid growth over the same period.
- Countries with high trading-to-volatility ratios likewise tended to grow faster, after controlling for conventional economic, political and policy variables associated with growth differentials for various periods and country samples. Volatility per se does not seem to be related to growth, but rather the ease with which financial instruments can be traded.
- Financial-market development seems to complement—rather than

substitute for—bank finance, both of which seem to promote growth independent of each other. Higher levels of development of the banking system are associated with faster growth no matter what the state of development of the stock market, and vice-versa, for reasons that are not yet well understood. Although most corporate investment in emerging-market countries is financed through bank loans and retained earnings, both (along with the debt-equity ratio) are positively associated with stock market liquidity.

Such findings suggest that international financial flows may play a substantially more critical role in the growth process than previously thought. They can contribute disproportionately to market liquidity, especially in the presence of "noise traders" such as open-end mutual funds which *must* but and sell in response to new client investments and redemptions and maintenance of portfolio weights. They can force security prices into line with those prevailing on global markets. They can encourage upgrading of the legal infrastructure, trading systems, clearance and settlement utilities, information disclosure and accounting standards, and custody services. They can improve the process of corporate governance, perhaps in association with significant shareholdings by banks. And they can serve as a bellwether for local investors, who may find encouragement from a significant foreign presence in the marketplace.

References

Aliber, Robert Z., 1984, International banking: A survey, Journal of Money, Credit and Banking, November.

Bank for International Settlements, 1986, Recent Innovations in International Banking (Bank for International Settlements, Basel).

Baumol, William, J. Panzar and R. Willig, 1982, Contestability of Markets and the Theory of Industry Structure. (Harcourt Brace Jovanovich, New York).

Baums, T., 1996, Universal Banks and Investment Companies, in Germany, in: Anthony Saunders and Ingo Walter, eds., Financial System Design (Irwin-Professional, Oak Park, Ill).

Cable, J., 1985, Capital market information and industrial performance: the role of West German banks, The Economic Journal, pp. 118-132.

Caves, Richard, and Michael Porter, 1977, From, entry barriers to mobility barriers: conjectural decisions and contrived deterrence to new competition, Quarterly Journal of Economics, May.

Dermine, J., ed., 1993, European Banking After 1992, Revised Edition (Basil Blackwell, Oxford).

Edwards, J. and K. Fischer, 1992, An overview of the German financial system, Centre for Economic Policy Research Working Paper, November.

Ergas, H., 1986, Does Technology Matter? (Centre for European Policy Studies, Brussels).

Federal Reserve Board of Governors, 1986, The Separation of Banking and Commerce in American Banking History, Appendix A of P. Volcker's statement before the Subcommittee on Commerce, Consumer and Monetary Affairs of the House Committee on Government Operations, June.

Gnehm, A. and C. Thalmann, 1989, Conflicts of Interest in Financial Operations: Problems of Regulation in the National and International Context, paper prepared for the Swiss Bank Corporation, Basel.

Goldberg, L. and G. Hanweck, 1990, The development and growth of banking centres and the integration of local banking markets, The Review of Research in Banking and Finance, Spring, pp. 85-105.

Goldberg, M., R.W. Helseley and M.D. Levi, 1988, The location of international financial centres, Annals of Regional Science, pp. 81-94.

Goldberg, M., R.W. Helseley and M.D. Levi, 1989, The location of international financial centre activity, Regional Studies, pp. 1-7.

Hayes, S. III, A.M. Spence and D.v.P. Marks, 1983, Competition in the Investment Banking Industry (Harvard University Press, Cambridge, Mass).

Herring, R.J. and A.M. Santomero, 1990, The corporate structure of financial conglomerates, Journal of Financial Services Research, December, pp. 471-497.

Hoshi, T., A. Kayshap and D. Sharfstein, 1991a, The role of banks in reducing the costs of financial distress in Japan, Journal of Financial Economics, pp. 151-167.

Hoshi, T., A. Kayshap and D. Sharfstein, 1991b, Corporate structure, liquidity and investment, evidence from Japanese industrial groups, Quarterly Journal of Economics, pp. 33- 60.

Institute of International Bankers, 1994, Global Survey (Institute of International Bankers, New York).

Jensen, M. and R. Ruback, 1983, The market for corporate control: the scientific evidence, Journal of Financial Economics, 11, April, pp. 5-50.

Kane, E.J., 1987, Competitive Financial Reregulation: An International Perspective, in R. Portes and A. Swoboda, eds., Threats to International Financial Stability (Cambridge University Press, Cambridge).

Kim, S. B., 1990, Modus Operandi of Lenders-Cum-Shareholder Banks, Federal Reserve Bank of San Francisco, mimeo, September.

Kaufman, G., Ed., 1992, Banking in Major Countries (Oxford University Press, New York).

Krümmel, Hans-Jakob, 1980, German universal banking scrutinized, Journal of Banking and Finance, March.

Levich, R. and I. Walter, 1990, Tax driven regulatory drag: European financial centres in the 1990s, in: Horst Siebert (ed.) Reforming Capital Income Taxation (J.C.B. Mohr Paul Siebeck, Tuebingen).

Levine, Ross, 1996, Stock markets: a spur to economic growth, Finance and Development, March.

Mayer, C.P., 1992, Corporate Control and Transformation in Eastern Europe, paper presented at a SUERF conference on The New Europe: Evolving Economic and Financial Systems in East and West, Berlin, Germany, 8-10 October.

Neave, E., 1992, The Economic Organization of a Financial System (Routledge, London).

Newman, H., 1978, Strategic groups and the structure-performance relationships, Review of Economics and Statistics, August.

Panzar, J.C. and R.D. Willig, 1981, Economies of scope, American Economic Review, May.

Pastré, O., 1981, International bank-industry relations: an empirical assessment, Journal of Banking and Finance, March.

Pozdena, R.J., 1989, Do banks need securities powers? Federal Reserve Bank of San Francisco Weekly Letter, 29 December.

Prowse, S.D., 1990, Institutional Investment Patterns and Corporate Financial Behaviour in the U.S. and Japan, Board of Governors of the Federal Reserve System, Working Paper, January.

Reed, H.C., 1981, The Preeminence of International Financial Centres. (Praeger, New York).

Röller, W. 1990, Die Macht der Banken, Zeitschrift für das Gesamte Kreditwesen, 1 January.

Rybczynski, T.N., 1989, Corporate restructuring, National Westminster Bank Review, August.

Saunders, A., 1990, The Separation of Banking and Commerce, New York University Salomon Centre, Working Paper, September.

Saunders, A. and I. Walter, 1993, Universal Banking in America (Oxford University Press, New York,).

Schonfield, A., 1965, Modern Capitalism: The Changing Balance of Public and Private Power (Oxford University Press, New York).

Schott, J.J., 1994, The Uruguay Round   (Institute for International Economics, Washington, D.C.).

Sheard, P., 1989, The main bank system and corporate monitoring and control in Japan, Journal of Commercial Banking and Organization, pp. 399-422.

Smith, G.D., and R. Sylla, 1992, Wall Street and the Capital Markets in the Twentieth Century: An Historical Essay, New York University Salomon Centre Working Paper, September.

Smith, R.C., 1993, Comeback: The Restoration of American Banking Power in the New World Economy (Harvard Business School Press, Boston).

Smith, R.C. and I. Walter, 1990, Global Financial Services (Harper & Row, New York).

Smith, R.C. and I. Walter, 1992, Bank-Industry Linkages: Models for Eastern European Restructuring, paper presented at a SUERF conference on The New Europe: Evolving Economic and Financial Systems in East and West, Berlin, Germany, 8-10 October.

Steinherr, A. and C. Huveneers, 1992, On the Performance of Differently Regulated Financial Institutions: Some Empirical Evidence, Université Catholique de Louvain, Working Paper (mimeo.), February.

Task Force on the International Competitiveness of U.S. Financial Institutions, Subcommittee on Financial Institutions, Committee on Banking, Finance and Urban Affairs, U.S. House of Representatives, 1990, Report of the Task Force, November.

United States Treasury, 1992, Modernizing the Financial System: Recommendations for Safer, More Competitive Banks (Department of the Treasury, Washington, D.C.).

Walter, I., 1985a, Barriers to Trade in Banking and Financial Services. London, Trade Policy Research Centre.

Walter, I. (ed)., 1985b, Deregulating Wall Street (John Wiley & Sons, New York).

Walter, I., 1988, Global Competition in Financial Services (Harper & Row, Cambridge, Mass).

Walter, I., 1993, The Battle of the Systems: Control of Enterprises and the Global Economy (Institut für Weltwirtschaft, Kiel, Germany).

Walter, I. and R.C. Smith, 1989, Investment Banking in Europe: Restructuring for the 1990s (Basil Blackwell, Oxford).

Walter, I. and T. Hiraki (Eds.), 1993, Restructuring Japan's Securities Markets (Business One/Irwin, Homewood, Ill).

White, L.J., 1991,The S&L Debacle: Public Policy Lessons for Bank and Thrift Regulation (Oxford University Press, Oxford).

Financial Sector Reform and
Privatization in Transition Economies
J. Doukas, V. Murinde and C. Wihlborg (Editors)
© 1997 Elsevier Science Publishers B.V. All rights reserved

Chapter 7

$L51$ $P34$

THE REGULATORY AND PUBLIC POLICY AGENDA FOR EFFECTIVE INTERMEDIATION IN POST SOCIALIST ECONOMIES

$G21$

$G10$ $G28$

Anthony M. Santomero
The Wharton School, 2336 Steinberg Hall-Dietrich Hall, University of
Pennsylvania, Philadelphia, PA 19104-6367, USA

7.1   Introduction

The financial structure appropriately has become a focus of attention in countries that were once part of the socialist bloc. Policy-makers have come to recognize that financial markets and institutions are essential for a modern market economy. Yet, these policymakers and regulators are completely new to the scene, and woefully unaware of the requirements for efficient financial intermediation.

One should not be surprised by this lack of experience. In a planned economy, banks as we know them do not exist. Their notion of banking, in fact, is quite alien to our own. Calvo and Coricelli (1993) summed up the socialist view of banking this way:

"In a centrally planned economy (CPE), bankers are a mixed breed of accountants and public notaries... (B)anks' role in screening financially viable firms from non-viable ones is relatively minor, if at all relevant. Firms, as well as banks, are state owned. Therefore, managers have no control over firms' revenues, let along profits:.. (T)he firm will get new bank credit to buy new outputs. Banks continue to lend because they are ordered to do so... (T)he creation of new loans does not require previous loans to be served. Consequently in CPE's firm creditworthiness is taken for granted as long as managers comply with the dictates of the central program." (p.33)

And, just to accentuate the alien nature of the entities they conclude with:

"Little firm-specific information needs to be collected by the bank extending credit, since no firm-specific collateral is involved in the credit transaction". (p.33)

By contrast, market-based economies view financial intermediaries as providing a dramatically different service to the capital market participant. According to this view, the financial sector is central to the smooth functioning of a market-based economy. It facilitates savings and its efficient use by investors, transforming excess current income of one agent into demand for current output for investment purposes by other parts of the economy.

Financial intermediaries, and most particularly banks, perform a significant portion of the services provided by the financial sector. Particularly in the early stages of financial development, the banking sector tends to provide the most substantial fraction of these services (McKinnon, 1973; Corbett and Mayer, 1991). They do so by combining two functions within a single institution, i.e. they accept deposits for transactions or savings, and use these funds to invest in investment opportunities requiring capital.

This conversion of savings into investment through bank lending is successful only if the institutions involved effectively and efficiently carry out this charge. However, this is not an easy task. It involves the ex-ante evaluation of proposed investment opportunities, borrower monitoring throughout the project's life cycle, and the determination of the actual outcome associated with the projects financed using the borrowed funds.

Particularly in developing economies, there are always too many borrowers seeking credit for a set of highly heterogeneous projects, offering all kinds of contracts for future repayment in return. In most cases the situation is made worse by financial repression and regulated interest rates. Beyond this, the proposed projects are often misrepresented; the funds are often misallocated; and the investments' returns are often misstated ex-post by the entrepreneurs involved. And, even in the best of both worlds, the investment projects themselves are risky endeavours. Results may prove unsatisfactory due to no fault of either the borrower or lender. In short, bad things happen to good projects. To researchers in the field, these inefficiencies in the market are a clear situation in which contracting between borrower and lender can be said to occur in the presence of asymmetric imperfect information.

7.2   The environment for effective intermediation

It is in this world that banking firms exist, and it is incumbent upon regulation and the legal system to foster an environment in which they can survive. The environment of laws and regulations surrounding these institutions must be constructed in a manner that permits them to evaluate investment opportunities as effectively as possible, enforce contractual relationships with borrowers in the most incentive compatible way, and allows them both a reasonable chance to determine investment outcome, and, if necessary, recourse to collateral in the event that these contractual commitments cannot be met. In short, the financial landscape must include a clear set of financial standards, a clear contractual legal environment, and clear property rights - all with the expectations that such an environment will enhance the efficiency of credit decision-making and the flow of savings into the highest present value investments available in the real economy.

Unfortunately, this is not the present condition in the formerly planned economies (FPEs). As Udell and Wachtel (1995) report, the status of banking law, the commercial legal code, and bankruptcy laws in FPEs are far from ideal. In fact, in virtually none of the eight countries surveyed in NatWest (1994) could the banking environment be characterized as acceptable. Therefore, the result is less than ideal. The banking industry in most of the FPEs is in desperate shape. Reluctant politicians, worried about closure without deposit insurance and the real possibility of bank runs, have been feverishly looking for a way out of the morass.

Most industry representatives, and academics alike, have continued to voice the need for structural reforms in three critical areas of financial reporting, contract law, and bankruptcy rights and remedies, as the only long-run solution. To them, a movement toward an efficient capital market requires greater transparency in financial reporting, free and enforceable contracting, and the very real possibility of collateral foreclosure for the lending market to function effectively (Sarcinelli, 1992). What is envisaged is a financial system in which institutions can make investment decisions in an environment that more closely approximates the first best solution of full and symmetric information facing both entrepreneurs and lenders alike, in which behaviour is contractible and contracts enforceable.

This implies that reporting systems and standards are key ingredients in any viable structure, with contract law and commercial codes in place to ensure the enforceability of financial contracts. Both of these are necessary ingredients to a sound loan market. Finally, clear definitions of property rights, collateral rights, and bankruptcy remedies need to be established, so that violations of contract terms have well known and viable implications. While the first two areas appear to have advanced relatively rapidly, the issue of bankruptcy codes and lender recourse to collateral is significantly further behind.

However, even if these steps are completed, there is no assurance that the banking institutions will perform their stated function in an appropriate manner. Once the environment for lending is improved, there is a clear need to establish a regulatory framework in which these financial institutions will operate. As we solve the banks' problem of evaluation and monitoring of the borrower relationship, there is an equal, if not greater, need to establish a framework for depositors and shareowners of financial institutions to likewise evaluate and monitor their financial institutions.

How is this accomplished? To many, the answer is straightforward. A regulatory regime needs to be established to permit the clear evaluation of bank assets, the monitoring of bank behaviour, and the enforceability of remedies in the face of bank default. Essentially, some would argue, the banking environment needs to be established in a symmetric manner with that which is proposed for the non-bank sector (Udell and Wachtel, 1995; and Perotti, 1994).

Yet, this view does not have universal support. Many are quick to point out that bank balance sheets are less transparent than their non-financial counterparts, and the "overhang" from the previous regime more serious (OECD, 1992). In addition, depositors are less able to pierce the corporate veil, particularly in the FPE context. This has led some to recommend higher capital for banking firms, and the establishment of a formal deposit insurance system to assure bank stability and protect uninformed depositors. In general, these recommendations come from those that view banks as somewhat unique institutions that require special regulations (Herring and Litan, 1995). Their objectives, however, are the same as those proposing commercial code revisions. The goal is to establish a set of rules and regulations that enhance the workings of the market-based system. In short, they are attempts to remediate the imperfections in the market, not substitute for market-based signals.

Stiglitz, however, has caused somewhat of a stir lately. In both Stiglitz (1989) and Stiglitz, Jaramillo-Vallejo, and Park (1994), he has come out in favour of a system that is less free-market based than many others would recommend. Relying on the existence of imperfect information in even the best of circumstances, he has argued in favour of selective government intervention in the financial structure of developing economies, including the use of various types of credit allocation schemes, as well as expanded government oversight of credit institutions. As Edwards (1995) characterizes the Stiglitz perspective, information problems in the credit market have two central consequences.

"First, since financial institutions know it is difficult to monitor them when information is limited, they are tempted to act recklessly, either undertaking excessively risky actions or committing fraud. And, second, since the public is aware of the incentive problem facing financial institutions it entrusts them with fewer resources than it would under the hypothetical case of full information". (Edwards, 1995, p.202).

In short, in the presence of imperfect information, financial institutions assume excessive risk and provide insufficient funds for capital formation. Therefore, a move toward a market-based system, even when the current structure is admittedly ineffective and grossly inefficient, may not be desirable. To Stiglitz, the inefficiencies of the second best world of an imperfect credit market may be large enough to make government intervention and credit allocation a preferred solution to the current situation. What we are seeing, in short, is a call to arms to all those who favour non-market credit decision-making and an expanded role for proactive government policy.

Those opposed to this policy prescription argue in favour of policies that would improve the functioning of the market, rather than replacing it with a government bureaucracy and its attendant shortcomings. They believe that management is more likely to be responsive to stakeholders in a market based system than in one in which the government plays a larger role. This point of view is neatly captured by Edwards (1995).

"In designing regulatory legislation for the financial sector, it is important to recognize that, to a large extent, the inadequate availability of information can be reduced significantly through actions mandated by the government but undertaken by the private sector itself. The use of credit-rating agencies and outside auditors to monitor the accounts of financial institutions are only two examples of quasi self-regulation. The long history of failed government initiatives in this direction strongly suggests that overregulating the financial sector, especially intervening through direct government actions, can be disastrous. It can negatively affect the efficiency of the capital market, while at the same time creating rent seeking and heightening corruption". (Edwards, 1995, p.202).

However, this is not to say that proponents of this view offer a laissez-faire government regime with no regulation. Rather, they argue that appropriate regulation requires an appreciation of the potential role of financial institutions in the capital market and how it can be enhanced by a supportive regulatory regime. Toward this end, let us review in further depth the current understanding of the functions performed by financial intermediaries with an eye toward a regulatory regime which can enhance their ability to perform these functions rather than replacing them with a greater government role.

7.3   Reviewing the role of financial intermediaries

The current academic view of the role of financial intermediaries is that they serve two primary functions. First and foremost, they are generators or creators of assets. These assets are obtained either from the government to finance deficits or from the private sector. In the latter case, banks are expected to screen the set of borrowing opportunities presented to them, using the expertise and specific-capital that is unique to this sector (Diamond, 1984; Bhattacharya and Thakor, 1993). Projects found worthy are financed and monitored until repayment. This secondary phase of the lending function, on-going servicing and monitoring is critical for a number of reasons. It is well known that once the loan is made, it is frequently illiquid and difficult to value without substantial effort (Gorton and Pennacchi, 1990; Santomero and Trester, 1997). Therefore, monitoring its performance and estimating its current value are crucial elements in the intermediation process. In addition, such oversight by firms who are responsible for financing the investment project often leads to higher returns from the endeavour, as investors respond to on-going monitoring by increasing effort and maintaining closer adherence to the proposed purpose of the loan (Allen and Gale, 1988). For both reasons, the existence of a monitoring institution improves the project returns accruing to the stakeholders of the intermediary itself.

The second function of the intermediary sector is the channeling of savings resources to a higher purpose. This is achieved in two distinct ways. For transaction balances, the financial sector needs to develop the capacity to use idle balances, even while it installs a viable and efficient payment system. From the perspective of the institution, financial intermediaries provide depository services as a mechanism to finance the lending activity outlined above. Yet, the fact that these banks are central to the clearing process suggests a need for regulatory concern and oversight, viz, maintaining the integrity of the payment system (Goodfriend, 1989). For FPEs, this is an enormous challenge, but one that already has been identified and is currently being addressed. For standard savings balances, the consumer must see that the return warrants the risk and the delayed consumption. The institutions must offer standard financial assets to the public which fairly compensate depositors. The benefits offered to the savings sector must include positive returns for deferred consumption, a return to risk-taking, and perhaps some liability transfer services, i.e., payment-clearing services.

As an intermediary, the financial institution provides both of these key functions simultaneously, i.e. it makes loans and accepts deposits. However, the maturity length of assets usually differs substantially from the average maturity of liabilities. Therefore, the standard asset transformation function includes maturity transformation as well as resource mobilisation. While these can be viewed as mostly complementary services, at times the use of relatively liquid liabilities to finance illiquid and longer-term risk assets generates an inherent instability into the system (Diamond and Dybvig, 1983; Gorton, 1988). Yet, it is central to providing the economy its value-added activity of mobilising savings assets into productive real investment.

Regulation and market intervention aimed at encouraging appropriate bank risk-taking and risk evaluation activity must be imposed in a way that supports these two key functions and improves the sector's ability to provide needed capital to capital-constrained firms. Given the above description of functions performed by the sector, a clear case can be made in answer to the question of why some regulatory oversight of the financial sector is appropriate.

7.4   Why financial institutions warrant oversight

As can be seen from the above discussion, financial institutions are structurally vulnerable because they finance the holding of imperfectly marketable direct claims with liabilities that are viewed as redeemable at par. In addition, they provide the valuable service of maturity transformation which is mutually beneficial to borrowers and savers but which may, nonetheless, place the financial institution itself in jeopardy (see

Kareken and Wallace, 1978; Jacklin, 1987; Santomero, 1992).

In doing so, imperfect information about the project financed and the value of the bank's claim is likely to be a fundamental characteristic of most of the direct claims held by these institutions. This imperfect information of most of the non-government direct claims held by financial institutions means that the market does not provide direct or accurate information about the value of a financial firm's assets. Therefore, holders of indirect claims (liability holders) cannot readily evaluate the solvency of the institution to affirm that the market value of their assets exceeds the promised value of their aggregate liabilities (Berger and Udell, 1992; Santomero and Trester, 1997).

Depositors and many other liability holders place funds in these institutions fully expecting to be able to withdraw their deposits whenever they choose. Frequently, their investment horizon is uncertain and cannot be clearly established at the outset. Accordingly, the financial institution is left in the awkward position of investing in long-term, imperfectly marketable assets funded by liabilities with a perceived short, but uncertain maturity. If withdrawals are purely random, as they are likely to be most of the time, they may be statistically predictable. However, if liability holders become concerned about the solvency of the institution, withdrawals may become systematic and jeopardize the liquidity and solvency of the entire institution (Gorton, 1988; Jacklin and Bhattacharya, 1988).

For this very reason, the management of an institution which hold imperfectly marketable assets may wish to be less than completely forthcoming. They may attempt to exercise control over information critical to estimating the value of their assets, and they may be tempted to conceal information regarding the deterioration of value. This may be done in the hope that delaying the release of information will give assets time to recover and thus avert giving liability holders an incentive to run.

Investors, of course, are aware that the financial institution's management has both the incentive and capacity to conceal a decline in value of the imperfectly marketable direct claims. They are also aware that these same institutions are usually highly leveraged, so that a relatively small percentage decline in the value of an institution's direct claims results in a much larger percentage decline in its net worth. For this reason, as Calomiris and Kahn (1991) illustrate, many depositors require that much of their deposits be held in demand form. If bad news casts doubt on the value of the institution's direct claims, these creditors have a mechanism to withdraw their resources from the troubled firm. This may be accomplished quickly, as soon as they observe an action which reduces their estimate of the institution's net worth, despite assertions by the institution's management that the firm is solvent.

If creditors cannot demand immediate repayment of their claims at par, the institution would not be seriously damaged by the loss of liability holders' confidence. With time to make a convincing case, the financial institution might be able to persuade creditors that its net worth is truly positive. Even if it could not, a solvent institution can liquidate direct claims without suffering loss. But, if investors can present their claims for immediate redemption at par, they may force the financial institution to make a hurried liquidation of imperfectly marketable direct claims at a loss. Alternatively, they may force the institution to borrow at rates sharply higher than it customarily pays or they may call in loans before the borrower's investment matures.

Runs, once begun, tend to be self-reinforcing. News that the depository institution is selling direct claims at distressed prices or is borrowing at very high rates will further undermine the confidence of current and potential depositors. Even those who believe that, with sufficient time the financial institution would be able to redeem all its liabilities, have a motive to join the run. They have reason to fear that the costs from the hurried liquidation of direct claims in response to the run by other creditors might render such an institution insolvent. This is the story that Diamond and Dybvig (1983) relate so forcefully.

Sophisticated investors know that illiquidity losses tend to get larger as the run goes on because the most marketable direct claims are sold first. They also know that as an institution's net worth approaches zero, the depository institution's managers may be tempted to take increasingly desperate gambles to stay in business (Herring and Vankudre, 1987; Kane, 1985). Thus, the perception of possible insolvency resulting from a decline in asset quality, whether true or not, can become a self-fulfilling prophecy by inducing creditors to take actions that erode the institution's net worth.

This vulnerability to runs is more than the strictly private concern of an individual depository institution and its customers. It becomes a public policy concern when a loss of confidence in the solvency of one institution may lead to a contagious loss of confidence in other institutions. Contagion may occur through three channels: (1) financial institutions lose reserves because cash drains from failing institutions are not redeposited in other institutions; (2) institutions that have or are suspected to have claims against failing institutions are then vulnerable in the second tier of the crisis; and (3) creditors at other institutions suspect that their institutions are exposed to the same shocks as the failing institution, and run without concern other than the legitimacy of their suspicion. This danger is particularly acute for commercial banks operating in the payments-clearing system in some countries where intra-day extensions of interbank credits are large relative to the settling depository institution's capital (Humphrey, 1987).

This potential for contagion in the interbank market is heightened by the lack of timely data on interfirm exposures. When one institution gets into trouble, it is often very difficult for another institution to determine its aggregate exposure to the problem firm, let alone the exposures to other institutions on which it may hold claims. Non-bank creditors do not have access to timely information. Hence, any existing concerns about a particular institution's solvency would be heightened if another institution were to fail and one suspected that the two institutions had substantial interbank dealings (Faulhaber, Phillips and Santomero, 1990).

Finally, a failure may also be contagious if other financial institutions are believed to have positions similar to the failing desposity institution, and therefore to have been weakened by the same economic disturbances (Gorton, 1988). This is a particularly serious problem when a large depository institution fails. The larger the institution, the greater the likelihood that its failure will attract public attention and undermine confidence in the financial system in general, and in similar large financial institutions in particular. Moreover, failures of large institutions are usually attributable to economic disturbances which affect the value of large categories of assets, rather than to embezzlement or other idiosyncratic causes. Since large institutions compete in the same national and international markets, they face generally similar cost and demand conditions and tend to have similar portfolios (Mayer, 1975).

7.5   A regulatory structure to assure financial stability

While the potential for contagion is clear, it does not necessarily follow that it needs to be a significant factor in a financial crisis. Financial sectors in developed economies have established a financial safety net, an elaborate set of institutional mechanisms for protecting the financial system, which has largely succeeded in preventing contagious runs in their financial sector. Most of these countries have developed a regulatory structure that prevents the amplification of shocks through the financial system. This safety net can be viewed as a set of preventive measures that can and should be triggered at various stages in the evolution of a financial crisis. These structures must be established in FPEs, as well. The simplest method of explanation of this preventive mechanism is to begin with an exogenous disturbance.

The earliest stage of financial crisis involves a financial institution's exposure to a shock which could jeopardize its solvency. This may occur because adverse changes in the economy have increased the probability of a shock. Alternatively, it may be the result of a decline in the value of assets, which was forced upon the institution by previous government policy or chosen by its managers, who had made conscious decisions to accept the risk. In any case, the institution's capital position declines. If the occurrence of a shock causes creditors to question the solvency of an institution, a run may occur which can lead to the contagious transmission of liquidity problems, and perhaps solvency problems throughout the financial system, as discussed in the preceding section.

An appropriate regulatory structure is designed to stop this sequence of events at a number of points, and preserve the integrity of the financial structure and the health of the real economy. The components of a safety net are best described in terms of functions, because the agencies which perform a particular function vary across countries and some functions are shared among agencies within a particular country.

- The Chartering Function should begin the process. It should be set up so as to screen out imprudent, incompetent or dishonest institution managers who would be likely to take on excessive insolvency exposure.
- In the event that some managers attempt to expose their institutions to shocks that could jeopardize their solvency, the Prudential Supervision Function should prevent it. This set of regulations limits the degree of risk that managers can absorb in their portfolio.
- In the event that prudential supervision does not prevent an institution from assuming excessive insolvency exposure and a damaging shock occurs, the Termination Authority should terminate the license of the institution before it becomes insolvent and causes excessive loss to creditors.
- Even if the Termination Authority acts too late to prevent losses, the explicit or implicit Insurance function provided by official or private sources may prevent creditors, most often depositors, from running.

- Even if the depository institution closes $_t$ abruptly, the Insurance function may prevent contagion by sustaining the confidence of the creditors at other institutions which are thought to be similar.
- If runs occur at other institutions, the Lender of Last Resort Function may enable solvent institutions to meet the claims of liability holders, avoiding forced asset liquidations and depressed prices.
- If other failures occur, the Monetary Authority can prevent a shift in the public's demand for cash from reducing the volume of reserves available to the financial system as a whole, thereby confining the damage to the institutions affected directly by the original shock.

In the major industrialized countries, the various circuit breakers that comprise financial safety nets have been generally successful in preventing a problem at one institution from damaging the system as a whole. In the United States, for example, the safety net which was constructed in the 1930s has virtually eliminated the contagious transmission of shocks from one depository institution to the rest of the system. In the crisis associated with the 1987 market decline, the central bank made it clear that this security would also be offered to other members of the financial industry. Likewise in Scandinavia, the safety net was tested at the opening of this decade and was able to stabilise a vulnerable financial system.

Governments clearly have an interest in maintaining the integrity of the financial sector, its assets, its unique capacity to provide risk capital to the industrial sector, and last but not least, its clearing and settlement system capability (Bernanke and Gertler, 1989, 1990). They also rely on it as a venue for macroeconomic policy. Governments therefore believe that they can and must play a role in improving the stability of the system through structures and support mechanisms which enhance the depth of the market.

7.6   The costs of the regulatory structure

However, in an important sense, any regulatory regime can be <u>too</u> successful. An overly broad safety net which de facto replaces private sector assurances with government guarantees has three very negative effects on the integrity of the financial sector. First, if the liability holders are confident that they will be protected against any loss, they have less incentive to monitor and discipline the behaviour of institutions that hold their resources. This is why the EU Deposit Insurance Directorate has set minimum deposit insurance coverage at the relatively low level of 50,000

ECU. Second, if government officials have any substantial impact on the fundamental lending decisions, they may view this as an opportunity to allocate credit to unworthy but potentially well connected borrowers. This may be viewed as a throwback to the vices embedded in the former FPE structure, where financial decisions were based on political expediency. In any case, the effect is that the integrity of the credit process deteriorates, as does the quality of the assets held by the financial sector. This is, then, further complicated by a third side effect of over-zealous government intervention, i.e., an erosion of both predictability and accountability within the system. Both bank and industrial management find that decisions are determined by an essentially political process which they can predict and for which they can not realistically be held accountable. In the extreme case, we are de facto back to the Calvo and Coricelli (1993) quote at the opening of this paper. Even beyond this, since liability holders do not demand greater compensation when their institutions take greater risks in the new market-based system, both bank and non-financial firm managers will feel free to assume more risk in the hope of achieving higher expected returns.

The preceding section emphasized the rational for regulating and supporting financial institutions, namely a concern over the possibility of damaging risk-taking with detrimental effects on the system as a whole. However, there are equally dangerous effects from excessive government involvement in the decisions made by the financial sector. By definition, a greater government role in the sector reduces the accountability of management. In the name of the public good, the financial condition of these institutions is frequently obfuscated and lending decisions influenced by political considerations. In the limit, this type of government involvement completely removes decisions from the marketplace and market discipline. Indeed, the intervention has made matters worse by preventing the triggering of market response functions. In essence, regulation itself has generated a need for regulation by eliminating the potential for market discipline and accountability by managers (Kareken and Wallace, 1978).

It is often contended, as Stiglitz, Jaramillo-Vallejo and Park (1994) have recently, that public interest is best served by politically motivated lending to specific firms or industries. However, in doing this, market forces are being thwarted and market discipline removed. There is little incentive for the establishment of a rational allocation of resources, the primary goal for moving to a market-based economy. Even at the operating level, government intervention thwarts the goal of appropriate asset allocation. There is little reason to demand repayment if loans are the result of government decision-making and not economics. Finally, there is little cause to worry if management knows that the institution itself is supported by government subsidy, oversight and the safety net.

The result is a bad institutional structure, not the development of rational, efficient intermediaries. Lending is not made for the public good, but for political expediency. Everywhere in the process, incentives are set up to prevent efficient utilization of the society's scarce capital. And, in the end, the government will be forced to intervene again to guarantee the creditors of the ill-fated institutions. This is the story of virtually every governmentally supported financial sector. The government intervenes because the financial sector, broadly defined, had not devoted sufficient attention to asset quality. This failure of management occurs throughout the lending process from loan approval procedures, to loan monitoring, to collection. In many cases, loan concentration in allegedly key sectors had been fostered by public policy, so the lack of diversification was not viewed as alarming. If large borrowers were having financial difficulties, these same firms were often granted extensions and concessions. It was, after all, a set of discussions that had been made for non-economic reasons of public policy or political expediency.

The resultant system reverts back to or at least in the direction of, the FPE structure which we so decry. In the end, one is left with a financial sector that has not achieved the desired goal of efficient asset creation and funds allocation. The economy will achieve sub-par performance because scarce capital is being squandered on projects that may have had negative returns from the start.

Proponents of government involvement in decision-making would argue with this characterization. They have asserted that if the professional bureaucracy were properly trained, the outcome would exceed the private sector outcome. However, as was discussed above, the efficient allocation of financial resources is exceedingly difficult even in the best circumstances. We have found, throughout history, that Plato's "philosopher-king" rarely appears. It is equally unlikely that the all-knowing bureaucratic class will emerge. Such a class may be present in the Asian economies, defined today as the miracle economies or Asian Tigers. However, even this characterization is being subjected to increased scrutiny as of late (Edwards, 1995).

In the end, the challenge is to build a support system for the financial sector that insures its stability but does not supersede its authority. The goal of regulation ought to be to offset negative externalities without creating too many new ones in the process (Udell and Wachtel, 1995).

7.7   Government's role in supporting financial innovations

There may also be a role for the government beyond its attempt to build an appropriate safety net around an inherently fragile system. In fact, it may be able to foster improvement and innovation in a sector that must be transformed to catch up to the rest of the world. Advances in computer hardware and software, telecommunication, and financial theory have led to a rapid increase in the pace of financial innovation in this sector in market economies. Such changes can be attributed to attempts by the private sector to respond to opportunities that exist in the marketplace.

Merton (1989), Santomero (1989), and others have identified several forces driving the innovation process. First, innovations have responded to market demands for risk-sharing, risk-pooling, hedging and intertemporal or spatial transfers or resources that are not currently available. Second, innovations have satisfied continuing needs for lower transactions costs or increased liquidity. Third, innovations have reduced asymmetric information between trading parties and improved the monitoring of the performance of principals by agents. Fourth, innovations have facilitated the avoidance of tax, regulatory and accounting constraints.

Active investors in world capital markets have seen substantial benefits from this period of change. Such innovations have provided greater opportunities for entrepreneurs to obtain capital, and offer a mechanism to insure that corporate managers are more accountable to shareholders. It is worth considering whether or not regulators and policymakers can facilitate this process in the FPE environment.

Entrepreneurs generally introduce financial innovations but, in some more important instances, governments have successfully taken an active role in the innovation process. For example, the US government played a leading role in securitizing mortgages so that what had been a very segmented set of local markets became a highly integrated national market. And, the United Kingdom made an important contribution to the array of investment opportunities by issuing indexed bonds, thus providing investors with a hedge against risk of general inflation which no private party could credibly supply. In each case, the government entered the market with a new product which established a standard for subsequent private sector innovation. This role of the government within the financial system is often neglected, but it offers important potential benefits (see Jaffee and Renaud, 1998, in this volume). Encouragement of financial innovations can add substantial value to both the financial sector and the broader economy.

However, there are also some cases where the government may need to play a role in slowing the speed with which innovations are introduced as soon as they are privately profitable, without regard to their effect on the financial infrastructure. This can be yet another variant of the public goods problem: although it is in everyone's interest to have a secure, reliable financial infrastructure, the entrepreneur who introduces a financial innovation will usually lack an incentive to consider the possible impact of the innovation on the financial infrastructure. Limits may occasionally be necessary, but they should be *transient* (Merton, 1990).

Regulatory attempts to constrain innovations should be made with extreme caution. Indeed, as a general matter, innovation should be encouraged. To the extent that innovations are a response to market forces, attempts to prohibit innovations may simply cause foreign and most domestic capital to flee offshore. Domestic firms, and consequently the growth of the real sector, may suffer. Although some innovations waste resources and diminish social welfare, this is not inevitably the case. When the financial sector is filled with inefficiencies due to an outdated financial structure such as exists in FPEs, even innovations motivated by short-term gain may enhance the efficiency of the economy.

7.8   The price of inefficient regulation

Clumsily applied, any of the regulatory interventions described in the preceding sections can produce dysfunctional results and undermine both the performance and viability of financial institutions. For example, if the prudential function is used as an asset allocation system, all of the ills addressed above will inevitably follow. This led Western Europe to retreat from this method of subsidized financing that had been common prior to the 1970s. The procedure was rife with politics and special interest, and ultimately did not appear to have the desired outcome. In the end, it transferred wealth from either the users of financial services or the government to the stakeholders of the preferred sector. Moreover, because the designated firms or industries were protected from new entrants, firms in these categories and the financial sector that supported them were likely to be less innovative in serving the changing needs of their customers. The world has seen any number of such cases including ill-conceived large scale government projects, or targeted industries which have led to staggering losses to lending institutions. These, in turn, had to be covered by other participants in the financial markets and, in some cases, the government itself. The macroeconomic effects of such policies are that they result in a lower capital stock and standard of living for the economy as a whole.

Similarly, regulations which place restrictions on the kinds of assets in which financial institutions are permitted to invest require them to hold assets which they would otherwise avoid. Alternatively, they may be prohibited from acquiring assets which they would prefer. Overly restrictive enforcement of these policies may also reduce the flow of risk capital to the real sector and reduce overall real sector investment. In each case, the allocation of capital will be distorted, relative to the competitive equilibrium, and the economy will be less productive than it could be.

In addition, the general level of supervision may also impose heavy direct costs on financial institutions in terms of auditing costs, filing requirements and examination fees. These side effects of regulation may reduce overall efficiency and cause regulated institutions to lose market share. Excessive regulation can and has rendered some financial services completely uneconomical in some jurisdictions.

Badly administered termination and insurance policies have costs. Delays in terminating insolvent institutions may result in a misallocation of funds, as desperate managers take increasingly risky gambles in order to prevent closure. Because shareholders are protected by limited liability, they may perceive high-risk activities as their only hope of salvation. Likewise, ineptly administered government guarantees may distort incentives for risk-taking in both the real sector and its financial counterparts. In addition, it may result in enormous transfers of wealth from conservatively managed institutions to risky institutions, and potentially, from taxpayers to creditors of involved firms. The thrift crisis in the United States provides dramatic evidence of the enormous potential costs of a badly managed insurance system and a failure to close insured institutions when they become insolvent (Kane, 1985).

The provision of lender-of-last resort assistance to *insolvent* institutions also has potential costs. This activity may undercut what would otherwise be a favourable signal to the market, thus weakening the ability of both the regulatory and monetary authority to deal with systemic shocks. It also may permit incompetently managed or excessively risky institutions to continue misallocating funds long after they would have been forced to close by market forces. And, perhaps worst of all, it may lead to expectations of future bailouts and intensify political pressures for such bailouts.

In the end, there is no substitute for appropriate proactive-market regulation. Badly administrated support structures have ways of exacerbating an already difficult situation. And, direct, centralized control of the financial structure and the lending process is doomed to failure because of all the negative incentive effects that are unleashed by such a system. They have been tried and abandoned in Western Europe. They have been touted, but have been relatively ineffective in Asia. It appears unlikely that they have much merit for Eastern Europe.

7.9   Summary and conclusions

The FPEs are at a unique point in their economic history. The advent of a market economy has led to dramatic change. Nowhere is the need for change greater than in the financial sector, and the behaviour of banking institutions. These firms must convert from de-facto government agencies to credit evaluators, borrower monitors, and loan collectors. To perform these functions, substantial change has begun to transform the accounting, legal system and property/bankruptcy law to be supportive of the new market economy. An equal change needs to occur in financial institution regulation. Financial system reform must be embarked upon in a manner that enhances the banks' ability to perform their new role. While they will not do so perfectly - because they function in an imperfect information environment - efforts should be made to have them approach their normative goal.

To remediate the problems associated with market imperfections a regulatory structure along the lines proposed here needs to be constructed. This includes a set of functions, procedures and controls which form the basis of a safety net for the system as a whole, not individual firms (Herring and Litan, 1995).

To some, this is not enough. They argue that permitting banks to function in an imperfect market may lead to inferior economic performance. They propose, instead, direct government intervention to improve the ability of the financial sector to allocate capital within the economy. From the time of Adam Smith, policymakers have been looking for mechanisms to replace the market. Arguments have been offered that a market-based solution ignores important social factors, externalities as they are now called. However, the replacement must be better than the alternative (Udell and Wachtel, 1995). To be first-best solution, a government run financial sector must be able to obtain and process all of the information absorbed in market prices and arrive at a socially desirable outcome. A bureaucratic structure must be established which is both knowledgeable, professional, and altruistic to obtain these results (Edwards, 1995). In truth, this cannot really be expected from any human endeavour.

We are, therefore, left to a second-best world. Here, we must choose between two systems. One is bureaucratically based, where the FPE structure is replaced by well meaning bureaucrats trying to effect socially desirable capital allocation without market prices or by entering the market to enhance or alter market signals. The other is market based, with carefully crafted pro-market regulation and a delicately applied financial institution safety net. Experience from North America and Western Europe clearly favours the latter. Without doubt, previous experiences in Eastern Europe with centralized decision making offer little to attract us to the government intervention model. The prudent course for FPEs appears to be toward constructive pro-market regulation of the financial sector, not centralization.

As is evident from the discussion above, even market-based regulations involve trade-offs between stability and market discipline. However, it would be a mistake to remove the latter. In the end, no stability is offered by the removal or manipulation of market signals and the discipline of the price system. The appearance of stability offered by centralization is only an illusion.

Notes

This paper is a product of the Wharton Financial Institutions Center, which is funded by a grant from the Alfred P. Sloan Foundation. An earlier version of the paper was prepared for the 5th Annual European Financial Association Meetings, Innsbruck, Austria, June 17-20, 1996. The author wishes to thank J. Doukas, V. Murinde and C. Wihlborg for helpful comments on an earlier draft.

References

Allen, F. and D. Gale, 1988, Optimal security design, Review of Financial Studies, 1, 3, pp. 229-263.
Berger, A. and G. Udell, 1992, Securitization, risk and the liquidity problem in banking, in: M. Klausner and L. White, eds, Structural Change in Banking (Irwin Publishing, Homewood, IL).
Bernanke, B. and M. Gertler, 1989, Agency costs, net worth, and business

fluctuations, American Economic Review, 79, 1, pp. 14-31.

Bernanke, B. and M. Gertler, 1990, Financial fragility and economic performance, Quarterly Journal of Economics, 105, 1, pp. 87-114.

Bhattacharya, S. and A.V. Thakor, 1993, Contemporary banking theory, Journal of Financial Intermediation, 3, pp. 2-50.

Bonin, J. and I. Szekely, eds., 1994, The Development and Reform of Financial Systems in Central and Eastern Europe (Edward Elgar Publishers, Cheltenham).

Calomiris, C. and C Kahn, 1991, The role of demandable debt in structuring optimal banking arrangements, American Economic Review, 81, 3, pp. 497-513.

Calvo, G. and F. Coricelli, 1993, Output collapse in Eastern Europe: the role of credit, IMF Staff Papers, 40, 1, pp. 32-52.

Calvo, G. and J. A. Frenkel, 1991, Credit markets, credibility and economic transformation, Journal of Economic Perspectives, 5, 4, pp. 139-48.

Caprio, G., D. Folkers-Landau, T. Lane, eds., 1994, Building Sound Finance in Emerging Market Economies (International Monetary Fund and World Bank, Washington, D.C.).

Cecchi, D., 1993, Creation of financial markets in (previously) centrally planned economies, Journal of Banking and Finance, 17, 5, pp. 819-47.

Corbett, J. and C. Mayer, 1991, Financial reform in Eastern Europe, progress with the wrong model, Oxford Review of Economic Policy, 7, 4, pp. 57-75.

Dewatripont, M. and J. Tirole, 1993, Efficient governance structure: implications for banking regulation, in: C. Mayer and X. Vives, eds., Capital Markets and Financial Intermediation (Cambridge University Press, Cambridge), pp. 12-35.

Diamond, D. W. and P. H. Dybvig, 1983, Banks runs, deposit insurance and liquidity, Journal of Political Economy, 91, pp. 401-419.

Diamond, D. W., 1984, Financial intermediation and delegated monitoring, Review of Economic Studies, 51, pp. 393-414.

Edwards, S., 1995, Crisis and Reform in Latin America: From Despair to Hope (Oxford University Press, Oxford).

Faulhaber, G., A. Phillips and A. Santomero, 1990, Payment risk, network risk, and the role of the Fed., in: D.B. Humphrey, ed., The US Payment System: Efficiency, Risk and the Role of the Federal Reserve, 197-213 (Kluwer Academic Publishers, London).

Fry, M. J., 1995, Money, Interest, and Banking in Economic Development (Johns Hopkins University Press, Baltimore).

Goodfriend, M.S., 1989, Money, credit, banking and payment system policy, in: D.B Humphrey, ed., The US Payment System: Efficiency, Risk and the Role of the Federal Reserve, 247-77 (Kluwer Academic Publishers, London).

Gorton, G., 1988, Banking panics and business cycles, Oxford Economic Papers, 40, 4, pp. 751-81.

Gorton, G. and G. Pennacchi, 1990, Financial intermediaries and liquidity creation, Journal of Finance, 45, 1, pp. 49-71.

Herring, R.J. and P. Vankudre, 1987, Growth opportunities and risk taking by financial intermediaries, Journal of Finance, 42, 3, pp. 583-99.

Herring, R.J. and R.E. Litan, 1995, Financial Regulation in the Global Economy (The Brookings Institution, Washington, D.C.).

Humphrey, D., 1987, Payments system risk, market failure, and public policy, in: E.H. Solomon, ed., Electronic Funds Transfers and Payments: The Public Policy Issues (Kluwer-Nijhof, Boston), pp. 83-109.

Jacklin, C., 1987, Demand deposits, trading restrictions, and risk sharing, in: E.C. Prescott and N. Wallace, eds., Contractual Arrangements for Intertemporal Trade (University of Minnesota Press, Minneapolis), pp. 26-47.

Jacklin, C.J. and S. Bhattacharya, 1988, Distinguishing panics and information based bank runs: welfare and policy implications, Journal of Political Economy, 96, 3, pp. 568-92.

Jaffe, D. and B Renaud, 1998, Strategies to develop mortgage markets in transition economies, in: J. Doukas, V. Murinde and C. Wihlborg, eds., Financial Sector Reform and Privatization in Transition Economies (North Holland, Amsterdam), pp. 69-94.

Kane, E.J., 1985, The Gathering Crisis in Federal Deposit Insurance (MIT Press, Cambridge, MA).

Kareken, J. and N. Wallace, 1978, Deposit insurance and bank regulation: a partial equilibrium exposition, Journal of Business, 51, 3, pp. 413-38.

Mayer, T., 1975, Preventing the failures of large banks, in: Compendium of Major Issues in Bank Regulations, Senate Committee on Banking, Housing and Urban Affairs, Washington, DC.

McKinnon, R., 1973, Money and Capital in Economic Development (The Brookings Institution, Washington, D.C.).

Merton, R.C., 1989, On the application of the continuous-time theory of finance to financial intermediation and insurance, The Geneva Papers on Risk and Insurance, 14, 52, pp. 225-61.

Merton, R.C., 1990, The financial system and economic performance, Journal of Financial Services Research, pp. 263-300.

NatWest Securities, 1994, Privatization in Central and Eastern Europe: Look Before You Leap (NatWest, London).

OECD, 1992, Bank restructuring in Central and Eastern Europe: issues and strategies, Financial Market Trends (France), 51, pp. 15-30.

Perotti, E., 1994, A taxonomy of post-socialist financial systems: decentralized enforcement and the creation of inside money, Economics of Transition, 2, 1, pp. 71-81.

Santomero, A.M. and J.J. Trester, 1997, forthcoming, Financial innovation and bank risk taking, Journal of Economic Behavior and Organization.

Santomero, A.M., 1989, The changing structure of financial institutions: a review essay, Journal of Monetary Economics, 24, 2, pp. 321-28.

Santomero, A.M., 1991, The bank capital issue, in: M. Fratianni, C. Wihlborg and T. Willett, Eds, Financial Regulation and Monetary Arrangements after 1992, (North Holland Press, Amsterdam) pp. 61-77.

Santomero, A.M., 1992, The banking firm in: P. Newman, M. Milgate, and J. Eatwell, eds., The New Palgrave Dictionary of Money and Finance, (Stockton Press, New York), pp. 141-3.

Sarcinelli, M., 1992, Eastern Europe and the financial sector: where are they going?, Banco Nazionale del Lavoro Quarterly Review, 183, pp. 463-92.

Saunders, A. and A. Sommariva, 1993, Banking sector and restructuring in Eastern Europe, Journal of Banking and Finance, 17, 5, pp. 931-57.

Stiglitz, J.E., J. Jaramillo-Vallejo, and Y.C. Park, 1994, The role of the state in financial markets, in: Proceedings of the World Bank and Annual Conference on Development Economics Supplement, Washington, D.C.

Stiglitz, J.E., 1989, Financial markets and development, Oxford Review of Economic Policy, 5, 4, pp. 55-68.

Szego, G., ed, 1993, Banks and capital markets in formerly centrally planned countries: their role in establishing a market economy, Journal of Banking and Finance, 17, 5, Special Issue, September.

Udell, G.F. and P. Wachtel, 1995, Financial system design for formerly planned economies: defining the issues, Financial Markets, Institutions and Instruments, 4, 2, pp. 1-60.

Financial Sector Reform and
Privatization in Transition Economies
J. Doukas, V. Murinde and C. Wihlborg (Editors)
© 1998 Elsevier Science Publishers B.V. All rights reserved

175 −

$9\,2$

Chapter 8 $G\text{-}2\backslash$ $G\text{-}3\,2$

$G\,3\,4$

UNIVERSAL BANKING: POLICY ISSUES
FOR EMERGING MARKET ECONOMIES

$P\,3\,4$

J. Kimball Dietrich
School of Business, University of Southern California, Los Angeles, CA 90089-
1421, USA

Kelvin Pan and Clas Wihlborg, Department of Economics, School of Economics
and Commercial Law, Göteborg University, Vasagatan 1, S411 80, Göteborg,
Sweden

8.1   Introduction

Commercial banking is among the most regulated business activities in
every country of the world. However, three distinct models of the scope of
commercial bank activities have emerged: the first model is typical in the
United States and the United Kingdom. Commercial banks focus on making
credits (loans) to non-banking firms. In the second model, banks provide
both equity and debt financing to corporations, and underwrite and sell
corporate securities issues to the public: this is commonly known as the
German "universal banking" model. In a third intermediate version banks
invest in both debt and equity of corporations but they do not to sell or
underwrite securities: this is the Japanese model which separates investment
and commercial banking along the United States model but allows bank
ownership of equity as in Germany. The different models of banking are in
some cases explained by regulation as in the USA and Japan. An important
aspect of the different models is that they are associated with different
mechanisms for changes in corporate control and management. Bank
regulation is only one facet of a battery of laws and regulations defining the
mechanisms for corporate control, however. Therefore, a country allowing
universal banking as in Germany is not certain to obtain the same system of
corporate control as Germany.

The prototype banking regulatory schemes are all imbedded in highly
developed market economies. The emerging market economies (EMEs) in

the former Soviet Union, Eastern Europe, and China are writing banking laws and developing bank regulatory schemes in an entirely different context. First, most of these economies had or have no privately owned banks: the banking industry consists of various subdivisions of the former central banks, finance ministries, or central planning institutions. Banks evolving from these government institutions will be under enormous political pressure to achieve temporary economic or long-term political objectives. In many of these countries, these banks have been forced to underwrite the losses of state-owned enterprises to maintain employment, exacerbating inflationary pressures. Discussion of banking laws regarding institutions subject to political pressure must be different from that of privately owned banks pursuing private interests as in the developed economies.

The economic development of the EMEs is based on newly privatized state enterprises and start-up operations. These firms will undoubtedly be involved in complex joint ventures, many involving foreign partners and experimental projects, which have substantial risk. Smaller and riskier businesses contrast with the stable, large name-corporations associated with the Japanese bank centered "keiretsu" or the German universal banking system and their influence on corporate control. The potentially dynamic character of industrial development in EMEs will require a system for financing and corporate control providing strong incentives for owners and managers to pursue economically sound objectives. Business failure should be much more common in EMEs, which are composed of new or newly privatized firms which are rapidly adopting new technologies in new markets with borrowed experience in business practice and modern production and marketing.

The EMEs are developing new financial systems without a historical development essential to the explanation of the institutional realities of the developed economies. No logical analysis would produce the U.S. system of state and federal banking regulation distributed at the national level among three banking regulators (the Federal Reserve, the Federal Deposit Insurance Corporation, and the Office of the Comptroller of the Currency in the Treasury Department). The Glass-Steagall act separating commercial and investment banking is also a regulatory solution explained by the Great Depression and political pressures in response to specific events in the USA. The regulatory structure of developed economies may not be relevant to the EMEs.

A factor influencing the creation of a new regulatory structure is that EMEs share with the developed market economies access to phenomenal changes in the technology of transmission and processing of information. Observers dispute the long-run significance of this technology on the evolution of financial institutions, but no one disputes that there will be a major impact. The common assumptions of economies of scale in the provision of financial services in the form of transaction processing, information gathering and distribution, and trading of financial instruments are no longer accepted without questions. Smaller financial institutions compete effectively and decentralized trading is commonplace. Distributed processing is changing our concepts of information management and efficient organization structure. Banking supervisors in EMEs must be careful to avoid adoption of constrictive regulations, such as limited access to the clearing system, adopted from models developed in irrelevant historical environments.

This paper applies recent research in the area of the financial economics of banking on the economic efficiency of differing bank powers to assess issues concerning universal banking in EMEs. In Section 8.2 we review research in universal banking and recently developed theories explaining banks' equity ownership in non-financial firms. In Section 8.3 we develop a model wherein the return to bank monitoring is enhanced by equity-lending. Corporate control arguments for equity holdings are reviewed in Section 8.4 making the point that it is not primarily universal banking that distinguishes one corporate governance system from another. Finally, in Section 8.5, the role of competition in universal banking systems is discussed and the results are applied to the situation of the EMEs.

8.2   Review of the issues in universal banking

A survey of recent literature concerning universal banking reveals the importance of precision in use of terms. Two of the most sophisticated papers, discussed below, focus on two entirely different attributes of universal banking: Berlin, Kose and Saunders (1996) are concerned with banks owning debt and equity ownership jointly, whereas Rajan (1992) emphasizes the underwriting of corporate securities. These two aspects of universal banking in Germany are separate economic issues: equity ownership by banks provides banks with opportunities to exercise a degree of direct corporate control. Japanese banks have this same opportunity. Underwriting of securities may allow banks to exploit privileged or low-cost information advantages which are different than those stemming from corporate control. Japanese banks are not able to underwrite securities while most continental European banks are.

The recent academic debate about universal banking has been dominated by the issue of separation between commercial banking and investment banking. Saunders (1994) contains a collection of papers on universal banking. With one exception the papers deal with the separation issue.

Rajan (1992) provides a clear picture of the economic problems addressed in the literature on the separation issue. Rajan models the value of banks who both lend and underwrite securities using information developed during the period before the firm issues securities. The analysis focuses on the incentives of the "house" bank to exploit its information advantage relative to outside investment bankers who must spend manpower and time in achieving the level of information possessed by banks. The information advantage creates a monopoly position of the housebank with the result that it cannot credibly communicate the quality of its client to the market. This cost of the information advantage of the house bank is balanced by "economies of scope" in the use of information when the bank acts both as a lender and an underwriter.

Rajan expands his analysis to investigate the effects of competition in the corporate loan market (which finances activity prior to the public issue), economies of scope, and permission for banks to own equity in underwritten public corporations. These complexities make it possible for inefficiencies in the previous analysis to be mitigated. In particular, a combination of bank equity ownership with bank underwriting may overcome the problem of bank credibility and may produce an efficient solution.

It is possible, as in the United States, for banks to underwrite corporate equity issues without establishing a controlling position. This can be accomplished by requiring underwriting activities through separate entities and limitations on the time of ownership of shares is allowed. These limitations, if obeyed, eliminate any economic advantage stemming from scale or scope economies in Rajan's model.

Krosznen and Rajan (1994) investigate whether banks in the USA prior to the 1930s exploited a monopoly position to underwrite security issues with the purpose of paying back the bank's loans. They are unable to detect evidence of this potential conflict of interest.

Most of the analysis below addresses the issue of banks' holding equity in non-financial firms. Based on Boot and Thakor (1994) our point of reference is that banks generally are reluctant to hold equity. Therefore, explicit advantages of equity investment must be demonstrated to explain this aspect of universal banking. Boot and Thakor explain why banks prefer to lend by holding senior debt in firms; in combination with banks' information advantage, seniority provides banks with incentives to induce a reorganization of firms in distress. With junior debt, banks would force firms approaching distress to close down "too early" imposing deadweight losses. With senior debt the bank can hold out longer before forcing liquidation or reorganization, and if a firm is viable the bank expecting to remain a senior debt-holders will prefer reorganization. The argument that banks are reluctant to hold equity is substantiated by the absence of banks' equity ownership in, for example, the UK where there are no restrictions on it.

There are few explicit models providing a rationale for banks' equity stakes in firms. Berlin, Kose, and Saunders (1996) develop a model of a bank which can make debt and equity investments in a risky firm which must rely on a third party supplier for essential inputs according to a fixed price contract. The essential feature of this analysis is that the bank can credibly signal the firm's true state to the supplier in order to induce the supplier to renegotiate the supply contract in cases of adverse outcomes only if the bank owns equity in the firm. The analysis allows the bank to renegotiate its equity claim on the firm by reducing its share of profits in cases of distress thus sharing the supplier's losses from the firm's distress. By varying its equity position the bank can align its incentives to varying degrees either with equity holders or with third party stake-holders. The bank's information advantage implies that its equity position has signalling value.

By having a fixed claim on the firm, the bank induces the firm's management to accept a more risky investment strategy. On the other hand, when the bank can veto the firm's investment strategy, the bank must have a mixture of debt and equity in order to induce the firm to accept the first best investment strategy. These results both stem from the firm's owners' (including the bank if it has control) ability and incentive to shift risk to fixed claimants. John, John, and Saunders (1994) analyze the effects of banks' equity stakes on the risk-taking of firms. They distinguish between cases when the bank takes a controlling role in investment decisions, when banks can veto investment decisions, and when banks have no direct influence. The first two cases correspond to different degrees of equity involvement by the bank in the firm. An equity stake allows the bank to influence the risk directly through its influence on firms' investment decisions. It is shown that the bank holding only debt is overly conservative. A larger bank-equity stake implies a more efficient investment policy.

The papers referred to above explore narrow specifications of the universal banking issue based on information asymmetries. Berlin, Kose and Saunders (1996) emphasizes the bank information signalling problem to third party stakeholders in the firm concerning the firm's investment risk in the absence of bank equity ownership. Rajan (1992) analyzes the bank credibility problem to the securities market when it already has debt and has an information advantage. Other important aspects of the economics of bank operations emphasized in recent work are not included in these analyses.

Leland and Pyle (1977) argue that banks may capture the value of privately obtained information by signalling in terms of their own capital structure. The above studies focus on bank owners without consideration of their overall cost of capital as it relates to the ability of the bank to signal the quality of its loan portfolio. Deposit insurance and state guarantees of the banking system reduce banks incentives to provide markets with this kind of signal, however.

The focus on information asymmetries in the literature cited above does not allow consideration of another important role of commercial banks; the production and use of the information in monitoring the performance of borrowers as stressed by Diamond (1984). Practically and intuitively, the monitoring role of banks is extremely important as can be seen in the complexity of the loan negotiation process and the resulting detail in many loan agreements. One interpretation of banking activities is that the output is information services, although this output is "sold" in the form of lending, deposit, and underwriting services. Thus, it is important to analyze banks' incentive to produce information i.e. to monitor firms' activities, management quality etc.

Additional considerations not examined further in this paper should be noted and may vitiate possible advantages of universal banking in developed financial markets. First, the evidence of economies of scale and scope in commercial banking is mixed. Bank economies apparently occur at relatively small scale of bank operations, but at the level of major national banks discussed in the cases of Japan and Germany the evidence is less clear.[1] Furthermore, recent evidence on bank performance suggests that size alone is no guarantee of information advantages with enormous losses and bankruptcies occurring in the largest bank and thrift institutions.

Another consideration in accepting results favoring specific regulation is the complexity of the financial structure of corporations relative to the simple models used in the papers discussed above. For example, Spatt and Sterbenz (1993) discuss changes in incentives when the firm capital structure includes debt, equity, and warrants and trading occurs in those instruments. The precarious balancing of capital structure and bundling of financial claims necessary to achieve first best investment policies suggests that the stylized models discussed above may simplify the effect of bank underwriting and investment powers on efficiency too much to be useful guides to policy.

Finally, banks have the potential to play an important role in the "markets for corporate control" as well. This consideration is especially relevant for universal banks owning large equity-stakes in firms. These stakes make direct exercise of control possible. We discuss these issues after analyzing incentives of banks to monitor and gather information for this purpose.

8.3 A model of incentives to monitor with universal banking

Bank monitoring of corporate performance is an important function of banks. Monitoring and information gathering about firms, projects, and management are multifaceted phenomena. Their general purpose is to identify factors influencing the probability of distress, as well as the rate of return on investments. Here, we assume that the information is used to influence firms' management to run efficient operations by means of threats of foreclosure, threats of withholding funding, or direct exercise of control when the bank has an equity stake.[2]

With this view of bank monitoring, it will increase corporate productivity if effective, in other words, effective monitoring will raise expected returns from investments. This increased productivity must be compared to the costs of monitoring. Diamond (1984) has demonstrated that financial intermediaries (banks) can economize on the costs of monitoring, providing a rationale for banks' economic existence. This section addresses the effects on bank monitoring of universal banking, defined here to consist of allowing banks to make both debt and equity investments in risky firms. We describe the production of monitoring in very simple terms, assuming that monitoring is a one dimensional activity. Monitoring activities are costly and they "produce" reduced probability of distress, as well as higher project returns.[3]

We begin with a simple model of bank and firm profitability under two regimes, *CB* for commercial banking without equity stakes and *UB* for universal banking with equity stakes. π_{CB} are commercial bank profits on one dollar invested by a firm, π_{UB} are the profits of a universal bank holding a share β of the firm's equity, and π_F are the investing firm's project return before repayment of the loan. $\pi_{\frac{N}{F}}$ are the firm's net profits after loan repayment. The loan share in the project is δ and the interest rate is $(R_L - 1)$.

$$\pi_{CB} = Max(\delta R_L - C(m),\ \pi_F - C(m)) \tag{8.1}$$

$$\pi_{UB} = Max(\delta R_L + \beta(\pi_F - \delta R_L) - C(m),\ \pi_F - C(m)) \tag{8.2}$$

$$\pi_{\frac{N}{F}} = Max\ (\pi_F - \delta R_L,\ 0) \tag{8.3}$$

In (8.1) and (8.2), $C(m)$ are the costs of monitoring. (8.1) and (8.2) are identical when $\beta = 0$. It is therefore sufficient to work with equation (8.2) that incorporates all cases.

It is assumed that there are two states of the world. The project return is high with probability p in which case the project's return is $\pi_{\frac{H}{F}} > \delta R_L$. The project's return is low with probability $(1-p)$ in which case return is $\pi_{\frac{L}{F}} < \delta R_L$. This amount must be paid to the bank in any case.

The expected profits of the universal bank are

$$E[\pi_{UB}] = p(\delta R_L + \beta(\pi_{\frac{H}{F}} - \delta R_L) - C(m)) + (1-p)(\pi_{\frac{L}{F}} - C(m)) \tag{8.4}$$

The firm maximizes expected profits with respect to monitoring effort (m) at a given loan rate.[4]

$$dE[\pi_{UB}]/dm = (dp/dm)[\delta R_L + \beta(\pi_{\frac{H}{F}} - \delta R_L) - \pi_{\frac{L}{F}}] +$$

$$d\pi_F/dm[p\beta + (1-p)] - dC(m)/dm \tag{8.5}$$

The corresponding derivative for the commercial bank is obtained by setting $\beta = 0$. In (8.5) the effect on the probability of success of increased monitoring can be expressed in terms of the effect of monitoring on project return. It is assumed that the increased probability of the high outcome results from a shift to higher project returns as a result of monitoring as follows:.

$$(dp/dm) = (dp/d\pi_F) \cdot (d\pi_F/dm) \tag{8.6}$$

where

$$(d\pi_F/dm) = (d\pi_F^H/dm = (d\pi_F^L/dm).$$

In other words, increased monitoring has the same effect on project return in the two states, while increasing the probability of the high outcome.

Using (8.5) and setting the derivative of the bank's profit derivative in (8.5) equal to zero, the bank's optimal monitoring effort is derived when the following equality holds:

$$(d\pi_F/dm)[(dp/d\pi_F)((\delta R_L - \pi_F^L) + \beta(\pi_F^H - \delta R_L)) + p\beta +$$

$$(1-p)] = dC/dm \tag{8.7}$$

The left hand side is the marginal profit increase from monitoring and the right hand side is the marginal costs of monitoring. The latter costs are assumed to be increasing. From (8.7) follows that the marginal profit increase is higher for the universal bank, since the terms $\beta, \pi_F^H - \delta R_L$, and $\delta R_L - \pi_F^L$ are positive. Thus, if the marginal cost of monitoring is independent of β then the equity stake contributes to monitoring effort.[5]

In the above model it has been assumed that the share of debt financing is the same in the two cases. Thus, the share of project-financing supplied by the commercial bank was less than the share provided by the universal bank. Although this might be realistic, it is desirable to evaluate monitoring effort when the two kinds of banks supply the same share of project financing. In this case the project's capital structure changes when β increases while in the previous case the debt-equity ratio was constant.

Set $\delta_{CB} = \delta + \beta(1-\delta)$ in (8.7). In this case the commercial and the universal banks supply the same amount of financing for the project but in different forms. The following equilibrium condition is derived:

$$(d\pi_F/dm)[dp/d\pi_F)(\delta_{CB}R_L - \pi\tfrac{L}{F}) + \beta(\pi\tfrac{H}{F} - R_L)) + p\beta + (1-p)] =$$
$$(dC/dm) \tag{8.8}$$

Equation (8.8) shows that as long as $\pi\tfrac{H}{F} > R_L$ the marginal profit increase from monitoring will increase with the equity stake (β) of the bank's financing.

The analysis here indicates that universal banks have a stronger incentive to monitor projects than commercial banks restricted from holding equity. This result holds also if monitoring affects the probability of the high outcome while leaving the project outcomes unchanged. Setting $d\pi_F / dm = 0$ in (8.5), the following equilibrium condition for monitoring is obtained when the share of loan financing is constant:

$$dp/dm[(\delta R_L - \pi\tfrac{L}{F}) + \beta(\pi\tfrac{H}{F} - \delta R_L)] = dC/dm \tag{8.9}$$

Assuming instead that the share of project financing is constant the following expression is obtained:

$$dp/dm[(\delta_{CB} R_L - \pi\tfrac{L}{F}) + \beta(\pi\tfrac{H}{F} - R_L)] = dC/dm \tag{8.10}$$

when the bank's share in total project financing is constant. In both cases, the marginal profit increase from monitoring increases with β. The marginal profit increase is greater in (8.9) for the case when an increase in β implies an increase in the bank's share in the project. The reason is that when comparing the parentheses multiplied by β in (8.9) and (8.10) $(\pi\tfrac{H}{F} - \delta R_L) > (\pi\tfrac{H}{F} - R_L)$.

In conclusion, under the assumption that monitoring increases the probability, of the high outcome, the marginal profitability of monitoring increases with the bank's equity stake. Thus, the equilibrium equity stake of the bank is positive. The equilibrium equity stake is higher when the bank's equity stake increases at the expense of other equity-holders' stake in (8.7) and (8.9) than when the bank's share in total financing is constant in (8.8) and (8.10).

Finally, we comment on some assumptions made. One assumption was that costs of monitoring are the same for the two types of banks. Since universal banks have an equity stake and possibly board membership, their monitoring costs would at least not be higher than the costs for commercial banks. Other aspects of corporate control were ₜneglected as well. These aspects are discussed in the next section.

Second, the debt-equity structure of the project was exogenous in one case while the bank's total stake was exogenous in the other. Empirical observations in the 1980's indicated that in strongly bank-oriented financial systems firms' debt equity ratios are higher than in Anglo-Saxon systems without universal banking. In model terms $\delta_{CB} < \delta_{UB}$. If so, universal banks supply larger proportions of both debt and equity financing. However, recent evidence in Rajan and Zingales (1995) indicates that debt equity ratios are constant across systems. This implies that banks' equity stakes substitute for other shareholders' stake.

Third, the advantage of universal banks derived in the model would dissipate if other suppliers of financial resources have a strong incentive to monitor. We return to this possibility in the next section when corporate control issues are discussed.

Fourth, the incentive of management to exert effort thereby increasing the probability of the high outcome was not considered. In Dietrich, Pan, and Wihlborg (1996) a model is developed wherein effort depends on management's equity stake and monitoring has the function of reducing diversion of project returns to management and the entrepreneur. In this model, the effects of bank's equity holding on the probability of success are ambiguous. It can be said, however, that the case favoring banks' equity holdings are weakened considerably when (1) a bank's equity stake reduces the incentives of an entrepreneur to exert effort, and (2) the bank's monitoring effort does not increase the expected returns on projects but redistributes these returns among stake-holders.

8.4   Universal banking and corporate control

A bank's equity stake if sufficiently large enables the bank to exert control over management. If the bank through its monitoring has inside information about the probability of distress, and if management can influence this probability, then board representation and associated direct control over management provide an additional channel for the bank to affect the probability of distress. Specifically, as the probability of distress increases it is in a large shareholder's power to fire management and install a new team. Through this channel, the bank with the equity stake can reduce the probability of bad outcomes and distress further than in the model in Section 8.3.

Holding a sufficiently large equity stake providing ability to select the management team implies that the bank with inside information has an option that can be exercised when distress approaches to bring in a new management team. For this option to be valuable the bank must have inside information not only about the incumbent "bad" management team but also about potential better teams. Such information is available for a shareholding bank that sits at the center of an industrial group. A group of firms with a common large shareholder with an information advantage about managers essentially form an internal labor market for management competence. Japanese "keiretzus" can be thought of as such internal markets for a pool of managers. In Germany also, each commercial bank has a group of firms in which they exert control over management.[6] In Sweden, there are groups of firms associated with each major bank that indirectly hold equity through related institutions. There is mobility of managers within these groups but little mobility among the groups (see Dahmén, 1970, and Eliasson, 1991).

A remarkable feature of the bank-industry groups is that the banks generally hold rather small equity stakes in the firms. For example, in Germany universal banks hold substantial stakes in only 39 of the 171 largest corporations and in theses cases most stakes represent less than 15 percent of the equity (see Franks and Mayer, 1996). Family ownership dominates business firms in Germany. In Sweden, banks hold no equity. Controlling equity stakes are instead held by investment firms that are related to banks by having major shareholders in common (see Berglöf and Sjögren, 1995). Bank equity holdings in non-financial firms in these cases confirm the observation, noted in Section 8.2, that banks are reluctant to hold large equity stakes. Thus, it seems that when universal banks take an important part in corporate control, it is not primarily the equity stake that allows control. Instead, there are a number of associated characteristics of the corporate control mechanism which jointly provide the conditions for bank-industry groups.

Apart from some shareholdings by banks or related firms, different classes of shares are given different voting rights in countries with bank-industry groups. In Sweden, A-shares have one vote, while B shares sometimes have one one-thousandth of a vote. In Germany, differentiated voting rights are accomplished indirectly by "pyramiding".[7] In Japan, cross-ownership is common.

The differentiation of voting rights, pyramiding and cross-ownership have the consequence that hostile take-overs are practically non-existent in countries with bank-industry gropus. It is also common in these countries that management by legislation and/or corporate charters has a direct say in take-overs. In general, take-overs defences are strong (see Franks and Mayer, 1996). As a result, if there are take-overs, they are friendly. Similarly, changes in management are friendly and organized within each group. In fact, the internal labor market for managers would not function well if take-overs were a threat. The reason is that the "pool" of managers within an internal labor market in a bank-industry group must be given a certain degree of job-security within the group in exchange for loyalty to the group. The implicit arrangement between the managers and the group or the dominant owners within the group would breakdown if hostile take-overs were possible.

According to this view of the bank-industry group as a corporate governance system the groups can function even without banks holding equity as the Swedish experience shows. The essential characteristics of the bank-industry group are that management is not subject to the threat of hostile take-overs and that owners exert substantial control in a group of firms. Equity holding banks is one way to build such groups but there are other ways.

In countries where corporate governance systems do not rely on internal labor markets for management, banks do not participate actively in the "market for managers" and do not hold equity even if they are allowed to, as in the UK. In the UK and the USA the market for corporate control is also a market for managers. Take-overs and management changes occur in external and competitive markets, in particular in the equity markets. We cannot here make a claim that one type of "market for managers" is more efficient than another. What is essential is that there exists a market or a mechanism for informed changes in management. Banks' equity holdings can contribute to the creation of "internal markets" for control. If a market for control is limited by regulation of bank equity investments, then other mechanisms for the development of external and internal markets for control must not be hindered by regulation, if efficient allocation of management is to be achieved.

8.5 Problems unique to emerging market economies

The consideration of specialized versus universal banking in the previous sections has been in the context of developed financial markets. The issues raised in the existing literature and in the above results must be reviewed against the backdrop of the realities of EMEs. Several points are relevant when considering expansion of bank authority to make equity investment in EMEs.

First, the high risks of business enterprises require critical evaluation to assure the efficient allocation of scarce savings in rapidly growing economies. Banks can provide critical review and evaluation of business plans when properly motivated. Furthermore, confidentiality of that information to assure benefits to entrepreneurs may be essential to stimulate the risk-taking involved. Campbell (1977) argued for restrictions on equity ownership by banks to prevent banks from participating in the gains to private information. Our analysis of monitoring effort, on the other hand, indicates that universal banking could play an important role in supplying risk-capital when well-developed securities markets are lacking and entrepreneurs lack sufficient funds for a venture. The universal bank would be more willing to supply funds than a commercial bank because of its higher return on monitoring effort, assuming that monitoring raises the expected return on projects.

Risky projects undertaken by non-public firms in highly growing and developing economies may well require carefully structured loan agreements which include collateral in order to screen for the best projects, as suggested by Chan and Thakor (1987).[8] Credible collateral pledges by entrepreneurs in the presence of bank equity financing would introduce new classes of financial claims unless banks were to pledge collateral as well. While the economics of these complex financial arrangements are not obvious, it would seem clear that these new types of claims would move the analysis into a world far more complex than that discussed.

The major concerns of regulators in the EMEs should be efficient allocation of savings to productive investment and the creation of regulatory structures that provides mechanisms for changes in ownership and management when inefficiencies arise. We argued that banks' equity participation in firms can provide a mechanism for the creation of internal well-informed markets for managers within bank-industry groups but there are alternative mechanisms for informed management change.

The development of aggressive competition in the financial sector and a flexible regulatory structure that enhances competition among contractual and institutional arrangements are important considerations for policy makers. Given doubts that the exploitation of scale and scope economies require large universal banks, the availability of new technologies facilitating competition from smaller firms, and the substantial threat of anti-competitive forces stemming from the political strength of former state enterprises, a wide distribution of corporate control is desirable. It can be debated whether the German and the Japanese systems for corporate control are superior to alternatives but we see no reason to follow the US and UK example of prohibiting equity ownership in banks provided competition in the financial sector can be obtained. The investors in EMEs face information problems of unknown magnitudes and types. Contractual and institutional arrangements will develop to overcome problems caused by information asymmetries and uncertainty if not prevented by regulation. There are no strong economic arguments for prohibiting particular institutional arrangements for lending, monitoring and corporate control. In designing regulatory schemes, policy makers in EMEs should be creating an environment stimulating competition, innovation and risk taking without subsidizing losses from inefficiency and bad luck.

Notes

1. Dietrich (1991) finds no evidence of economies of scale in a study of banks in the EC countries. Altunbas and Molyneux (1996) argue that there are cost advantages related to size, but attributable to economies of scope in the German system of universal banks. Lang and Welzel (1996) support this view in a study of German banks.
2. Monitoring may also have the objective of reducing the diversion of profits to management, as argued below and explored in Dietrich, Pan, and Wihlborg (1996).
3. The economic role of monitoring could be described in other ways. We return to this issue below.
4. The results are not influenced by assuming that the loan rate is endogenous and compensates the bank for an exogenous probability of project failure, while an endogenous component of this probability depends on monitoring.
5. $dm/d\beta$ can be derived from (8.7) in the following way. Set G (m,β) = the right hand side in equation (8.5). Then $dm/d\beta = - (dG/d\beta)/(dG/dm)$. Under the assumptions that $(d^2C)/dm^2 \geq 0$, $d(dp/d\pi)/dm = d(dp/dm)/d\pi$ < 0 and $d\pi^2/dm^2 < 0$ it can be shown that $dm/d\beta > 0$.
6. Baums (1994) notes that bankers on Germany's boards contribute to creating an institutionalized market for managers.
7. Franks and Mayer (1996) note that tiers of ownership are common.

190   *J. K. Dietrich, K. Pan and C. Wihlborg*

8.   It is an important task in EMEs to define property rights to real estate
     and other property in such a way that a collateral against loans can be
     pledged credibly.

References

Altunbas, V. and P. Molyneux, 1996, Economies of Scale and Scope in European Banking, Applied Financial Economics, 6, 4, pp 367-375

Baums, T., 1994, The German banking system and its impact on corporate finance and governance, in M. Aoki and H. Patrick, eds., The Japanese Main Bank System; Its Relevance for Developing and Transforming Economies (Oxford University Press, Oxford).

Benston, G.J. , 1990, The Separation of Commercial and Investment Banking: The Glass-Steagall Act Revisited and Reconsidered (Oxford University Press, New York).

Berglöf, E. and H. Sjögren, 1995, Combining arm's length and control oriented finance evidence from main bank relationships in Sweden, Working Paper, ECARE, Brussels.

Berlin, M., J. Kose and A. Saunders, 1996, Bank equity stakes in borrowing firms and financial distress, Review of Financial Studies, 9, Fall, pp. 889-919.

Boot, A. and A.V. Thakor, 1994, Financial system architecture, Working Paper, Indiana University.

Campbell, T.S. ,1979, Optimal investment financing decisions and the value of confidentiality, Journal of Financial and Quantitative Analysis, XIV, 5, pp. 913-924.

Chan, Yuk-Shee and A.V. Thakor, 1987, Collateral and competitive equilibria with moral hazard and private information, Journal of Finance, XLII, 2, pp. 345-363.

Dahmén, E., 1970, Entrepreneurial Activity and the Development of Swedish Industry ,1919-1939 (Richard D. Irwin Inc., Homewood, Ill).

Diamond, D.W., 1984, Financial intermediation and delegated monitoring, Review of Economic Studies, LI, pp. 393-414.

Dietrich, J.K., 1991, Consequences of 1992 for Competition in Financial Services: Banking, in: Wihlborg, C. M. Fratianni, and T.D. Willett eds., Financial Regulation and Monetary Arrangements after 1992 (North Holland, Amsterdam).

Dietrich, J.K., K. Pan, and C. Wihlborg, 1996, Capital structure and universal banking with endogenous effort and bank monitoring, Gothenburg Studies in Financial Economics, Göteborg University.

Franks, J. and C. Mayer, 1996, European capital markets and corporate control, in: Bishop, M. and J. Kay, eds., European Mergers and Merger Policy (Oxford University Press, Oxford).

Gorton, G. and R. Rosen, 1992, Corporate control, portfolio choice, and the decline of banking, Finance and Economics Discussion Series, Federal Reserve Board, Division of Research and Statistics, Division of Monetary Affairs, Washington D.C.

Harm, C., 1995, The role of universal banks in overcoming financial cosntraints, PhD dissertation, Stern School of Business, New York.

Jensen, M.C., 1986, Agency costs of free cash flow, corporate finance, and takeovers, American Economic Review, pp, 323-329

John, K., T. A. John and A. Saunders, 1994, Universal banking and a firm risk taking , Journal of Banking and Finance, 18, pp. 307-323.

Kolari, J. and A. Zardkoohi, 1987, Bank Costs, Structure and Performance (Lexington Books, Lexington, Mass.).

Krosznen, R.S. and R.G. Rajan, 1994, Is the Glass-Steagall act justified? A study of the U.S. experience with universal banking before 1933, American Economic Review, 84, 4, pp. 810-832.

Lang, G. and P. Welzel, 1996, Efficiency and Technical Progress in Banking: Empirical Results for a Panel of German Corporate Banks, Journal of Banking and Finance, 20, 6, pp. 1003-1023.

Leland, H.E. and D.H. Pyle. 1977, Informational asymmetries, financial structure, and financial intermediation, Journal of Finance, XXXII, No 2, May, pp. 371-387.

Myers, C. Stewart and N.S. Majluf, 1984, Corporate dinancing and decisions when firms have information that investors do not have, Journal of Financial Economics, 13, pp. 187-221.

Rajan, R.G., 1992, A theory of the costs and benefits of universal banking, Working Paper 345, Center for Research in Security Prices, Grad. School of Business, University of Chicago.

Roe A., 1992, Financial sector reform in transitional socialist economies, Seminar Report No 29, Economic Development Institute (The World Bank, Washington D.C.)

Santomero, A.M., 1984, Modeling the banking firm, Journal of Money, Credit and Banking, XVI, 4, 2, pp. 576-644.

Spatt, C.S. and F.P. Sterbenz, 1993, Incentive conflicts, bundling claims, and the interaction among financial claimants, Journal of Finance, XLVIII, 2, June, pp. 513-528

Financial Sector Reform and
Privatization in Transition Economies
J. Doukas, V. Murinde and C. Wihlborg (Editors)
© 1998 Elsevier Science Publishers B.V.

$2/4$

$(l\, \S,\ \text{Sweden})$

Chapter 9

$G/2$

EMERGING STOCK MARKETS: LESSONS FROM INDUSTRIALIZED COUNTRY HISTORY

$N\,20$

R.J. Sweeney
Georgetown School of Business, Georgetown University, Rm. 323 Old North Bldg.,
37th and "O" Sts., NW, Washington, DC 20057, USA

9.1   Introduction

Many emerging market economies have stock markets, often several markets. The range of institutions in these markets is very wide, including government regulators and regulations. Whether through focusing on other goals or even through ignorance, the designs of many of the institutions seemingly ignore some lessons of history. This paper looks at the evolution of two stock markets, in the U.S. and Sweden, for their lessons for pressures on the institutional evolution of emerging stock markets (ESMs). It also looks at evidence on the historical cost-benefit tradeoffs from "international diversification"; the benefits can be much oversold, and in particular the 1985-1993 boom for ESM stocks predictably contains the seeds of bust. Some of these lessons are briefly--and tentatively!--applied to Poland's stock market.

9.2   Evolution of stock markets

To some extent, the evolution of stock market institutions in the U.S. and Sweden was driven by the demands of the market place. For example, the New York Stock Exchange began with outdoor trading on the curb of a street in what became New York's financial district. Up until the Great Depression (1929-1941 in the U.S.), U.S. stock markets were only lightly regulated at the Federal level. In the wake of the Crash of 1929 and the Great Depression, the Securities and Exchange Commission was founded and granted substantial regulatory powers that have periodically been increased; a key element in the design of stock-market regulators and regulations has been to maintain public confidence in the integrity of U.S. financial institutions, and of stock markets in particular.

Over the past two decades, the over-the-counter (OTC)[1] market has grown to rival the importance of organized exchanges, particularly those OTC stocks traded through the computerized NASDAQ system. Thus, U.S. regulations have allowed enough slack that new market institutions can arise in response to market demands; importantly, these new institutions provide important competition for traditional organized exchanges.

Most countries are going to be interested in regulators and regulations that maintain the public's confidence in the integrity of stock markets. There is a trade-off, however. Over-regulation increases costs of doing financial business and hence increases the overall cost of capital for the economy's firms. Further, over-regulation will hinder the development of new market institutions in response to market demands, thus reducing financial-market efficiency. If regulation stifles new institutions, market demand for changes will not disappear but will find other outlets; for example, regulations on exchanges and brokers may push large trades off exchanges and take them out of the hands of brokers. Trades in domestic securities may easily and rapidly come to be dominated by foreign stock markets if foreigners are allowed to purchase domestic securities; an example is the domination of the Vienna exchange for large Hungarian companies' shares.

In the first half of the 1890s, Sweden's stock market was open one day per month, with only a single brokerage house making the market in all of the stocks on the exchange on that one day each month that the exchange was open. In the second half of the 1890s, a second brokerage house began to make markets and the stock market was then open a second day per month. The majority of stocks with prices reported in newspapers had only one month with a transaction price reported, no stock had a transaction price in every month of the decade. Table 9.1 shows that of the 477 stocks that traded during the decade, only 34 had trading prices reported for the last month of the decade (Sweeney 1996a). Further, in Table 9.1 of the 77 bank/credit and insurance companies that traded over this period, only 13 traded in the last month; this reflects the tendency for many such Swedish firms to be small, local and illiquid. Of the top ten firms in terms of number of reported trading prices over the 120 months, the most active firm traded 101 times, the tenth most active firm, 54 times. Table 9.2a and Table 9.2b give a flavor of the fact that of many firms for which there are no trading prices in the first half of the decade there suddenly appear trades in the second half, and with some frequency of trades. Clearly, the Swedish market was thin and illiquid at the start of the 1890s, though showing signs of becoming more active by the end of the decade.

TABLE 9.1
Number of Swedish stocks with
trading prices in December 1899

Category	Number of companies traded in 1890-1899[a]	Number of companies with Dec. 1899 observation[b]
Total	477	34
Bank/credit	52	11
Insurance	25	2
Transportation/ communications	68	10
Manufacturing, industry etc.[c]	291	10
Steamships, shipping	41	1

Source: Sweeney (1996a).

Notes: (a)   Within categories, a company is included if newspapers reported at least one trading price in the decade 1890-1899.

(b)   Companies for which newspapers included a reported trading price for December 1899.

(c)   This is a catch-all category.

TABLE 9.2A
Trading activity in Swedish stocks, first half of 1890s

		1890												1891											
Year	Month	J	F	M	A	M	J	J	A	S	O	N	D	J	F	M	A	M	J	J	A	S	O	N	D
C	1																								
O	2																								
M	3																								
P	4																								
A	5																								
N	6																							1	
Y	7																								
	8																								
	9																								
	10																								
	11																								
	12														1									1	
	13																								
	14											1													
	15																								
	16			1																					
	17				1																			1	
	18			1																				1	
	19		1																						

TABLE 9.2A

Trading activity in Swedish stocks, first half of 1890s (Continued)

	1890												1891											
	J	F	M	A	M	J	J	A	S	O	N	D	J	F	M	A	M	J	J	A	S	O	N	D
20															1									
21							1	1	1		1						1		1				1	
22										1				1		1				1				
23																								
24																								
25																								
26															1									
27			1								1				1									
28																1								
29		1																						
30	1	1	1																					
31	1	1	1		1	1	1	1	1	1	1	1		1	1	1	1	1	1	1				
32																								
33																								
34																								
35																								
36																								
37																								
38																								

R. J. Sweeney

TABLE 9.2A

Trading activity in Swedish stocks, first half of 1890s (Concluded)

	1890												1891											
	J	F	M	A	M	J	J	A	S	O	N	D	J	F	M	A	M	J	J	A	S	O	N	D
39	1	1							1	1	1			1	1							1	1	
40	1		1																					
41												1												
42	1		1							1	1					1		1						
43																								
44																								
45																								

Source: Sweeney (1996a)

TABLE 9.2B
Trading activity in Swedish stocks, second half of 1890s

COMPANY	1898 J	F	M	A	M	J	J	A	S	O	N	D	1899 J	F	M	A	M	J	J	A	S	O	N	D
1				1						1	1				1	1	1	1				1	1	1
2																								
3										1	1		1	1	1	1	1	1	1			1	1	1
4														1	1						1			
5					1											1								
6		1	1	1			1		1						1									
7				1																				
8			1		1			1	1	1					1	1	1			1	1		1	1
9																1								
10	1									1														
11		1	1	1	1		1		1	1													1	
12				1								1												
13	1		1				1						1											
14								1	1															
15	1	1		1	1			1		1	1			1	1	1		1	1					1
16							1				1												1	1
17			1		1					1	1				1	1								
18		1		1																				
19	1				1																			

TABLE 9.2B

Trading activity in Swedish stocks, second half of 1890s (Continued)

	1898												1899											
	J	F	M	A	M	J	J	A	S	O	N	D	J	F	M	A	M	J	J	A	S	O	N	D
20		1	1	1	1	1	1		1		1		1	1	1	1	1		1	1	1	1		
21	1	1	1	1	1	1	1						1	1	1	1	1							
22		1			1					1					1									
23		1								1		1				1						1	1	1
24			1	1	1	1	1	1	1	1	1	1	1	1	1	1	1	1	1	1	1	1	1	1
25	1					1	1		1	1	1		1		1									1
26		1	1		1	1	1		1	1	1	1	1	1		1								
27	1				1	1	1	1	1		1	1	1	1	1									
28		1		1		1	1	1	1	1	1		1		1	1	1	1	1	1	1	1		1
29									1	1						1								
30								1	1	1	1	1	1	1	1	1	1	1	1	1	1	1	1	1
31	1	1	1	1	1	1	1	1	1	1	1	1	1	1	1	1	1	1	1	1	1	1	1	1
32	1	1	1	1	1	1	1	1	1	1	1	1	1	1	1	1	1	1	1	1	1	1	1	1
33	1			1	1		1	1	1							1				1	1			
34						1																		
35				1	1	1	1	1																
36	1			1	1	1																		
37	1	1	1	1	1	1	1	1	1	1	1	1	1	1	1	1	1	1	1	1	1			1
38	1	1	1	1	1	1	1	1	1	1	1	1	1	1	1	1	1	1	1	1	1	1	1	1

TABLE 9.2B

Trading activity in Swedish stocks, second half of 1890s (Concluded)

	1898												1899											
	J	F	M	A	M	J	J	A	S	O	N	D	J	F	M	A	M	J	J	A	S	O	N	D
39	1	1	1	1	1	1	1	1	1	1	1	1	1	1	1	1	1	1	1	1	1	1	1	1
40																								
41												1												
42																								
43				1	1	1					1			1		1	1	1		1		1	1	1
44		1														1	1	1						
45	1	1	1		1				1		1		1				1	1		1	1			

Source: Sweeney (1996a)

By the period of the first world war, more than twenty Swedish firms traded at least once a month (save for rare occasions) in reasonably thick and liquid markets, allowing creation of a meaningful stock-market index (Frenberg and Hanson 1992a, 1992b). Between the two periods, Sweden had undergone substantial growth, urbanization and internationalization (Wihlborg 1990). Table 9.3 shows comparative per capita growth rates; after the property-rights reforms of 1864, Sweden began to grow at substantial per capita rates over the century from 1870 to 1973. There were also substantial shifts in the producing-sector composition of GNP and in employment over time, of the type to be expected with industrialization and real per capita growth: a declining contribution from agriculture and rise in industry and later in services. Table 9.4 shows the decomposition of GNP across final-use sectors; Sweden enjoyed substantial shares going to investment over long periods. The growth of the stock market in terms of size, number of issues, number of shares traded, liquidity and thickness roughly corresponds to these macro trends, though of course causality between the real and financial sectors is likely bi-directional. Thus, much of the "underdevelopment" of the Swedish stock market in the 1890s endogenously disappeared as Sweden became industrialized.

From the 1980s to the early 1990s, Sweden imposed a 1 percent turnover tax on the seller of any share in Sweden. This succeeded in driving most of the larger trades in large Swedish companies to the London Stock Exchange;[2] the Stockholm exchange kept the largest number of Swedish companies, mainly small companies, and London had the greater Swedish-crown value of trading in shares of Swedish companies. The turnover tax was increased to 2 percent, reenforcing these pressures and trends. Then the turnover tax was abolished: the Stockholm market regained some but (note well) not all of its lost volume in Swedish stocks. These results could have been anticipated from other evidence. For example, there is substantial evidence that when international trade in a country's securities is allowed, arbitrage keeps values of its shares much the same in the home country and abroad: an example is the pricing of Japanese shares on the Tokyo Stock Exchange (TSE) and of the ADRs[3] on these shares on the New York Stock Exchange (NYSE)[4].

Some work suggests that government interventions in financial markets may improve their performance, hasten their development or hasten the development of the nonfinancial sector of the economy. For example, Demetriades and Luintel (1996) present evidence that government regulation of banks in South Korea increased the volume of bank credit and through this channel increased the real growth rate of the nonfinancial sector; however, in an earlier paper on India they find that intervention appears to have had oppositie effects (see Demetinades and Luintel, 1994). Murinde and Eng (1994) find evidence to support the view that efforts by Singapore's government to stimulate the growth and sophistication of its financial sector, primarily banking, succeeded and also stimulated growth of Singapore's nonfinancial sector.

This evidence is relevant to stock-market issues, even if not directly, because government actions in one part of the financial system may spill over to other parts. For example, some observers believe German regulations favoring universal banking relative to U.S. regulations are responsible in part for the relative underdevelopment of German stock markets--though obviously not of the German economy. Note that Poland has adopted banking laws on the German model.

Lessons from the evolution of stock markets

It seems that ESMs that appear underdeveloped will endogenously develop as the economy does; regulatory efforts to hasten, retard or in general guide this development may be unwise. Further, taxes on stock markets will tend to drive away trade in the securities, to other countries if this is possible, perhaps to negotiated and perhaps unreported transactions otherwise. Indeed, regulations will eventually stunt an ESM unless these conform to conditions on the most cost-effective exchanges or trading systems.

9.3   International diversification

In the post-1985 period, there was a boom in ESM stocks, lasting into 1994; even including the many busts across countries in 1994, many ESMs showed remarkably large rates on return over the period, as the International Finance Corporation's *Emerging Stock Markets Fact Book* shows. Further, over this period, the sample correlations of rates of return in many ESMs were small and statistically not significantly different from zero relative to other ESMs and to developed countries stock indices. Taken at face value it appeared that a well diversified portfolio of stocks from ESMs offered a high rate of return with very little risk (diversification eliminates most of the risk); adding such a portfolio to another portfolio diversified across large, developed economies would increase expected return and reduce risk.

204
204 · R. J. Sweeney

TABLE 9.3
Annual growth rates per capita, 1820-1985, constant prices

	1820-70	1870-1913	1913-50	1950-73	1973-79	1950-60	1960-70	1970-80	1980-85	1950-80	1950-85
Denmark	0.9	1.6	1.5	3.3	1.8	2.6	3.5	2.1	2.5	2.8	2
Finland	(n.a.)	1.7	1.7	4.2	2.0	4.0	4.3	3.1	1.9	3.8	3
Norway	1.0	1.3	2.1	3.1	3.9	2.8	3.6	4.6	2.6	3.6	3
Sweden	0.6	2.1	2.2	3.12	1.5	2.6	3.7	1.8	2.2	2.7	2
Australia	(n.a.)	0.6	0.7	2.5	1.3						
Austria	0.7	1.5	0.2	5.0	3.1						
Belgium	1.9	1.0	0.7	3.6	2.1						
Canada	(n.a.)	2.0	1.3	3.0	2.1						
France	1.0	1.5	1.0	4.1	2.6						
Germany	1.1	1.6	0.7	5.0	2.6						
Italy	(n.a.)	0.8	0.7	4.8	2.0						
Japan	0.0	1.5	0.5	8.4	3.0						
Netherlands	1.5	0.9	1.1	3.5	1.7						
Switzerland	1.7	1.2	1.5	3.1	-0.2						
UK	1.5	1.0	0.9	2.5	1.3						
USA	1.4	2.0	1.6	2.2	1.9						
Arithmetic average	1.1	1.4	1.2	3.8	2.0						

Sources: Wihlborg (1990)
Notes: missing data for some periods

TABLE 9.4

Distribution of Gross National Product by final use, selected countries, long periods (based on totals in current prices)

	Private consumption (1)	Government consumption (2)	Gross domestic capital formation (3)	Capital exports or imports (4)	Gross national capital formation (5)
United Kingdom					
1. 1860-79	82.7	4.8	9.4	3.1	12.5
2. 1880-99	81.9	5.8	8.4	3.9	12.3
3. 1900-14	78.6	7.4	8.7	5.3	14.0
4. 1921-29	82.0	8.9	6.8	2.3	9.1
5. 1950-58	66.9	9.4	15.5	0.7	16.2
Germany (boundaries of the period)					
6. 1851-70	81.6	4.0	13.7	0.7	14.4
7. 1871-90	73.1	5.9	18.9	2.1	21.0
8. 1891-1913	68.7	7.1	13.0	1.1	24.1
9. 1928	76.1	7.2	18.2	-1.5	16.7
10. 1950-59	58.7	14.4	23.7	3.1	26.8
Italy					
11. 1861-80	87.3	4.2	10.0	-1.5	8.5
12. 1881-1900	84.4	4.8	10.8	0	10.8
13. 1901-10	78.4	4.2	15.9	1.4	17.3
14. 1921-30	78.5	5.6	18.1	-2.2	15.9
15. 1950-59	68.2	12.0	20.8	-1.0	19.8

TABLE 9.4
Distribution of Gross National Product by final use, selected countries,
long periods (based on totals in current prices) (Continued)

		Private consumption (1)	Government consumption (2)	Gross domestic capital formation (3)	Capital exports or imports (-) (4)	Gross national capital formation (5)
Denmark						
16.	1870-89	92.0		9.8	-1.8	8.0
17.	1890-1909	88.8		13.5	-2.3	11.2
18.	1921-30	87.8		11.9	0.3	12.2
19.	1950-59	68.6	12.5 (9.6)	18.9	0	18.9
Norway						
20.	1865-74	83.8	3.8	11.3	1.2	12.5
21.	1875-94	84.7	4.8	11.9	-1.4	10.5
22.	1895-1914	83.6	6.6	14.7	-4.9	9.8
23.	1915-24	78.1	8.5	18.9	-5.5	13.4
24.	1925-34	77.5	8.7	14.4	-0.6	13.8
25.	1950-59	60.0	12.5 (8.9)	29.9	-2.4	27.5
Sweden						
26.	1861-80	85.3	4.4	10.8	-0.5	10.3
27.	1881-1900	85.0	5.4	11.2	-1.6	9.6
28.	1901-20	81.6	5.8	13.1	-0.5	12.6
29.	1921-40	75.0	8.6	15.8	0.6	16.4
30	1941-59	64.8	14.3	21.0	-0.1	20.9
31	1950-59	61.9	16.8 (11.9)	21.2	0.2	21.4

TABLE 9.4

Distribution of Gross National Product by final use, selected countries, long periods (based on totals in current prices) (Concluded)

	Private consumption (1)	Government consumption (2)	Gross domestic capital formation (3)	Capital exports or imports (-) (4)	Gross national capital formation (5)
United States (official concept)					
32 1869-88	76.7	3.6	20.6	-0.9	19.7
33 1889-1908	73.6	4.4	21.4	0.5	21.9
34 1909-28	74.7	4.9	18.4	2.0	20.4
35 1929-38	77.9	9.4	12.3	0.4	12.7
36 1946-55	66.4	15.4	17.3	0.9	18.2
37 1950-59	63.7	17.9 (7.5)	17.9	0.5	18.4

Source: Wihlborg (1990)

R. J. Sweeney

TABLE 9.5

Value of diversified stocks bought in 15 countries, as registered by the latest official quotations obtained during the first half of 1929

	Amount originally invested in Jan 1914 ($)	Market value first half 1929 ($)	Percentage of increase	Percentage of decrease
Austria............	12,302.88	3,212.36		73.88
Belgium............	12,500.99	10,890.60		12.88
Denmark............	11,827.60	10,055.05		14.99
England............	12,500.00	75,106.19	500.84	
France............	12,694.43	7,507.20		56.62
Germany............	11,861.77	10,761.90		9.29
Holland............	12,856.06	21,369.60	66.14	
Hungary............	12,467.00	2,798.58		77.55
Italy............	12,834.97	5,517.95		57.00
Norway............	11,860.75	19,455.76	64.03	
Spain............	11,496.40	13,778.75	19.85	
Sweden............	12,488.00	12,569.55	0.65	
Switzerland............	11,753.51	14,963.15	27.08	
Total 13 countries............	159,447.36	207,986.67	30.44	
Canada............	12,464.60	56,864.00	356.23	
United States............	12,457.00	34,918.37	180.30	
	24,921.60	91,782.37	268.29	
Grand total 15 countries....	$184,368.96	$299,769.04	62.59	

Source: Stern (1929)

Table 9.6
Investment in diversified stocks of 15 different countries

Country	Jan 2 1914 ($)	Oct 14, 1924			April 2, 1928		
			% of increase	% of decrease		% of increase	% of decrease
Austria	$ 12,302.88	$ 1,292.91		89.50	$ 2,772.08		77.46
Belgium	12,500.99	6,046.05		51.63	9,215.57		26.28
Denmark	11,827.60	8,494.68		28.18	12,877.92	8.88	
England	12,500.00	16,125.00	29.00		39,816.00	218.53	
France	12,694.43	3,980.19		68.65	7,553.20		40.50
Germany	11,864.77	3,558.10		70.01	11,314.16		4.64
Holland	12,856.06	12,865.90	0.07		18,624.78	44.87	
Hungary	12,467.00	11,519.34		7.60	13,366.62	7.21	
Italy	12,834.97	7,778.85		39.40	8,320.06		35.17
Norway	11,860.75	10,827.79		8.71	15,004.34	26.51	
Spain	11,496.40	10,544.80		8.28	15,381.89	33.79	
Sweden	12,488.00	13,928.48	11.53		16,629.52	33.16	
Switzerland	11,753.51	11,402.25		2.98	17,473.65	48.67	
Canada	12,464.60	20,862.50	67.37		49,347.70	295.90	
U S A	12,457.00	16,359.00			28,709.00	130.46	
Total	$184,368.96	$155,585.84	31.32	15.61	$266,406.49	44.50	

Source: Stern (1929)

These data may be highly misleading with respect to the gains from international diversification. In 1929, Siegfried Stern published a book showing how an internationally diversified portfolio over the major countries' stocks and bonds would have done from 1914 to either 1924 or 1929 (a 10- or 15-year holding period). For the 10-year holding period, the results show little support for international diversification. An investor would have been better off holding U.S. and Canadian stocks and bonds (or pure portfolios of either stocks or bonds) than diversifying internationally (Stern 1929); see Tables 9.5 and 9.6. The reason of course was World War I. The stock and bond markets in defeated nations (Germany, Austria-Hungary) showed disastrous results, as did markets in many of the victors (Belgium, France). It is quite possible that severe, highly correlated disturbances may hit emerging market economies in the future. In other words, the cheery outlook for ESMs based on 1985-1993 data may be due simply to using too short a sample.[5]

In addition to the losses on stock portfolios over Stern's periods, investors in many countries faced a sudden and large decrease in liquidity and thickness of stocks markets during WWI. Stock prices obtained from newspaper reports for five large, blue-chip German companies over the decade 1910-1919 show a complete lack of reported trades during WWI; this reflects the German government's decision to close stock markets for the duration of the war. Of course there were private, non-exchange trades of these stocks in Germany and likely outside, but in an environment of greatly reduced liquidity and thickness; and of course the informativeness of such prices was greatly reduced (Sweeney 1996b).

Lessons from the history of international diversification

1985-1993 ESM data should be treated as a major episode, like the 1914-1924 period, with the truth that these data represent some average of important boom and bust periods. Instead, much comment seemed to assume that the 1985-1993 data were best forecasts of the future.

9.4   Applications to the Polish stock market

A major concern in the mind of those designing the Polish stock market, its regulator and its regulations, was to build and maintain the public's confidence in the stock exchange and by extension financial institutions in general and even the free enterprise system. This concern was reasonable and wholly understandable for a country making a transition to liberalized markets from the communist command system. The emphasis was on transparency, fairness to all market participants, and reduction of volatility.[6] Some of the institutions and regulations in the Polish market may conflict with market desires, however, and the costs of these conflicts may rise over time; this suggests that Poland may want to consider periodically revising regulations and even fundamental institutions such as how trades are carried out.

Because the Polish stock exchange in effect trades only once a day, and all stocks trade at the same instant, the market lacks the liquidity and price-informativeness of markets with more continuous trading, for example, the U.S. NYSE and NASDAQ markets. In particular, traders on the Polish exchange receive only one price-quantity observation per day on each stock, and can take advantage of the information in today's 11 a.m. price only 24 hours later (Kowalski, 1995). This suggests that there will be a demand for institutions that allow Polish stocks to be traded more continuously and that provide more information revelation through more observed price-quantity points. Further, limits to how far a stock's price can move in one day (Kowalski 1995) also reduce the liquidity and information provided by the exchange, suggesting that the limits might be counterproductive on net.

Poland is adapting to market pressures. The Warsaw Stock Exchange (WSE) has multiple "floors"; on the first floor, the original stringent standards for listings still apply, but on other floors the standards are relaxed, allowing smaller and newer firms to be listed. Perhaps more importantly for the longer term, an over-the-counter market is scheduled to be launched in early 1996. These moves should increase liquidity and information revelation. These moves also respond at least in part to a long queue of companies wanting access to the stock market, and the number of brokers that want to join the Warsaw Stock Exchange.

There are two fundamentally different approaches to institutional change in stock markets. The first approach uses regulators to design institutions that are optimal in light of a given set of goals that are presumably derived from society's concerns. The regulators may, however, be inept or may substitute for society's concerns the concerns of special interest groups or the regulators themselves; this is "government failure." The second approach allows institutions to develop endogenously in the market. These institutions may be socially sub-optimal because they are dominated by groups or individuals whose concerns do not match society's; this is market failure. The evidence across a wide part of economics suggests that government failure is as dangerous as market failure, though the consequences differ across cases. Balancing these costs suggests that governments might want to consider running regulated stock markets but also allowing less regulated ways for trading stocks, to see what the freer market has to say about revising regulations for the more controlled market, and to see what the more controlled market has to say about the need to impose regulations on the freer market. These empirical observations may be useful to regulators but also to the public in generating more informed debate about the costs and benefits of particular regulations.

Notes

For helpful comments and discussions, thanks are due to Qaizar Hussein and Clas Wihlborg, and to participants in the Poznan Conference on Financial Reform in Emerging Market Economies, especially Christopher J. Green, Tadeusz Kowalski, Victor Murinde and Vello Vensel. Mats-Ola Forsman and Molly Moosbrugger provided helpful research assistance on this project. This paper was written at the Gothenburg School of Economics and research on it was partially supported by Georgetown University and Georgetown Business School summer grants. This paper was presented at the Conference on Financial Reform in Emerging Market Economies, at the Poznan University of Economics, Poznan, January 20-21, 1996.

1. An over-the-counter stock market is one where trade in shares does not take place on an organized exchange such as the New York stock exchange, but rather among brokers and customers without going through an exchange. OTCs are often regulated and thus have rules from this source; an OTC may also be organized and have its own regulations adopted by members. In the U.S. market, an important subset of shares are traded electronically on the so-called NASDAQ system, where orders placed and actual trades are shown on members' computer screens.

2. Lybeck (1991, p. 167) cites unpublished Stockholm Stock Exchange estimates that "two-thirds of the turnover on the 16 most widely traded Swedish shares takes place in London."

3. ADRs are American Depository Receipts. A financial intermediary buys shares in a Japanese company on the Tokyo exchange and sells ownership rights, though not the shares themselves on say the New York Stock exchange.

4. Christopher J. Green helpfully points out similar evidence for the seventeenth century for Amsterdam and London.
5. This is not the only possible problem with interpreting these data. Among others, there is also the effect on inferences of allowing the holding period to increase; Marcus, Solberg and Zivney (1991) argue that this effect reduces individual stocks' variations and also reduces the relative benefits of international diversification.
6. Poland chose stock-market institutions quite different from Germany's, but as noted above chose banking laws similar to Germany's. A number of other EMEs have been similarly eclectic in borrowing financial laws, institutions and regulations.

References

Demetriades, P.O. and K.B. Luintel, 1996, Financial repression in the South Korean 'miracle' (University of Keele Working Paper, Keele).
_____, and _____, 1994, 'Financial repression,'financial deepening and economic growth: Evidence from India (University of Keele Working Paper, Keele).
Murinde, V. and F.S.H. Eng, 1994, Financial development and economic growth in Singapore: Demand-following or supply-leading? Applied Financial Economics, 4, pp. 391-404.
Frennberg, P. and B. Hanson, 1992a, Swedish stocks, bonds, bills and inflation, Applied Financial Economics, 2, pp. 79-86.
_____, and _____, 1992b, Computation of a monthly index for Swedish stock returns 1919-1989, Scandinavian Economic History Review, 40, pp. 3-27.
Kowalski, T., 1995, The Polish stock market. Presentation to the Georgetown Business School Workshop in Finance and Accounting, 1995.
Lybeck, J.A., 1991, On political risk--The turnover tax on the Swedish money and bond markets, or How to kill a market without really trying, in: Sarkis J. Khoury, ed., Recent Developments in International Banking and Finance (Elsivier Science Publishers, Amsterdam).
Marcus, R.D. D. Solberg and T.L. Zivney, 1991, A reexamination of the benefits to international diversification, in: Sarkis J. Khoury, ed., Recent Developments in International Banking and Finance (Elsivier Science Publishers, Amsterdam).

Stern, S. 1929, Fourteen Years of European Investments (The Bankers Publishing Company, New York).

Sweeney, R.J., 1996a, Stock market evolution in Sweden: From 1890 to 1995 (Georgetown Business School Working Paper, Washington D.C.).

_____, 1996b, Stock market shocks in Germany: From 1890 to 1953 (Georgetown Business School Working Paper, Washington D.C.).

Wihlborg, C., 1990, The Scandinavian models for development and welfare (Gothenburg University Department of Economics Working Paper, Gothenburg).

Part Three

The Financial Sector and the Macroeconomy

Financial Sector Reform and
Privatization in Transition Economies
J. Doukas, V Murinde and C Wihlborg (Editors)

217 — 39

Chapter 10

REGULATORY CHANGE AND THE
ALLOCATION OF FINANCE:
The Role of Business Conglomerates in
Chile, 1983-1992

Niels Hermes and Robert Lensink
Department of Economics, University of Groningen, PO Box 800, 9700 AV,
Groningen, The Netherlands

10.1 Introduction

This paper investigates how changes in the financial institutional framework
in Chile during the 1980s have had an impact on the decisions of financial
institutions, especially banks, with respect to the allocation of financial
resources over different groups of firms. The regulatory changes included
the reduction of the implicit deposit insurance, which had been developed
during the 1970s, and limitations on the extent of financial ties between
financial and non-financial firms. In particular, the paper focuses on the
impact of these institutional changes on the allocation of funds between
firms belonging to business conglomerates - or Grupos in the Chilean
context - as compared to firms not belonging to such conglomerates.

The regulatory changes affecting the organisation of firms in Grupos
may have had an impact on the allocation of resources, because lending
decisions based on intra-conglomerate linkages could lead to market
segmentation. The reason is that firms not belonging to a conglomerate have
reduced access to loans, since banks may have less information about
investment projects of these firms. Moreover, the regulatory changes may
have had an impact on the efficiency of resource allocation. The existence
of such business conglomerates may be one way of mitigating information
problems in capital markets, since financial institutions, e.g. banks, are
usually closely linked to such conglomerates. Such links may have an
important impact on how banks decide to issue and allocate new loans,

because they reduce the information asymmetry between borrower and lender. Limitations on financial ties between financial and non-financial firms as in the Chilean case, may therefore have increased informational problems reducing allocational efficiency in Chile in the 1980s.

The analysis in this paper focuses on the effects of the changing institutional framework on the pattern of resource allocation. First, groups of firms are distinguished based on the extent to which banks hold information on their activities. Second, investment behaviour of groups of firms is compared. In particular, it is expected that internal sources of finance are more important in determining investment patterns of firms for which banks hold relatively less information as compared to firms for which they hold relatively more information. It is assumed that banks' information about firms depends on their relatedness to a business conglomerate: banks will have more information on firms related to a conglomerate. In contrast to most papers using the above method, this paper explicitly focuses on the effects of regulatory changes, hypothesizing that differences between Grupo and non-Grupo firms with respect to the sensitivity of their investment for fluctuations in internal funds available will diminish after the implementation of the changes, indicating reduced market segmentation.

The issue discussed in this paper is of a more general interest, because business conglomerates appear to be an important feature in many developing countries, that are in the process of changing their financial institutional framework. By investigating the impact of regulatory changes on patterns of allocation of financial resources in Chile, this paper may yield useful lessons for implementing such reforms elsewhere.

The paper is organised as follows. Section 10.2 discusses the reasons for the existence of industrial conglomerates emphasising the impact of such structures on investment and financial decisions of firms. Moreover, it provides a description of the existence and importance of conglomerate structures in Chile, as well as of the regulatory changes of the 1980s aimed at reducing the interrelatedness between banks and firms. Section 10.3 describes the data that have been used in the empirical analysis. Section 10.4 presents the results of the econometric analysis testing for the impact of the regulatory changes on allocation. Section 10.5 summarises and concludes the paper.

10.2 Conglomerates, investment and corporate finance: theory and descriptive evidence for Chile

10.2.1 Conglomerates, investment and information problems in capital markets

In many developing countries (but also in some developed countries, e.g. Japan) a substantial part of productive activities appears to be organised in so-called business conglomerates, referred to as Grupos in the Latin American context.[1] One of the basic characteristics of this form of industrial organisation is that there are strong linkages between different firms participating within the Grupo. In many cases a Grupo owns a large number of industries in various sectors. Normally, it also owns one or more financial institutions, such as banks, and investment and insurance companies.

The creation and existence of business conglomerates in developing countries may be explained on the grounds of existing market failures. Market failures are prevalent in these countries (Stiglitz, 1989). Domestic markets in most of these countries are relatively small and are characterised by high instability due to rapid structural changes. Moreover, markets to directly hedge risks and uncertainty are in most cases practically non-existent. The institutional structure of the business conglomerate reduces the adverse impact of these market failures on resource allocation and output.

This also holds in the case of financial markets. In developing countries these markets are generally underdeveloped (and/or repressed due to government interference). This stimulates the creation of Grupos, in which internal relations between banks and firms are developed and tightened to increase access of firms to outside financial sources, i.e. financial sources other than retained earnings.

From the point of view of banks, tight relationships with borrowers have advantages. Usually, banks are confronted with information problems, since the borrower will be better informed about the risks and returns of investment projects, i.e. information is divided asymmetrically among borrowers and lenders. In this situation, varying the interest rate is not the optimal policy, since adverse selection and moral hazard may occur, which leads to increasingly risky lending portfolios and - at least after some point - to falling expected rates of return on loans (Stiglitz and Weiss, 1981). Therefore, banks may ration credit to borrowers for whom the perceived riskiness of activities is higher. Close ties with borrowers, such as those existent within the Grupo structure may mitigate information problems of banks. The close relationships between industrial firms and banks within a Grupo structure increase the amount of information available to evaluate the riskiness of investment projects. In short, the Grupo structure may contribute to improving effective screening and monitoring. It helps to resolve the agency problem between the bank and its borrowers. The result will be that firms related to banks within a Grupo may face less credit rationing when looking for resources to finance their investment projects as compared to firms outside such Grupo structures for which banks hold less information. In other words, the creation of Grupos leads to market segmentation in capital markets.

Following the above line of thought, one expects to find differences in patterns of financing of investment between Grupo related firms and firms without connections to Grupos. In particular, since Grupo related firms are generally confronted with less severe credit rationing, the timing of their investment plans will be less restricted by the availability of internal funds. Firms without close connections, however, may face effective constraints to attract outside funds and are more dependent on internal sources when they want to finance their investment plans. Such constraints may disrupt their desired investment pattern.

In recent years, a large body of empirical literature has investigated the issue of information problems in financial markets and their impact on investment decisions of firms in developed countries (see, among others, Fazzari, Hubbard and Petersen, 1988; Devereux and Schiantarelli, 1990; Whited, 1992; and Chirinko and Schaller, 1995). These studies analyse the importance of measures of internal funds or liquidity as an explanatory variable of annual investment outlays. Theory would suggest that if there are no information problems, availability of internal funds does not affect investment behaviour (Modigliani and Miller, 1958). The above mentioned empirical studies approach this issue by dividing firms into groups for which it may be expected that differences exist with respect to the severity of information problems banks are confronted with. Thus, firms may for example be divided into large and small, and old and young firms; the first of these pairs are those firms for which information severity is assumed to be low(er). Next, these studies compare the impact of internal funds on investment of these different groups of firms to see whether there is evidence for the hypothesis that measures of internal funds are less important as determinants of investment of those firms for which banks may hold more information (i.e. larger and/or older firms). If imperfections in capital markets exist, then it is expected that differences occur in financial constraints for different classes of firms; firms for which the information problem is more severe have less easy access to external finance, revealing itself in a higher level of the coefficient of the internal funds variable in the investment function of these firms. In general, these studies find empirical support for the hypothesis of existence of information problems based on this empirical test (Hermes and Lensink, 1998).

Only a few studies have followed the above described strategy of empirical research to investigate differences in investment and its finance for firms within and outside business conglomerates. Hoshi, Kashyap and Scharfstein (1991) provide evidence for the importance of conglomerates in explaining differences in investment finance between related and non-related firms in the case of Japan. Van Ees and Garretsen (1994) analyse the importance of informal networks, rather than formal linkages within conglomerates, to explain differences in firms' access to capital markets in the Netherlands. These studies find support for the hypothesis that informationally disadvantaged firms (i.e. firms outside conglomerate structures) rely more on internal funds when they invest.

To our knowledge, studies by Harris, Schiantarelli and Siregar (1994), and Siregar (1995) are the only ones investigating the issue of the relevance of business conglomerates in influencing resource allocation, and the impact of financial reforms on this. These studies look at the case of Indonesia in the 1980s; they do not find conclusive evidence for the hypothesis that after the reforms market segmentation based on whether or not firms belong to a conglomerate has been reduced.

In this context, this study extends the scarce empirical literature on the impact of financial reforms on changes in the allocation of financial resources by concentrating on the issue of market segmentation in capital markets based on the existence of business conglomerates in the case of Chile. Preceding the empirical research in Section 10.3 and 10.4, we present below further details on Chilean business conglomerates and clarify why the issue studied here is of particular relevance to the Chilean case.

10.2.2 Chilean Grupos and the changing institutional environment

Traditionally, Grupos have been existent and important in Chile - politically as well as economically - since the late nineteenth century. In the pre-Allende period - i.e. before 1970 - they were mainly based on strong family ties and social group structures and consisted of a wide range of enterprises, among them financial institutions. These old Grupos were led mainly by conservatism and aimed at gaining political influence to an important extent. After the military coup of 1973, which marked the turn from state intervention and economic repression to capitalism and economic liberalisation, several new Grupos were created in addition to the existing ones. During the 1970s, Grupo activities were focused on gaining economic, instead of political power. In this decade, Grupos were characterised by strong relationships between banks and real sector firms. This was strongly stimulated by the fact that in the process of privatisation banks were privatised sooner than firms in other sectors (Paredes and Sánchez, 1994, p.19). In particular, the Grupos built extensive networks of relations with different kinds of financial institutions such as mutual funds, investment companies, real estate companies, finance companies, etc. Such financial relations were far more extensive as compared to those of the 1950s and 1960s.

The economic and financial powers the Grupos (both old and new) built up during the 1970s were overwhelming. Paredes and Sánchez (1994, p.1) mention that in 1980 Grupos controlled around 30 per cent of the total economy. According to estimates by Dahse (1979), Grupos controlled 80 per cent of the equity of the Chilean national banks at the end of the 1970s. Moreover, in 1978 the six largest Grupos owned 54 per cent of the equity in the 250 largest Chilean companies; in 1980 they controlled 50 of the 100 largest firms, holding 62 per cent of their total assets. Grupo Cruzat-Larraín and Grupo Vial, the two largest Grupos of the country, together controlled 43 per cent of these assets (Dahse, 1983, pp.49-51). Due to their close connections with banks, Grupo related firms had relatively easy access to credit markets. They were also able to attract loans to cover the losses during a time when these losses were building up rapidly in the early 1980s, following the domestic economic crisis.

Unfortunately, the enormous growth of financial transactions carried out within the Chilean Grupos - as well as those transactions outside these Grupos but carried out by Grupo related financial institutions - was one of the main reasons for the financial collapse of the Chilean financial markets in the early 1980s. It took major interventions by the central bank to rescue the Chilean financial system from a total break down (Larraín, 1989). Most observers agree that the combination of weak prudential regulation and the dominance of Grupos in the Chilean economy has been an important cause of the explosive growth of financial transactions, especially during 1977-1981 (Edwards and Cox-Edwards, 1991; Velasco, 1991; Hermes, 1995).

They argue that the way the regulatory authorities acted during the 1970s led to the creation of an implicit deposit insurance. On the one hand, on several occasions after 1977 the authorities announced that insolvent financial institutions would not be rescued. On the other hand, insolvent institutions were actually supported by the authorities, which made the public - i.e. banks as well as deposit holders - to believe that deposit insurance was in fact present.

The implicit deposit insurance led banks to relax their efforts with respect to credit evaluation and stimulated them to take increased risks. This is explained by the fact that a deposit insurance can be viewed as a contingent subsidy, since the government insurance provides an arbitrage profit (Merton, 1977). When a bank increases its liabilities it can exploit the difference between the market value of the insurance and the price its pays for it (De la Cuadra and Valdès, 1992a, p.34).

It has been suggested that increased risk taking of banks due to installing a deposit insurance is even more pressing in the presence of Grupo structures (De la Cuadra and Valdès, 1992a, pp.41-45). This is the case, since Grupo banks have better opportunities to evade prudential regulation of the monetary authorities than have banks outside Grupos. The nature of holding structures within a Grupo are normally difficult to observe for outsiders; yet, the authorities should have detailed information about these structures to be able to evaluate the solvency and liquidity positions of the Grupo banks. One of the ways in which banks can make monitoring of internal lending activities more difficult is by splitting up a loan into smaller ones, and issuing them to newly (created) shell-companies, which in turn relend the small loan to the firm for which the loan was originally destined. As De la Cuadra and Valdès (1992a, p.45) put it: "...the supervisory powers of the superintendency reach only to the banks; it has no authority over the successive layers of holding companies that define the structure of the business group." This increases the information problems of the regulatory authorities, who, in the presence of a deposit insurance system, monitor bank behaviour in the name of the depositors.

The above line of reasoning is illustrated by the facts in Chile during the 1970s and early 1980s. Grupo banks more easily financed the losses of Grupo firms, which resulted from liberalisation of trade, domestic markets and the growing exchange rate overvaluation, to postpone bankruptcy in the hope that economic growth would help to overcome the financial problems of these firms in the near future. At the same time, the regulatory authorities appeared to be unable to effectively control the banks' activities. With the high real loan rates dominating the domestic financial markets during the several years in the 1970s, in combination with the presence of an implicit deposit insurance and weak prudential regulation, banks, and in particular the ones related to Grupos, were playing an unfair bet against the government (Villanueva and Mirakhor, 1990, pp.519-521). The resulting high growth of financial transactions contributed to the growing financial instability during the early 1980s.[2]

As a reaction to the problems with the domestic financial markets, the Chilean government decided to strengthen the regulatory system in the early 1980s. Initially, the main objective of these regulatory changes was to reduce the possibilities of intra-Grupo lending. The authorities were convinced that the large number of intra-Grupo financial transactions was one of the major sources of financial distress. In fact, these measures aimed at restricting possibilities for banks being the financial heart of the Grupos, a position they had obtained in the course of the 1970s. Moreover, the measures aimed to press banks to give more information about their activities, enabling deposit holders to better monitor bank behaviour.

The most important regulatory reforms of the early 1980s were the following:

- *March 1981*: limits on transactions with related individuals or parties, *i.e.* shareholders and employees of banks; transactions with these individuals and parties have to be reported on.
- *April 1981*: loan classification system (introduced in February 1980) is extended to include the 300 largest debtors on which banks have to report details to the regulatory institution (*Superintendencia de Banco e Instituciones Financieras, SBIF*).
- *August 1981*: new definition of the individual borrower; according to the new definition the debt of an individual includes that of all firms of which the individual owns or controls more than 50 per cent, plus the prorated share of debts in firms of which the individual owns or controls between 10 and 50 per cent.
- *February 1982*: loan classification system is extended to 400 largest debtors. Banks may also choose to report details of 85 per cent of their loan portfolio outstanding.

Notwithstanding the introduction of the above measures, the Chilean financial system collapsed in 1983. Due to a massive devaluation of the peso against the dollar in June 1982, foreign denominated debt became an almost insurmountably heavy burden, triggering the bankruptcy of many firms, and consequently of several commercial banks. Moreover, the international debt moratorium following the Mexican debt crisis in August of the same year added to the financial problems of both Chilean banks and firms, since this triggered immediate and severe liquidity and solvency problems.

In early 1983 the central bank decided to intervene by taking over non-performing debts of banks with severe financial problems and by liquidating insolvent institutions. Together with earlier interventions in the financial system during 1981, the central bank intervened in thirteen banks and six other financial institutions. Eight of these banks and the six other institutions were liquidated. The others were technically taken over by the central bank. Among the latter were the two largest banks of the country. The loan portfolio of the intervened institutions represented 60 per cent of all loans issued by the financial system (Larraín, 1989, pp.1-2). Later on during the 1980s, the government reprivatised the financial institutions that had been taken over by the central bank by selling shares to the public. In contrast to the privatisation of banks during the 1970s, however, the government explicitly aimed at spreading these shares over a large number of shareholders to reduce the potential dangers of creating too close connections between banks and real sector firms within Grupos.

The above described regulatory changes of the early 1980s were clearly reflecting the monetary authorities' belief that the extent of financial linkages between banks and firms within Grupos was one of the primary causes of the domestic financial crisis. This led them to concentrate their regulatory changes on enabling them to control and reduce such links. One might expect these measures to have an impact on the allocation of financial resources over firms in the course of the 1980s. In particular, differences with respect to credit constraints of non-Grupo versus Grupo-firms may have been reduced.

There may have been yet another effect on credit allocation, though. By introducing the above measures aiming at reducing the possibilities for banks to have close links with firms within Grupos, the mitigating effect of these links on information problems and its potential positive impact on the efficiency of resource allocation may have been reduced. In fact, the real problem in Chile in the 1970s and early 1980s may not have been the extent of the financial linkages, but the existence of the implicit deposit insurance. One may hold the view that if the latter problem could have been solved in an earlier stage, then the risk taking of banks would not have been as extensive as it appeared to be in practice, even in the presence of Grupos. The authorities seemed to have realised this. In November 1986 - as part of the new banking law - they introduced an explicit deposit insurance regime, in which basically small deposit holders are insured. Moreover, the authorities aimed at increasing the credibility of the insurance by explicitly stating the rules to be followed when banks would fail and become insolvent.[3] As already mentioned in the introduction, however, the basic aim of the empirical investigation of Sections 10.3 and 10.4 is to analyse the impact of the regulatory changes on the allocation of resources.

10.3   Data description

To analyse the impact of the regulatory changes on the allocation of resources, financial data have been used on a firm level. These data have been provided by the *Superintendencia de Valores y Seguros* (SVS), a government agency to which limited companies have to report their activities on a quarterly basis since 1981. For the present analysis annual data have been used. The data set consists of information on balance sheets, income statements and uses and sources of funds of firms from different sectors of the economy for the 1981-1992 period. For every year between 1981 and 1992 some 250 to 300 firms reported information to the SVS.

The following criteria have been adopted to construct the data set that has been used in the empirical part of this paper. First, firms have been selected that presented full information for all relevant variables during the 1982-1992 period in order to acquire a balanced data set. Second, firms have been eliminated from the data set when they were operating within the financial sector, public administration or social sectors. Thus, the firms in the data set are engaged in the agricultural, mining, manufacturing, construction, or services sector. Using these two criteria, 81 firms remained in the data set. After eliminating those firms reporting that they were in a state of liquidation, or for which data appeared to be unacceptable or inconsistent (such as reporting zero sales, and unacceptable large changes in fixed and total assets), 70 firms remained, of which financial data have been used in the estimations presented below. It is acknowledged that the data set used in this study is not necessarily representative of the corporate sector in Chile. It consists of relatively larger firms, which may have better access to capital markets than the average Chilean firm. Any result of the present research project must therefore be appreciated as indicative only.

Firms have been divided into those belonging to a Grupo and those active outside Grupo structures. This division is based on information provided by the SVS data. Apart from the financial data, there is also more general information in the SVS data set, including information on the amount of employees, number of shares, etc. Among the general information is also a reference to whether or not a firm belongs to a Grupo. If this reference is applied to the set of 70 firms, 38 firms can be classified as non-Grupo related firms, whereas 32 firms can be classified as Grupo related firms.

TABLE 10.1

Summary statistics of non-Grupo versus Grupo firms

	Total assets	Fixed assets	Invest-ment	Related investment	Profit	Sales	Internal sources
Non-Grupos							
average	5,702	2,579	0.117	0.146	0.051	0.989	0.393
median	2,876	731	0.077	0.039	0.058	0.747	0.188
Grupos							
average	38,660	20,283	0.122	0.243	0.085	0.503	0.291
median	12,935	4,575	0.093	0.146	0.086	0.457	0.207

Note: Total and fixed assets are in millions of 1985 pesos; investment and internal sources are divided by the capital stock; all other variables are divided by total assets.

Table 10.1 provides basic information on the characteristics of both Grupo and non-Grupo related firms. In general, the summary statistics presented in the table show that both groups of firms differ in a number of ways. First, it appears that the Grupo related firms are generally larger. In terms of total assets, the median value of Grupo related firms is four and a half times that of non-Grupo related firms. For the stock of fixed assets this is more than six times. Second, when looking at the ratio of investments in related firms to total assets, the table clearly shows that Grupo related firms hold substantially more of these investments, as might be expected. Third, non-Grupo firms have substantially higher sales to asset rates. Fourth, Grupo firms are more profitable than non-Grupo firms. Examination of annual average figures shows that non-Grupo firms were hit harder by the economic crisis of the early 1980s as compared to the Grupo firms. Finally, non-Grupo firms seem to have higher internal sources (divided by capital stock) available. Yet, the annual amount of these internal sources is rather volatile for non-Grupo firms (measured by its standard deviation); the median values may give more accurate information on the volume of internal sources for both groups of firms. The difference between the median values of both groups of firms appears not to be statistically significant.

10.4   Econometric investigation

10.4.1   The strategy of econometric investigation

In order to investigate the impact of regulatory changes in financial markets on the changes in the allocation of resources, the empirical methodology used to analyse the existence of informational problems in capital markets is also applied here. As dicussed in Section 10.2, one particular branch of empirical studies approach the issue of capital market imperfections by dividing firms into groups based on differences with respect to the severity of information problems banks are confronted with. Next, these studies compare the impact of internal funds on investment of these different groups of firms to see whether there is evidence for the hypothesis that measures of internal funds are less important as determinants of investment of those firms for which banks may hold more information. If imperfections in capital markets exist, then it is expected that differences occur in financial constraints for different classes of firms; firms for which the information problem is more severe have less easy access to external finance, revealing itself in a higher level of the coefficient of the internal funds variable in the investment function of these firms. In the context of this paper, if relatedness to a Grupo reduces information imperfections, this should be exposed by the fact that the coefficient for the internal sources variable in the investment equations is lower for Grupo firms than for non-Grupo firms.

The econometric analysis is carried out as follows. An investment equation is estimated, in which the dependent variable is annual gross investment, *i.e.* net investment plus depreciation. The estimation procedure is based on pooled regressions of individual firm data, using the least squares technique.[4]   All variables (dependent as well as independent) in the regressions presented below have been scaled by total capital stock one period lagged and have then been transformed into logs.[5] In order to be able to pool the information of individual firms, the *fixed effects technique* has been used. This technique assumes that the intercepts of individual firms differ, yet the slope coefficients are the same for all firms. To carry out fixed effect estimations, the data have been transformed. For each variable, the means of individual firm observations have been subtracted from the original observations. The least squares method has then been applied to the transformed data (Hsiao, 1986, pp.29-41). In the estimation procedure, outliers have been skipped based on extreme values of the residuals of the individual equations.[6]

10.4.2 Specification of the investment model

In the estimations three different specifications of the investment model have been applied, i.e. an accelerator type investment model, a Q-model of investment, and a combination of both these models. The accelerator type model is fairly standard in investment literature. It incorporates changes in total sales (DSAL) as the basic regressor that may explain investment behaviour. The idea is that investment decisions are based on observed patterns of past demand for final output. Therefore, a positive relationship is expected to be found between investment and the sales variable.

Other regressors that have been added to the model are the debt to capital (or leverage) ratio (DEBT) and investment one period lagged (GINV). The debt to capital ratio has been included to account for the effects of the cost of debt on investment. Investment outlays will be negatively affected by this ratio, since the higher the leverage, the higher the costs of financing investment with debt. This is due to the fact that creditors will increase the marginal price of loans when a debtor already has a high level of debt to capital (Harris, Schiantarelli and Siregar, 1994, p.38). One expects a negative relationship between investment and the debt indicator. Investment one period lagged is included to account for the stock adjustment process.

Furthermore, a measure of internal sources has been added. In the empirical literature, the standard measure for this purpose is cash flow (CF), i.e. net profit after taxes plus depreciation. The latter variable is of primary interest to the underlying analysis as the coefficients of this variable for both groups of firms will be compared to see whether there is evidence for information problems in capital markets which lead to differences in access to external finance. Thus, one should expect to find a positive relationship between investment and cash flow. However, the coefficient of the cash flow variable should be lower for firms for which the information problem in capital markets is assumed to be smaller (i.e. Grupo firms) due to the special institutional characteristics of business conglomeration.

Standard criticism of analysing the relationship between investment and measures of internal sources by using the above presented specification of the investment model points out that the measures of internal sources available may also proxy for the profitability of investment. According to this criticism, one should expect a positive relationship between internal sources and investment, since firms with more liquidity are doing well and thus have better possibilities to invest (Hoshi, Kashyap and Scharfstein, 1991, p.43). This may pose problems when one wants to interpret the cash flow coefficients in terms of representing capital market imperfections. Since this criticism may be valid, a Q model of investment is also applied in the empirical analysis. Tobin's Q (TOBQ) - a proxy measure for expected profitability of the firm - is used, instead of the sales variable, and along with the other regressors mentioned above, to account for the effect of the expected future profitability of investment on investment decisions.[7] Tobin's Q is defined as the market value of equity plus the book value of (short plus long-term) debt divided by the book value of total assets.

Finally, to account for both the accelerator and profitability aspects influencing investment, a specification is used which includes both the sales and the Q variable as regressors, together with the other regressors.

As has been described in Section 10.2 of this paper, the Chilean government changed the regulation during the early 1980s to reduce the possibilities of intra-Grupo lending. The new regulation adversely affected the opportunities of banks to serve as the financial heart of the Grupos. This may have reduced the information advantages they had with respect to lending to Grupo firms as compared to non-Grupo firms before the restrictions on intra-Grupo lending had been effectuated. In particular, it may have led to a reduced segmentation of capital markets as non-Grupo firms now have gained more equal access to loans. The impact of the change of regulation will not show until after some time, however, i.e. it may take some years for the new regulation to be really effective. Banks as well as firms need time to adjust their financial decisions to the changed institutional environment. If this is the case, it may be hypothesised that differences in the sensitivity of investment with respect to cash flow for Grupo versus non-Grupo firms exist during the first few years of the period under investigation, whereas these differences are reduced or even disappear later on.

The exact specification of the three investment models can be found in Tables 10.2 and 10.3, equations (10.1) - (10.3). Table 10.2 gives the estimation results for the entire 1983-1992 period; Table 10.3 gives the results when the period is split up in a pre-reform and post-reform period (see below). Equation (10.1) presents the results of the accelerator-type investment model. The model includes changes in total sales of the present period. All other variables are included with a lag of one period.[8] Cash flow is added one period lagged, based on the idea that in general a firm will finance investment in period t, using the cash flow that is generated one period earlier - i.e. that is available at the beginning of period t. In the regressions two cash flow variables are included. One variable is obtained by multiplying one period lagged cash flow with a dummy variable, which is one when observations refer to non-Grupo firms and zero when they refer to Grupo firms (CFNG). The other variable is obtained by multiplying one period lagged cash flow with a dummy variable, which is one when observations refer to Grupo firms and zero when they refer to non-Grupo firms (CFG). All equations have been estimated including year dummies to capture the impact of macroeconomic changes during the 1983-1992 period. Equations (10.2) and (10.3) present the Tobin's Q model of investment and a combination of both investment models, respectively.

To test for the effects of the changes in regulation on differences in access to external finance for both Grupo and non-Grupo firms, the three investment models presented in Table 10.2 have been re-estimated, this time including four instead of two cash flow variables (Table 10.3). There are now two cash flow variables for non-Grupo and two for Grupo firms. The cash flow variable for non-Grupo firms is multiplied with a dummy variable, which is one when observations refer to the 1983-1987 period and zero when they refer to the 1988-1992 period (CFNG 1983-87). Moreover, the cash flow variable for non-Grupo firms is multiplied with a dummy variable, which is one when observations refer to the 1988-1992 period and zero when they refer to the 1983-1987 period (CFNG 1988-92). The same procedure has been followed to construct the two cash flow variables for the Grupo firms (CFG 1983-87 and CFG 1988-92, respectively).

10.4.3 Discussion of the results

The estimation results of the accelerator model of investment are as follows when using data for the entire 1983-1992 period (Table 10.2). First, the results show that the accelerator model is satisfied, since the sales variable appears with a strongly significant positive coefficient. Second, investment one period lagged also appears with a positive sign and is strongly significant. Third, the debt to capital ratio appears not to be statistically significantly related to investment. Finally, and of particular interest in this analysis, the cash flow variable for both Grupo and non-Grupo firms appear with the expected sign in the investment equation and are both strongly significant. Although the coefficient of the non-Grupo firms is higher than that of Grupo firms, the difference between the levels of both coefficients appears not to be significant, however.

Equation (10.2) presents the results of the estimation of the Q model, using Tobin's Q one period lagged as the regressor, for the 1983-1992 period.[9] The outcomes show that the Q model of investment is a valid specification of investment behaviour of the firms in the data set during the 1983-1992 period. Tobin's Q is significant and has the right sign. In general, the overall outcomes of the estimations do not differ substantially when using the Q model instead of the accelerator model of investment. With respect to the cash flow variable, the outcomes show that the levels of the coefficients for Grupo and non-Grupo firms fall, but the difference remains insignificant. This is in line with the earlier findings of equation (10.1). Finally, the results remain unchanged when both the sales variable as well as the measure for expected profitability of firms is included in the investment equation. The estimation outcomes of this specification can be found in equation (10.3) in Table 10.2.

The central focus of the econometric investigation is whether the regulatory changes of the early 1980s have had an impact on market segmentation in financial markets. The outcomes of the estimations taking into account the changes in regulation, are as follows (Table 10.3). In general, the results with respect to the sales variable, Tobin's Q, the debt to capital ratio and investment one period lagged are consistent with those presented in Table 10.2. Of special interest is the behaviour of the four cash flow variables. In this respect, all three investment specifications give similar results. During the 1983-1987 period cash flow appears to be of more importance to the explanation of investment of non-Grupo firms than that of Grupo firms. This is shown by the fact that the cash flow coefficient for non-Grupo firms is significantly higher than that for Grupo firms. The cash flow coefficient for non-Grupo firms ranges between 0.175 and 0.212, whereas for Grupo firms it ranges between 0.106 and 0.132.

TABLE 10.2
Econometric results of the investment equation

Equation	(10.1)	(10.2)	(10.3)
CFG (-1)	0.141 (4.05)	0.114 (3.08)	0.119 (3.23)
CFNG (-1)	0.171 (4.76)	0.127 (3.27)	0.144 (3.79)
TOBQ (-1)		0.057 (1.91)	0.058 (1.98)
DEBT (-1)	-0.035 (-1.24)	-0.049 (-1.70)	-0.043 (-1.52)
D SAL	0.216 (3.74)		0.214 (3.72)
GINV (-1)	0.321 (6.85)	0.278 (5.70)	0.303 (6.35)
R^2	0.27	0.25	0.28
adj. R^2	0.13	0.11	0.14
N	472	472	472

Notes: The independent variable is gross investment. For an explanation of the abbreviations used, see the main text. All equations have been estimated with year dummies. Only dummies for 1988 and 1992 appeared to be significant. The estimations shown in the Table include these two dummies only. They have been omitted from the Table for presentation purposes. Estimations including all year dummies do not differ substantially from those presented in the Table. The t-statistics and R^2 have been corrected for the loss of degrees of freedom due to the inclusion of firm specific dummies. Adjusted t-values (between parentheses) and R^2 are presented in the Table. Estimations have been tested on the condition of normally distributed residuals, using the Jarque-Bera test statistic (JB). This test is chi-squared distributed with two degrees of freedom and should always be lower than 5.99 to be significant at the five per cent level. For all regressions presented in this Table, the test results show that the hypothesis of normally distributed residuals can be accepted at the five per cent level of significance. The White test is applied to test for problems of heteroscedasticity of residuals. In almost all cases the hypothesis of no problems of heteroscedasticity could be excepted at the one per cent level of significance. This indicates that there may still be some minor problems with respect to heteroscedasticity.

Abbreviations used:

CFG(-1)	=	cash flow of Grupo firms one period lagged
CFNG(-1)	=	cash flow of non-Grupo firms one period lagged
TOBQ(-1)	=	Tobin's Q one period lagged
DEBT(-1)	=	debt to capital ratio one period lagged
ΔSAL	=	change in total sales
GINV(-1)	=	investment one period lagged
N	=	number of observations

During the 1988-1992 period, however, the picture changes significantly. The coefficients of cash flow for both Grupo and non-Grupo firms seem to converge to levels around 0.12. In all three equations, the differences between the cash flow coefficients for both groups of firms are no longer significant.

The results presented in Table 10.3 provide support to the following hypothesis. Initially, existing information problems adversely affected the access of non-Grupo firms to outside finance, whereas Grupo firms experienced relatively easier access to such funds. Due to the changes in regulation, however, these information advantages and the resulting relatively easy access to loans of Grupo firms disappeared. The econometric outcomes suggest that during the second half of the 1983-1992 period there is no difference between Grupo and non-Grupo firms with respect to constraints on funds for investment. These outcomes may be interpreted as evidence for the fact that existing market segementation in financial markets was reduced due to the regulatory reforms; these reforms did not become effective until after some years, however.

TABLE 10.3

Econometric results of the investment equation: Different time periods

Equation	(10.1)	(10.2)	(10.3)
Grupos			
CFG (-1) 1983-87	0.132 (2.90)	0.106 (2.21)	0.109 (2.33)
CFG (-1) 1988-92	0.154 (2.82)	0.126 (2.27)	0.133 (2.45)
Non-Grupos			
CFNG (-1) 1983-87	0.212 (3.47)	0.175 (2.71)	0.186 (3.00)
CFNG (-1) 1988-92	0.151 (3.52)	0.104 (2.33)	0.123 (2.69)
TOBQ (-1)		0.057 (1.98)	0.059 (2.07)
DEBT (-1)	-0.034 (-1.19)	-0.048 (-1.66)	-0.042 (-1.49)
D SAL	0.215 (3.72)		0.213 (3.70)
GINV (-1)	0.319 (6.80)	0.276 (5.65)	0.301 (6.57)
R^2	0.27	0.25	0.26
adj. R^2	0.13	0.10	0.12
N	472	472	472

Notes: see Table 10.2.

10.5 Summary and conclusions

This paper has investigated the impact of regulatory changes on the allocation of financial resources in capital markets in Chile during the 1980s and early 1990s. In particular, the empirical analysis has focused on the effects of new regulations that aimed at weakening the tight relations with banks within business conglomerates, the so-called Grupos.

The issue of business conglomerates is an interesting one, since these conglomerates appear to be one of the important institutional characteristics in many developing countries. They may influence the allocation of financial resources through capital markets in two different ways. First, they may create a situation of market segmentation, in which firms not belonging to a conglomerate have more difficulties in obtaining access to external finance. Second, they may have a positive effect on the efficiency of allocation, since the close ties between firms and banks may reduce the information asymmetry between borrower and lender.

The hypothesis analysed in this paper is related to the first of these two issues. It has been investigated whether Chilean firms belonging to Grupos have easier access to debt finance from banks compared to firms outside these conglomerates. However, the change in regulations of the early 1980s may have reduced this kind of market segmentation. Since the possibilities of having tight relations with banks have been reduced after the introduction of these regulations in the early 1980s, this may have led to a more equal access to loans for both Grupo and non-Grupo firms.

To investigate this issue, the analysis has followed techniques used in existing empirical literature. In particular, the econometric investigation has focused on whether internal sources of finance are more important in determining investment patterns of firms without relations to Grupos as compared to firms with relations to Grupos. The outcomes of the econometric analysis revealed that when taking into account the regulatory changes, the outcomes show that in the 1983-1987 period there is indeed a significant difference between the levels of the coefficients of the cash flow variable for Grupo and non-Grupo firms: the coefficient for the latter firms is substantially higher. For the 1988-1992 period, however, the difference between the coefficients becomes insignificant.

These outcomes suggest that the relatedness to business conglomerates affected the access to capital markets of different firms. Grupo firms were less restricted in attracting debt finance when they wanted to invest compared to non-Grupo firms. The relatedness to a business conglomerate in which relations with banks were important did reduce information problems. The practice of credit rationing based on the may have been a remainder of the late 1970s, when the Grupos dominated activities in financial markets. The changes in regulation, which were introduced precisely to reduce this dominant role of Grupos in financial markets, appear to have reduced the existing segmentation in capital markets, at least from the second half of the 1980s. In conclusion, it appears the regulatory change has affected the allocation of financial resources in the expected direction.

As was mentioned before, however, the regulatory changes may also have adversely influenced the efficiency of allocation. By reducing the possibilities of banks having tight relations with firms, the positive effect of such relations on mitigating information problems in capital markets may have been diminished. Thus, due to the installment of controls and limitations on financial ties between financial and non-financial firms, informational problems may have increased rather than decreased and this may have adversely affected allocational efficiency. As was suggested in section 10.2, the real problem in Chile in the 1970s and early 1980s may not have been the extent of the financial linkages as such, but the existence of the implicit deposit insurance. The monetary authorities tried to tackle this problem by introducing an explicit deposit insurance regime in 1986, and by explicitly stating the rules followed when banks would fail and become insolvent, in order to increase the credibility of the deposit insurance regime. Yet, the entire package of regulatory changes of the 1980s may have been too strict on Grupo. More research into this area is needed to establish the contribution of the regulatory changes in Chile to efficient resource allocation.

Notes

The authors would like to thank Victor Murinde, Clas Wihlborg and participants of the Monetary and Financial Affairs working group of the EADI at the conference in Vienna, September 1996, for helpful comments on an earlier version of this paper.

1.   These conglomerates also exist in Asia and Africa. See, among others, Amsden (1989) and Jones and Sakong (1980) on Korea; and Johnson (1982 and 1985) on Japan. See also Leff (1978) for an early theoretical account specifying the rationale for business conglomerates and for additional references of case studies on conglomerates in developing countries (footnote 6, pp.662-663).

2. The details of the events related to these issues are beyond the scope of this paper. See De la Cuadra and Valdés (1992a) and Hermes (1995) for more indepth analyses of the facts that led to the financial instability of the early 1980s.
3. See De la Cuadra and Valdès (1992b) and Ramírez and Rosende (1992) for a more extensive discussion of the contents of the new banking law.
4. In some of the recent empirical work quoted the Generalised Methods of Moments (GMM) has been applied to analyse balance sheet data from a large number of firms. Although this method may be preferred since it uses the data more efficiently as compared to the least squares technique, GMM has not been applied here due to the fact that it is only useful when large data bases (i.e. data for more than 150-200 firms) are available.
5. Note that this introduces a minor bias in the data, since this leaves out observations with zero or negative values.
6. Only a few observations have been deleted from the data based on this procedure.
7. Several studies have followed this procedure. See, among others, Fazzari, Hubbard and Petersen (1988); and Devereux and Schiantarelli (1990).
8. The results with respect to the cash flow variable presented in the Table below remained unchanged when the debt to capital ratio of the current period, instead of the lagged ratio, was used.
9. Using Tobin's Q in the current period did not change the findings presented in the Table.

References

Amsden, A.H., 1989, Asia's Next Giant: South Korea and Late Industrialization (Oxford University Press, New York).

Chirinko, R.S., and H. Schaller, 1995, Why does liquidity matter in investment equations?, Journal of Money, Credit, and Banking 27, pp.527-548.

Dahse, F., 1979, Mapa de la extrema riqueza (Santiago Editorial Aconcangua).

Dahse, F., 1983, El poder de los grandes Grupos económicos nacionales, Contribuciones 18 (FLASCO, Santiago).

De la Cuadra, S., and S. Valdés, 1992a, Myths, and facts about financial liberalization in Chile: 1974-1983, in: P.L. Brock, ed., If Texas were Chile: A Primer on Banking Reform (ICS Press, San Francisco), pp.11-101.

De la Cuadra, S., and S. Valdés, 1992b, Banking structure in Chile, in: G.G. Kaufman, ed., Banking Structures in Major Countries (Kluwer Academic Publishers, Boston), pp.59-112.

Devereux, M., and F. Schiantarelli, 1990, Investment, financial factors and cash flow: Evidence from UK panel data, in: R.G. Hubbard, ed., Asymmetric Information, Corporate Finance, and Investment (University of Chicago Press, Chicago), pp. 279-306.

Edwards, S., and A. Cox Edwards, 1991, Monetarism and Liberalization: The Chilean Experiment (University of Chicago Press, Chicago).

Fazzari, S.M., R.G. Hubbard, and B.C. Petersen, 1988, Financing constraints and corporate investment, Brookings Papers on Economic Activity 1, pp. 141-206.

Harris, J.R., F. Schiantarelli, and M.G. Siregar, 1994, The effects of financial liberalization on the capital structure and investment decisions of Indonesian manufacturing establishments, World Bank Economic Review 8, pp. 17-47.

Hermes, N., 1995, Financial markets and the role of the government in Chile (Labyrint Publication, Capelle a/d IJssel).

Hermes, N., and R. Lensink, 1998, Banking reform and the financing of firm investment: An empirical analysis of the Chilean experience, 1983-1992, Journal of Development Studies (forthcoming).

Hoshi, T., A. Kashyap, and D. Scharfstein, 1991, Corporate structure, liquidity, and investment: Evidence from Japanese industrial groups, Quarterly journal of economics 106, pp. 33-60.

Hsiao, C., 1986, Analysis of panel data (Cambridge University Press, Cambridge).

Johnson, C., 1982, MITI and the Japanese Miracle: The Growth of Industrial Policy, 1925-1975 (Stanford University Press, Stanford).

Johnson, C., 1985, Political institutions and economic performance: The government-business relationship in Japan, South Korea and Taiwan, in: R.A. Scalapino, S. Sato, and J. Wanandi, eds., Asian Economic Development - Present and future, (University of California, Berkeley), pp. 63-89.

Jones, L.P., and I. Sakong, 1980, Government, Business, and Entrepreneurship in Economic Development: The Korean case (Harvard University Press, Cambridge Mass).

Larraín, M., 1989, How the 1981-83 Chilean banking crisis was handled, Policy research working papers 300 (World Bank, Washington D.C.).

Leff, N.H., 1978, Industrial organization and entrepreneurship in the developing countries: The economic groups, Economic Development and Cultural Change 26, pp. 661-675.

Merton, R.C., 1977, An analytical derivation of deposit insurance and loan guarantees: An application of modern option pricing theory, Journal of Banking and Binance 1, pp. 3-11.

Modigliani, F., and M.H. Miller, 1958, The cost of capital, corporation finance and the theory of investment, American Economic Review 48, pp. 261-297.

Paredes, R., and J.M. Sánchez, 1994, Grupos económicos y desarollo: El caso de Chile, unpublished paper (Universidad de Chile, Santiago).

Ramírez, G., and F. Rosende, 1992, Responding to collapse: Chilean banking legislation after 1983, in: P.L. Brock, ed., If Texas were Chile: A Primer on Banking Reform (ICS Press, San Francisco), pp.193-216.

Siregar, M.G., 1995, Indonesia's financial liberalization: An empirical analysis of 1981-1988 panel data (Institute of Southeast Asian Studies, Singapore).

Stiglitz, J.E., Markets, market failure and development, American Economic Review 79, pp. 197-203.

Stiglitz, J.E., and A. Weiss, 1981, Credit rationing in markets with imperfect information, American Economic Review 71, pp. 393-410.

Van Ees, H., and H. Garretsen, 1994, Liquidity and business investment: Evidence from Dutch panel data, Journal of Macroeconomics 16, pp. 613-627.

Velasco, A., 1991, Liberalization, crisis, intervention: The Chilean financial system, 1975-85, in: V. Sundararajan and T.J.T. Baliño, eds., Banking Crises: Cases and Issues (International Monetary Fund, Washington, D.C.), pp. 113-174.

Villanueva, D., and A. Mirakhor, 1990, Strategies for financial reforms: Interest rate policies, stabilization, and bank supervision in developing countries, IMF Staff Papers 37, pp. 509-536.

Whited, T.M., 1992, Debt, liquidity constraints and corporate investment, Journal of Finance 47, pp. 1425-1460.

Financial Sector Reform and
Privatization in Transition Economies
J. Doukas, V. Murinde and C. Wihlborg (Editors)
© 1998 Elsevier Science Publishers B.V. All rights reserved

241 $-$ 79

$P2\mathrm{l}$ $P24$

$P34$ $E60$

Chapter 11

FLOW-OF-FUNDS AND THE MACROECONOMIC POLICY FRAMEWORK FOR FINANCIAL RESTRUCTURING IN TRANSITION ECONOMIES*

Christopher J. Green
Department of Economics, Loughborough University, Leicestershire, LE11 3TU, UK

Victor Murinde
Department of Accounting and Finance, The Birmingham Business School, The University of Birmingham, Edgbaston, Birmingham, B15 2TT, UK

11.1   Introduction

Most transition economies in Eastern Europe were characterised by the pervasiveness of central planning and a large but inefficient industrial base. These conditions adversely influenced the growth of real output and generated substantial price distortions. To foster transition to a market economy, the prescriptions that have so far been dispensed in most of these economies generally comprise orthodox neo-classical as well as heterodox new - structuralist policies (see Murinde, 1993, on these schools of thought). Four areas have dominated the recent policy prescriptions, namely, price de-control (World Bank, 1993; Patterson, 1996); privatisation of state enterprises (Frydman, Pistor and Rapaczynski, 1996; Rondinelli and Yurkiewicz, 1996); legal and institutional reforms (Sachs, 1996); and financial reforms (Griffith-Jones and Drabek, 1995), especially with regard to the banking sector (Borish, Long, and Noel, 1996). Despite these recent policy reforms, transition economies are still characterised by slow growth of formal market arrangements, especially with respect to the financial sector.

If it is to be successful, financial sector reform in the transition economies must be underpinned by strategic policy choices at the macroeconomic level, in addition to corporate sector restructuring at the microeconomic level. In general, the transition economies have found themselves faced with three sources of inspiration for financial sector reform and macroeconomic policy design, namely, the recent experience of developing economies, the phenomenal performance of the newly industrialising countries (NICs), and the historical experience of the European economies (particularly in the 19th century). Existing macroeconomic and financial modelling work on the above wide-ranging experiences can be categorised into at least four genres. In the first genre, a theory of a small open economy underpins an economic and financial structure similar to that in developed, market economies. The economic structure is reflected in the distinguishing features of the financial system and the real sector of the models specified; for example, Turnovsky (1990) assumes perfect capital mobility, and Dornbusch and Fisher (1994) assume fixed real incomes but a more complete supply side. The second genre uses a descriptive approach rather than a formal model: notable examples are the country-specific studies in Roe et al. (1993). A third genre focuses on a single economic problem, say inflation, or isolates a distinct policy instrument for study, or just models the financial sector: for example, the studies reported in Fry (1995). The piecemeal approach employed in this genre makes it possible to undertake a detailed analysis of strategic sectors of an economy; however, this is achieved at the cost of assuming away some economy-wide issues. Finally, to a limited extent some studies have attempted to build country-specific econometric models for non-industrial countries; recent examples include Taylor (1990), FitzGerald (1993) and a collection of studies in Khan et al. (1991). While economy-wide models are potentially useful in studying policy transmission mechanisms, the data problems that plague transition economies do not make possible meaningful application of large models to these economies.

This paper aims to contribute to the ongoing effort to identify feasible strategies for financial sector reform and macroeconomic policy design in transition economies. The paper recognises the potential crucial role of financial sector reforms in influencing macroeconomic outcomes and in facilitating the general transition to a market economy. Conventional macroeconomic theory is applied to develop a macroeconomic model that captures the financial sector and other special features of transition economies, in line with the new-structuralist critique that the distinctive features of these economies must be incorporated into the analysis in order to render the model relevant to the problems of economic transition. The model is then deployed to isolate the potency of some individual instruments which typically form the policy packages applied during financial sector reforms in transition economies. Given the importance of the correct sequencing of these reforms (Rybczynski, 1991), knowledge of the potency of policy instruments is desirable for designing and implementing strategic policy shifts.

A number of novel ideas may be noted; at least four specific areas of departure from existing work should be mentioned. First, the model is explicit about the flow-of-funds among various sectors of a representative transition economy and thus has a complete stock-flow accounting structure; the structure is used to generate identities and functions that serve as the building blocks of the model. Thus, the intrinsic structure of transition economies is theoretically underpinned in line with the new-structuralist approach.[1] Second, in modelling the financial and goods markets, we take into consideration market dualism in transition economies as characterised by the co-existence of official and informal (curb) markets in loans (credit), foreign currency and goods.[2] For example, the model is innovative by introducing an exogenous official interest rate and an endogenous curb interest rate. Third, we introduce a supply-side that spells out the labour market conditions and the special role of imported inputs and curb-market working finance in the production function of transition economies; we highlight the existence of a part of the capital stock which is unproductive, and a labour force which has the wrong skills. Fourth, in modelling the money market, we endogenise money rather than the interest rate: this is because our model contains both the official and the curb-money market interest rate, and it is the latter which is a free-market rate. Policy-induced changes in the official interest rate form part of a typical financial sector reform package (see Caprio, Folkerts-Landau, and Lane, 1994). Finally, we assume a flexible exchange rate regime; however, our model is flexible enough to be solved for the fixed exchange rate regime. Our experience is that some countries in Eastern Europe have adopted a floating rate regime, although others have chosen a quasi-fixed rate pegged either to a single strong currency (especially the Deutsche Mark), or to a small basket of hard currencies.

The remainder of this paper is divided into five sections. In Section 11.2, we construct a stock-flow accounting structure of a representative transition economy, modelling the expenditure, monetary and external sectors before introducing a supply-side. An algebraic solution of the model is derived in Section 11.3 yielding a system of reduced-form equations; the solution hypothesises the short-run impact of given policy instruments on major macroeconomic targets namely real growth, inflation and balance of payments (BOP) equilibrium, under fixed exchange rates. In Section 11.4 we perform comparative statics analysis to gain insight into the channels through which financial sector reforms and related policy effects permeate the macroeconomy. The ultimate section, 11.5, sums up the results relating to single-equation and system-wide impacts of policy instruments on macroeconomic targets; this highlights how the model and its extensions could be applied to empirically study financial sector policy reforms in transition economies.

11.2   Flow-of-funds and model specification

In order to represent the intrinsic structure of transition economies, we develop a macroeconomic model from a simple accounting framework for a representative transition economy. The framework is shown in Table 11.1; rows represent income-expenditure flows (part 1) or stocks of assets and liabilities (part 3), and columns motivate the choice of broad sectors of the economy. Thus, a single row distributes the stock or flow of a variable over the supplying (+) and demanding (-) sectors, while a single column represents a sector's sources and uses of funds (flows) or its balance-sheet (stocks).

11.2.1 Expenditures

The expenditure components of the income-expenditure identity for a transition economy are modelled as follows. Real consumption expenditure *(C)* is postulated to depend on real income *(Y)* net of real tax revenue *(T)*; real wealth *(V)*; and the relative price of domestic and foreign goods *(Q*E/Q)*. The ratio *(Q*E/Q)* captures the foreign producer price *(Q*)* converted into domestic currency by multiplication by the spot exchange rate *(E)*, and the domestic component of the price level *(Q)*; where *E* is a weighted average of the official exchange rate and the parallel market exchange rate.   Hence, consumption behaviour is given by:

$$C = c(Y,T,V,Q*E/Q); \quad c_1 > 0; c_2 < 0; c_3 > 0; c_4 > 0 \qquad (11.1)$$

The nature of shortages in the goods market is such that Q is actually a weighted average of the domestic (producer) price level for goods produced in the official sector and the corresponding price level for goods produced in the parallel (informal) sector. The inclusion of $Q*E$ and Q in equation (11.1) reflects the fact that consumption includes both home and imported goods. Moreover, these two variables are used to tie down the basics of the dual economy; the parallel market in foreign exchange operates via $Q*E$ while the parallel market in goods operates via Q.

TABLE 11.1

A simplified inter-sectoral accounting framework of a macro-model for a transition economy

	Private & banks (PB)	Government (G)	Foreign (O)	Totals
1. Income-expenditure				
1.1 Income: Total	Y	-	$-X^o$	$Y-X^o$
Home	(Y_H)	-	-	
Foreign	(X)	-	$(-X^o)$	
1.2 Taxes	$-T$	T		
1.3 Consumption: Total	$-C$	$-C^G$	Z^o_c	$-C-C^G+Z_G$
Home	$(-C^{PB}_H)$	$(-C^G_H)$		
Foreign	$(-Z^{PB}_c)$	$(-Z^G_c)$	(Z^o_c)	
1.4 Investment: Total	$-I$	$-I^G$	Z^o_I	$-I-I^G+Z_I$
Home	$(-I^{PB}_H)$	$(-I^G_H)$		
Foreign	$(-Z^{PB}_I)$	$(-Z^G_I)$	(Z^o_I)	
2. Net acquisitions	S^{PB}	S^G	S^o	0
3. Assets & liabilities: Balance sheet accounts				
3.1 Capital	K^{PB}	K^G	-	K
3.2 Loans	L^{PB}/P	$-L^{PB}/P$	-	0
3.3 Domestic money	M^{PB}/P	$-M^{PB}/P$	-	0
3.4 Foreign money	-	F^{PB}/P	$-F^o/P$	0
Total: Real net worth	V^{PB}	V^G	$-V^o$	K

Memo: Total government spending $= G = C^G + I^{PB}$
       Total imports $= Z = Z^{PB} + I^{PB}$
       Total domestic net worth $= V = V^{PB} + V^{PB}$
       Retail prices $= P$

Real tax revenues depend on the level of real income and real imports, as well as the tax parameters for income and imports, respectively:

$$T = T(Y,Z, TY, TZ); \qquad t_1 > 0; \; t_2 > 0; \; t_3 > 0; \; t_4 > 0 \qquad (11.2)$$

where Z = real imports; TY = the marginal rate of income tax in the private sector; TZ = the marginal tax rate on imports. These taxes are relevant to almost all transition economies as part of the transition process to a market economy. As Ruggerone (1996) observes, tax issues seem to have been side-stepped in some recent theoretical work notwithstanding the special role of the tax system in the early stages of the transition process.

Real wealth of the private sector (V) consists of the productive component of private capital stock (K), money (M/P) and loans (L/P) in real terms (where M and L are deflated by the retail price index, P):

$$V = K + (M/P) + (L/P) \qquad (11.3)$$

The retail price index is a weighted average of domestic and foreign producer prices:

$$P = \alpha Q + (1-\alpha) Q^*E \qquad (11.4)$$

The productive component of the capital stock is given by:

$$K = (1-\zeta) KK \qquad (11.5)$$

where KK = the total capital stock; and ζ = the unproductive bias in KK, and satisfies the restriction $0 < \zeta < 1$. It is assumed that privatisation and financial reforms in the transition economies inevitably involve introduction of new technologies to replace obsolete components of the existing capital stock. As financial restructuring and transition to a market economy become more sustainable, the productive component of the capital stock increases and ζ falls to zero; ultimately, all total stock becomes usable for productive purposes and $K = KK$. In general, the real productive capital stock changes over time according to:

$$K_t = I_t + (1-\beta) K_{t-1} \qquad (11.6)$$

where I = real gross investment expenditure; β = the depreciation rate; and t = a time subscript.

It is reasonable to postulate that real gross investment expenditure has both domestic and foreign components and is a function of: real income and the official real interest rate, given by the difference between the regulated official nominal rate *(R)* and expected inflation $(\hat{Q}^e)$. Borish, Long and Noel (1996) point out that during bank and enterprise restructuring in the transition economies, many enterprises turn to state-owned banks for credit to allow them to defer restructuring. Indeed, as the experience in Romania indicates, the financing of small- and medium-sized enterprises (SME) creates huge demands on a constrained state banking sector, and ultimately SMEs may have to resort to the informal financial sector (Anton, Danciu and Mitu, 1996). In this context, we recognise that in most transition economies, business firms tend to rely on informal market loans to finance their short-term working capital, so we include the real curb-market interest rate $(NR - \hat{Q}^e)$ as an argument.[3] In addition, since investment goods include imports, we postulate that real gross investment expenditure is influenced by the relative prices of domestic and imported goods $(Q*E/Q)$. We include overseas aid (K_0) as an additional variable in the investment function to hypothesise a direct positive relationship between overseas aid inflows and direct investment which overseas companies bring during the transition period.[4]

$$I = I\ (Y, NR - \hat{Q}^e, R - \hat{Q}^e, Q* E\ /\ Q, K_0),$$
$$i_1 > 0;\ i_2 < 0;\ i_3 > 0;\ i_4 > 0;\ i_5 > 0 \tag{11.7}$$

Real government expenditure is exogenous, hence:

$$G = G^0 \tag{11.8}$$

On the basis of the transactions in the foreign sector within a flow-of-funds framework presented in Table 11.1, we postulate that the level of real exports *(X)* is a function of relative prices for domestic and imported goods. The official and informal markets in goods and foreign currency, characterised in the transition economies, are reflected in these prices:

$$X = x(Q*E/Q);\qquad x_1 > 0 \tag{11.9}$$

The behaviour of imports is assumed to be consistent with the consumption and investment functions, each of which include an import component. In addition a significant part of the government revenues in many transition economies is generated from import taxes. So, we include a tax on imports as an argument, hence:

$$Z = Z\,(Y,\ TZ,\ Q^*E/Q,\ V,\ (R\text{-}\hat{Q}^e),\ (NR\text{-}\hat{Q}^e));$$
$$z_1,\ z_2,\ >0;\ z_3\ <0;\ z_4,\ >\ 0;\ z_5,\ z_6 <0 \tag{11.10}$$

We linearize equations (11.2), (11.3), (11.7), (11.9) and (11.10) and solve equations (11.2), (11.7), (11.8), (11.9) and (11.10) in an income expenditure identity of the form $Y = C + I + G + X - Z$, including the definitions for V, T, P, and K; this yields after re-arranging:

$$Y = a_1\,Q^*E - a_2\,Q + a_3\,K_{-1} + a_4\,L - a_5\,R + a_6\,G$$

$$-\ a_7\,NR\ +\ a_8\,\hat{Q}^e + a_9\,K_0 - a_{10}\,TY - a_{11}\,TZ \tag{11.11}$$

with $a_1 = [i_4\,(1 + c_3 - z_5) + z_3 + x_1 + c_4 + (z_5 - c_3)(1\text{-}\alpha)]\theta^{-1} > 0;$

$\qquad\quad a_2 = [i_5\ (z_5 - c_3 - 1) + \alpha\,(z_5 - c_3) - z_4 - c_4]\ \theta^{-1} < 0;$

$\qquad\quad a_3 = [c_3\,(1 - \beta)\text{-}z_5\,(1\text{-}\alpha)]\theta^{-1}\ > 0;$

$\qquad\quad a_4 = [c_3 - z_5]\ \theta^{-1} > 0;$

$\qquad\quad a_5 = [c_4 + i_3(z_5\text{-}1\text{-}c_3)]\ \theta^{-1}\ < 0;$

$\qquad\quad a_6 = (1)\ \theta^{-1} > 0;$

$\qquad\quad a_7 = [i_2\,(z_5 - 1 - c_3 + z_6)]\theta^{-1} < 0;$

$\qquad\quad a_8 = [i_2\,(1+c_3\text{-}z_5) + i_3\ (1+c_3\text{-}z_5) - z_6]\ \theta^{-1} > 0;$

$\qquad\quad a_9 = (i_5)\ \theta^{-1}\ > 0;$

$\qquad\quad a_{10} = \text{-}(c_2\ t_3)\ \theta^{-1}\ < 0;$

$\qquad\quad a_{11} = \text{-}(c_2\ t_4\ z_5)\ \theta^{-1} < 0;$

and $\theta = (1\text{-}c_1 + z_1)(1\text{-}t_1) + i_1\ (z_5 - 1\text{-}c_3)\ > 0\,.$

The signs associated with $Q^*E(+)$ and $Q(\text{-})$ are unambiguous, as expected, in the sense that devaluation of the exchange rate tends to have a positive effect, while a rise in domestic producer prices tends to have a negative effect, on expenditures. In general, all the coefficients are unambiguously signed in that they are either positive or negative definite. In conformity with conventional economic theory, equation (11.11) represents a downward-sloping IS curve in the $(Y,\ NR)$ space; and shows income and curb-market interest rate combinations which keep the goods market in equilibrium, given prices.

11.2.2 The money market

In putting forward the four basic tasks of the transition from socialism in Eastern Europe and the former Soviet Union, Sachs (1996) has argued that the second task of economic reform is financial stabilisation; it involves the end of the pre-reform monetary overhang, high repressed and open inflation, and large fiscal deficits. In this context, we try to capture a joint monetary and fiscal process. Specifically, we characterise the money supply process in transition economies by specifying the government budget constraint facing these economies as follows:

$$G\text{-}T = \Delta M/P + \Delta L/P - \Delta F/P \tag{11.12}$$

The identity in (11.12) implies that fiscal and monetary policy instruments cannot be used independently. During the process of transition, the government may be forced into undertaking huge expenditures; for example during the recent process of re-unification of Germany, former Western Germany had to foot the expenses of facilitating economic reform. At the same time the sources of tax revenues for the government remain severely limited until the transition is completed. Thus the transition process is characterised by budget deficits, as government spending exceeds tax revenue. Stocks of assets cannot be constant as the deficit needs to be financed by printing money $(\Delta M/P)$, by borrowing from commercial banks $(\Delta L/P)$ or by drawing upon foreign reserves $(\Delta F/P)$.[5] Linearizing the terms in equation (11.12), and writing out the first differences (e.g. ΔM by $M_t - M_{t-1}$), gives:

$$G\text{-}T = M + L - F - \lambda_1 \, P - (M_{-1} + L_{-1} - F_{-1}) \tag{11.13}$$

Using (11.3) and (11.5) to eliminate T and P in equation (11.13) yields, after some re-arrangement, a money supply function:

$$M = b_1 \, G - b_2 \, Y - b_3 \, Q^*E + b_4 \, Q - b_5 \, L - b_6 \, F - b_7 \, TY - b_8 \, TZ + b_9 \, (M_{-1} + L_{-1} - F_{-1}) \tag{11.14}$$

The demand for real money balances (M^d/P) is a function of real income (Y), real wealth (V), and the real rates of return to money and loans. To capture the relative influence of these variables, we incorporate the relevant returns to money and loans by thinking of various economic agents as trading off the following asset substitutes: (i) real (rather than nominal) assets are substitutes for money, amidst high inflation; thus, expected inflation $(\hat{Q}^e)$ is a proxy for the opportunity cost of holding money; (ii) loans for working capital in the informal credit markets earn NR; in real terms, $(NR\text{-}(\hat{Q}^e))$; (iii) bonds or loans to government that earn R, which is the regulated official rate; in real terms, $(R - \hat{Q}^e)$. Thus, the demand for real balances is specified as follows:

$$M^d / P = l(Y, (R - \hat{Q}^e), (NR - \hat{Q}^e), V, Q)$$
$$l_1 > 0; l_2 < l_3 < 0; l_4 > 0; l_5 < 0 \qquad (11.15)$$

where restrictions are imposed on the coefficients l_2 and l_3 such that $l_2 < l_3 < 0$. These restrictions on the two interest rate elasticities, to be discussed below, reflect the role of official and informal finance. Substituting for V and P in (11.15), and linearizing, yields:

$$NR = d_1 Y - d_2 R + d_3 Q * E + d_4 Q - d_5 M + d_6 L + d_7 \hat{Q}^e + d_8 K$$
$$(11.16)$$

(11.16) thus represents the demand side of the money market, and amounts to a demand for money specification presented in (M, NR) space.

We assume financial dualism in transition economies as characterised by the co-existence of official and informal (curb) markets in loans (credit). While the official sector comprises the new financial institutions and markets that are being established as part of financial reforms, the informal counterpart comprises the lending and borrowing transactions of economic agents outside the official sector. Following Montiel, Agenor and Haque (1993: 10-11), we classify transactions in the informal credit markets into the following four categories:

1   Occasional lending category which involves lending by individuals and institutions with a surplus of funds; for example, friends and relatives serve as an important source of consumer credit and small business loans. The credit is extended at various terms; the most concessional terms being that the loan is available at no interest and with no collateral.

2   Regular moneylending activities involve lending by specialist individuals or institutions who use their own funds or borrow funds from banks in the official sector for onlending to borrowers in the informal sector. The moneylenders provide very expensive credit in terms of very high

(extortionary) interest rates; they also demand very expensive collateral relative to the value of the loan. The moneylenders have asymmetric information advantage over any competitor financier; hence they occupy a monopolistic position in the credit market. The typical borrowers are often those who are unable to obtain credit from the new financial institutions and markets.

3   A category of tied credit involves lending transactions by economic agents who tie credit to transactions in markets where primary activities lie; for example, loans by landlords to their tenants, credit by a supplier to a purchaser, advance payment by an employer to an employee. The informal collateral usually consists of the ongoing business relationship between the two parties; hence, the need for formal collateral is reduced and transactions costs and risks are minimised.

4   Group finance may involve various forms of cooperative efforts to generate loanable funds for individual credit needs.

The nature of the dual financial markets has important implications for the financial reforms addressed in our model, especially with respect to interest rate policy. Unlike its formal (official) counterpart, the informal financial sector is not subject to interest rate ceilings and reserve requirements. In terms of a single-period, the curb-market interest rate is assumed to have higher elasticity than the official interest rate; for example, the effect of a rise in the official real interest rate on the demand for real money balances is smaller than the effect of a rise in the curb-market rate. At the beginning of financial reforms, the experience of transition economies suggests some kind of financial repression in which the official interest rate is pegged, and credit rationing takes place; hence unsatisfied demand for credit in the official sector spills over to the informal sector. The curb-market interest rate is determined by the forces of demand and supply in the informal financial market, thus the rate rises with an increase in unsatisfied official-sector demand for credit. As the process of financial reform picks up, the official and curb-market interest rates are inversely related; as the official rate rises, more funds are deposited in official financial institutions for intermediation purposes, and as more demand for credit is met in the official sector, the curb-market rate falls due to diminishing spillage of unsatisfied demand to the informal sector. Successful financial restructuring is consistent with the expansion of the official financial sector to take over the activities hitherto carried out in the informal financial institutions and markets; the official and curb-market interest rates ultimately converge, and the former becomes a free market rate. It is assumed in our theoretical framework that the transition economies are working towards this goal.

We equate demand (11.16) and supply (11.14) to bring together the components of the money market; this gives an *LM*-type equation:

$$NR = w_1 \ Y + w_2 \ Q^*E + w_3 \ Q + w_4 \ \hat{Q}^e + w_5 \ L + w_6 \ K - w_7 \ R - w_8 \ G$$

$$+ \ w_9 \ TY + w_{10} \ TZ + w_{11} \ F - w_{12} \ (M_{-1} + L_{-1} - F_{-1}) \qquad (11.17)$$

where $w_1 = (d_1 + d_5b_2) > 0;$ $w_2 = (d_3 + d_5b_4) > 0;$ $w_3 = (d_4 - d_5b_5) > 0;$

$\qquad w_4 = d_7 > 0;$ $\qquad w_5 = d_6 + d_5b_6 > 0;$ $w_6 = d_8 > 0;$

$\qquad w_- = -d_2 < 0;$ $\qquad w_8 = -d_5b_1 < 0;$ $\qquad w_9 = d_5b_7 > 0;$

$\qquad w_{10} = d_5b_7 < 0;$ $\qquad w_{11} = d_5b_8 < 0;$ $\qquad w_{12} = -d_5b_9 < 0.$

In equation (11.17) almost all the coefficients are unambiguously signed: they are either positive or negative definite. However, the coefficient w_3 is signed using a restriction that $d_4 > d_5b_5$. The argument in w_3 is that through d_4 domestic prices affect the whole stock of money, whereas through d_5b_5 domestic prices only affect the size of the flow of new money through the government budget, hence $d_4 > d_5b_5$; and $w_3 > 0$. Overall, given Q, the *LM* curve determines combinations of *(Y, NR)* which keep the money market in equilibrium. Note that this too is a relationship between real income and the free (informal) market interest rate, official interest rates being taken as exogenuously given during the initial stages of the transition process.

11.2.3 The supply side

In exploring the dynamics of unemployment and inflationary finance at the early stages of economic transition, Ruggerone (1996) observes that what seems to have been neglected so far in recent macroeconomic modelling for transition economies is the interaction of inflationary finance and real variables during policy reforms. We attempt to address this issue by developing a specification in which inflation is underpinned by the supply side. Specifically, we build up the aggregate supply function from a production function and a simple but plausible set of labour market relationships. We postulate that for transition economies, production *(Y_p)* in the short-run is a function of labour inputs *(LB)*, the availability of curb-market loans for working capital needs *(WK)*, and imported materials input *(N)*. As earlier explained in equation (11.5), we incorporate the fact that transition economies are characterised by the existence of a part of the capital stock which is unproductive; this renders the capital stock fixed in the short-run. Given these features of transition economies, we specify the following production function:

$$Y_p = U(LB, N, WK), \quad u_1, u_2, u_3 > 0 \tag{11.18}$$

The assumption of fixed capital in the production function in the short run implies that:

$$(u_1 \, LB + u_2 \, N + u_3 \, WK) \, / \, Y < 1 \tag{11.19}$$

We also incorporate in our specification a central feature of the labour market in transition economies. We note that a fundamental feature of the centrally planned economies was full employment, with state enterprises hoarding unproductive labour (Svejnar, 1996). We argue that the current composition of labour in transition economies is such that part of the labour force, which was previously employed in government-owned corporations, has the wrong skills and have to be retrained to be able to work productively for private sector companies in a market economy. At the wage bargaining time, the supply of employable (productive) labour *(LBs)* is a function of the real wage-package $(W\text{-}\hat{Q}^e)$:

$$LBs = LBs \ (W/\hat{Q}^e, ST) \quad l_{s1}, l_{s2} > 0 \tag{11.20}$$

where ST = a shift parameter representing training in new skills for restructured enterprises during the transition to a market economy; $l_{s2} > 0$ i.e. since current labour has the wrong skills, training in new skills will increase the supply of employable labour. In the short run, our focus is on the variable $(W/\hat{Q}^e)$ and the associated coefficient l_{s1}.

On the demand side, the marginal physical products of labour, informal-market finance, and imported materials at wage bargaining time are derived and equated by producers to their expectations of: the expected real product wage $(We/\hat{Q}^e)$, the expected real price of curb-market finance $(NR^e - \hat{Q}^e)$ and the expected real price of imported materials $(Q^*E^e/\hat{Q}^e)$, respectively. Hence:

$$u_1 \ (Y_p^e/LB^e) = W^e/\hat{Q}^e \tag{11.21}$$

$$u_2 \ (Y_p^e/N^e) = Q^*_e E^e/\hat{Q}^e \tag{11.22}$$

$$u_3 \ (Y_p^e/WK^e) = NR^e - \hat{Q}^e \tag{11.23}$$

We linearize (11.18), (11.21) - (11.23) and solve to obtain a demand for labour (*LB^d*) equation:

$$L^d = A^{*-1} [(1-u_2-u_3) \, W_e/\hat{Q}^e + u_2 (Q^*_e E_e/\hat{Q}^e) + u_3 \, (NR^e - \hat{Q}^e) +$$
$$(u_2 + u_3 - 1) \tag{11.24}$$

where $A^* = u_1 + u_2 + u_3 - 1$. The labour market is assumed to clear through price (wage) adjustments or through quantity (queues) adjustment:

$$LB^d = LB^s \tag{11.25}$$

Thus, to obtain the contract wage package, we equate labour supply to labour demand *(l^d = l^s)* and re-arrange to yield:

$$W_e = [A^* \, (\tau_1 + u_3 - 1) \, \hat{Q}^e + u_2 \, (Q^*_e E_e) + u_3 \, (NR^e - \hat{Q}^e)]$$
$$(A^* \, \tau_1 + u_2 + u_3 - 1) \tag{11.26}$$

where $\tau_1 = l^{s1}$. Finally, to obtain short-run output and pricing, we solve for Y_p, *LB, N, K* using *actual* rather than *expected* prices. This yields a short-run aggregate supply function; for convenience in later manipulations, the function is expressed as a price equation, and include expected domestic as well as expected foreign prices:

$$Q = \phi_1 \, Y + \phi_2 \, Q^* E + \phi_3 \, NR + \phi_4 \, (Q^* E)^e + \phi_5 \, Q^e + \eta \tag{11.27}$$

where $\phi_1 = -A^*(A^* \, \tau_1 + u_3 - 1) > 0;$ $\phi_2 = u_2 \, (A^* \, \tau_1 + u_2 + u_3 - 1) > 0;$
        $\phi_3 = u_3 \, (A^* \, \tau_1 + u_2 + u_3 - 1) > 0;$ $\phi_4 = u_2 \, (A^* \, \tau_1 + u_2 - 1) > 0;$
        $\phi_5 = u_3 \, (A^* \, \tau_1 + u_3 - 1) > 0;$ η = supply-side shock.

11.2.4 The foreign sector

The flow-of-funds characteristics of the foreign sector are set out in Table 11.1 within a general intersectoral accounting framework for transition economies. It is assumed that at this initial stage of the transition process, some exchange controls are still in force and convertibility has not been attained at this stage, though the process of financial liberalisation has been set in motion. Exogenous capital inflows take the form of concessionary finance from donor agencies such as the International Monetary Fund, the World Bank, and the European Commission; the grant element character of these inflows renders them to be classified as aid; as discussed below these inflows may be wide ranging in content during the early stages of the transition considered in this paper.

On the basis of the foregoing, the basic flow of funds identity we adopt here for the foreign sector states that a change in foreign reserves (ΔF) is equal to the difference between export earnings (X) and import payments (Z), plus exogenous aid inflows and any possible net capital inflows in the form of investment from overseas companies (K_o)[6]:

$$\Delta F = X - Z + K_o \tag{11.28}$$

We do not specify the accumulation of foreign reserves to be sensitive to the interest rate; hence we omit the interest rate variable in (11.28). Rather, we argue that during the transition process, an increase in exogenous aid inflows seems to signal an improvement in credibility in economic reform, and foreign companies therefore gain more confidence and increase their investment flows into the reforming economy; thus the K_0 is defined to encompass overseas aid inflows and related inward investment from foreign companies. This specification of the external sector equation is consistent with the argument that at the moment the reform process in most transition economies is still a distant cry from complete trade liberalisation and the attendant responsiveness of capital flows to interest rate changes (Hillman and Ursprung, 1996).

We substitute equations (11.9) and (11.10) for X and Z into equation (11.28) to obtain, after linearizing and re-arrangement, the following reduced form for foreign reserve flows:

$$\Delta F = e_1 \ Q^*E - e_2 \ Y - e_3 \ Q - e_4 \ M - e_5 \ L + e_6 \ R + e- \ NR - e_8 \ K$$
$$- e_9 \ \hat{Q}e + e_{10} \ K_o \tag{11.29}$$

where $e_1 = (x_1 + z_3) + (1 - \alpha) z_5 - i_4 z_5 > 0;$ $e_2 = -z_1(1-t_1) + z_5 i_1 < 0;$
$e_3 = (-x_1 - z_4 + z_5 \alpha - z_5 \ i_5 < 0;$ $e_4 = e_5 = -z_5 < 0;$
$e_6 = z_5 + i_3 z_5 > 0;$ $e_7 = z_6 + i_2 z_5 > 0;$
$e_8 = -x_4 (1-\beta) < 0;$ $e_9 = -(i_2 z_5 + z_5 + i_3 + z_6) < 0;$
$e_{10} = 1.$

Thus the coexistence of the formal and informal markets in goods and foreign currency is incorporated in the equations for imports and exports. The parameter signs are definite.

11.3   The solution of the model

We solve the model to yield the estimating equations in terms of the major target and instrumental variables, carefully pointing out the coefficient signs in the reduced-form. Our motivation is to yield aggregate demand, aggregate supply and BOP equilibrium equations that fully incorporate the economic structure of transition economies.

11.3.1 Aggregate demand

We solve simultaneously equations (11.11) and (11.17) which correspond to conventional IS and LM. This yields, after some re-arrangement the following aggregate demand curve under fixed exchange rates:

$$Y = \pm f_1\, Q^*E - f_2\, Q \pm f_3\, I_{-1} \pm f_4 I_{-2} - f_5\, L \pm f_6\, R + f_7\, G - f_8\, F$$
$$+ f_9\, K_0 - f_{10}\, TY - f_{11}\, TZ + f_{12}\, (M_{-1} + L_{-1} + F_{-1})\qquad (11.30)$$

where, $f_1 = (a_1 - a_7\, w_1) > 0,\ possibly < 0;$ $f_2 = -(a_2 + a_7\, w_3) < 0;$
$\quad\quad f_3 = f_4 = (a_3 - a_7 w_6) > 0,\ possibly < 0;$ $f_5 = (a_4 - a_7 w_5) < 0;$
$\quad\quad f_6 = (a_7 w_7 - a_5) > 0,\ possibly < 0;$ $f_7 = (a_6 + a_7\, w_8) > 0;$
$\quad\quad f_8 = -(a_7\, w_{11}) < 0$ $f_9 = (a_9) > 0;$
$\quad\quad f_{10} = -(a_{10} + a_7 w_9) < 0;$ $f_{11} = -(a_{11} + a_7 w_{10}) < 0;$
$\quad\quad f_{12} = (a_7\, a_{12}) > 0;$

The flexible exchange rates variant of equation (11.30) is derived by splitting the Q^*E variable by approximation and re-writing the reduced form coefficients to yield:

$$Y = \pm j_1 Q^* \pm j_2 E - j_3 Q \pm j_4 I_{-1} \pm j_5 I_{-2} - j_6 L \pm j_7 R$$
$$+ j_8 G - j_9 F + j_{10} K_0 - j_{11}\, TY - j_{12} TZ + j_{13}(M_{-1} + L_{-1} + F_{-1})\qquad (11.31)$$

where $j_1, j_2 = f_1;\ j_i = f_{i-1}$ for $i = 3, \ldots\ldots 13.$

Almost all the coefficients are unambiguously signed such that they are either positive or negative definite; the exceptions are $j_1, j_2, j_4, j_5,$ and j_7. The signs $j_1,$ and j_2 are uncertain because a rise in foreign prices (as in a_1) could rise output, assuming the Marshall-Lerner type of elasticities hold, in which case j_1 and $j_2 > 0$; however, in the transition economies the direct and indirect effects of relative prices might be more predominant in their negative effects on aggregate demand such that j_1 and $j_2 > 0$. Regarding j_4 and j_5, the wealth effects on demand for money are offset by the wealth effects on consumption demand hence turning j_4 and $j_5 > 0$; however the coefficient may be positive or negative depending on whether or not the first-round effects persist. The sign for j_7 depends on whether, for interest rate reforms in transition economies, the orthodox effect outweighs the McKinnon (1973) and Shaw (1973) effect, or otherwise. Since lagged capital stock data may not be available in transition economies, we follow equation (11.6) and express incremental capital stock as $K_{t-1} = I_{t-1} + (1-\delta) K_{t-2}$, thus in order to exhaust the approximation of lagged capital stock, this equation has investment lagged once as well as investment lagged twice. We also impose restrictions such that expected prices are approximated by current prices in this equation.

Equation (11.31) is a conventional aggregate demand schedule in output-producer price *(Y, Q)* space. However, this formulation has the great convenience that the informal market interest rate is solved out of the system. This obviates the need for estimating this rate directly in an empirical implementation of the model. However, solutions of the model necessarily incorporate endogenous changes in the informal market rate.

In (11.31), the sign associated with *Q(-)* is unambiguous in the sense that it is negative definite: in conformity with economic theory, the aggregate demand curve is downward sloping in the *(Y,Q)* space. Regarding the rest of the model variables, only the variables for exchange rate devaluation, lagged investment, and official interest rate policy have signs which are theoretically indeterminate $(\pm)$. The indeterminate parameter signs represent competing hypotheses that need to be resolved empirically, as discussed in Section 11.4.

11.3.2 Aggregate supply

Our modelling procedure assumes that financial restructuring is the driving force of the process of economic transition. Thus, to obtain the supply-side equation that incorporates the effects of the financial sector under fixed exchange rates, we solve equation (11.27) simultaneously with the *LM* equation (11.17) thus removing endogenous *NR*. Using Cramer's rule to solve for *Q* yields, after some re-arrangement:

$$Q = g_1 Y + g_2 Q^*E + g_3 (Q^*E)^e + g_4 \hat{Q}^e + g_5 L + g_6 I_{-1}$$
$$- g_7 R - g_8 G + g_9 F + g_{10} TY + g_{11} TZ - g_{12} (M_{-1} + L_{-1} + F_{-1}) \quad (11.32)$$

where

$g_1 = N^{-1} (\theta_1 + \theta_3 \, w_1) > 0; \quad g_2 = N^{-1}(\theta_2 + \theta_3 \, w_2) > 0; \quad g_3 = N^{-1}(\theta_4) > 0;$

$g_4 = N^{-1}(\theta_3 \, w_4 + \theta_3 \,) > 0; \quad g_5 = N^{-1} (\theta_3 \, w_5) > 0; \quad g_6 = N^{-1} (\theta_3 \, w_6) > 0;$

$g_7 = N^{-1} (-\theta_3 \, w_7) < 0; \quad g_8 = N^{-1}(-\theta_3 \, w_8) < 0; \quad g_9 = N^{-1} (\theta_3 \, w_{11}) > 0;$

$g_{10} = N^{-1} (\theta_3 \, w_9) > 0; \quad g_{11} = N^{-1} (\theta_3 \, w_{10}) > 0; \quad g_{12} = N^{-1} (-\theta_3 \, w_{12}) < 0;$

and $N = (1 - \theta_3 \, w_3) > 0.$

The above equation conforms to the conventional aggregate supply curve which is upward sloping in the (Y, Q) space. The parameter signs are positive or negative definite.

The flexible exchange rates variant of equation (11.32) is derived by splitting the Q^*E variable by approximation and re-writing the reduced form coefficients to yield:

$$
\begin{aligned}
Q = & \, k_1 Y + k_2 Q^* + k_3 E + k_4 Q^*_{-1} + k_5 E_{-1} + k_6 Q_{-1} + k_7 L \\
& + k_8 I_{-1} - k_9 R - k_{10} G + k_{11} F + k_{12} TY + k_{13} TZ - k_{14} (M_{-1} + L_{-1} + F_{-1})
\end{aligned}
\tag{11.33}
$$

where $k_1 = g_1; \quad k_2, k_3 = g_2; \quad k_4, k_5 = g_3;$

$k_i = g_{i-2}$ for $i = 6, \ldots, 14.$

BOP Equilibrium To obtain BOP equilibrium, we solve equation (11.29) for ΔF simultaneously with the money demand and money supply functions. Endogenous money (M) and the curb-market interest rate (NR) are thus eliminated. Solving for ΔF yields, after some re-arrangement, BOP equilibrium, under fixed exchange rates:

$$
\Delta F = -h_1 \, Y \pm h_2 \, Q^*E - h_3 \, Q + h_4 \, L \pm h_5 \, R \pm h_6 \, I_{-1} - h_7 \, G + h_8 \, K_0 - h_9 \, \hat{Q}^e
$$

$$
+ h_{10} \, TY + h_{11} \, TZ - h_{12} \, (M_{-1} + L_{-1} F_{-1})
\tag{11.34}
$$

where $h_1 = S^{-1}[e_7 \, d_1 - e_2 + e_7 \, d_5 \, b_2 + e_4 \, b_2) < 0;$

$h_2 = S^{-1} [(e_1 + e_7 \, d_3 + e_2 \, d_5 b_3 + e_4 \, b_3)] < 0;$ possibly $> 0;$

$h_3 = S^{-1} [(e_7 \, b_4 - e_3 - e_7 \, d_5 \, b_4 - e_4 \, b_4) < 0;$

$h_4 = S^{-1} [(e_7 \, d_6 - e_5 + e_7 \, d_5 + e_4 \, b_5) > 0;$

$h_5 = S^{-1} [(e_6 - e_7 \, d_2)] < 0;$ possibly $> 0;$

$$h_6 = S^{-1}\left[+ (e_7\,d_8 - e_8)\right] \; < \; 0; \;\; possibly >0;$$

$$h_7 = S^{-1}\left[(-e_7\,d_5\,b_1 - e_4\,b_1)\right] \; < \; 0;$$

$$h_8 = S^{-1}\left[(e_{10})\right] \; > \; 0;$$

$$h_9 = S^{-1}\left[(e_7\,d_7 - e_9)\right] < 0;$$

$$h_{10} = S^{-1}\left[(e_7\,d_5\,b_7 + e_4\,b_7)\right] > 0;$$

$$h_{11} = S^{-1}\left[(e_7\,d_5\,b_8 + e_4\,b_8)\right] > 0;$$

$$h_{12} = S^{-1}\left[-(e_7\,d_5\,b_9 + e_4\,b_9)\right] < 0;$$

$$\text{and } S = 1 - b_6\,(e_7\,d_5 + e_4)\; > 0.$$

Under flexible exchange rates, the exchange rate adjusts endogenously so that $\Delta F = 0$. Thus, the exchange rate variable (E), rather than ΔF, becomes the endogenous or target variable. Thus we split the variable Q^*E by approximation and re-arrange terms to yield:

$$E = p_1 Y \pm p_2 Q^* + p_3 Q - p_4 L \pm p_5 R \pm p_6 I_{-1} + p_7 G - p_8 K_0$$
$$+ p_9 Q_{-1} - p_{10} F - p_{11} TY - p_{12} TZ + p_{13}(M_{-1} + L_{-1} + F_{-1}) \tag{11.35}$$

where:

$$p_1 = (-h_1 / -h_2) > 0; \quad p_2 = (-h_2 / -h_2) > 0; \quad p_3(-h_3 / -h_2) > 0;$$
$$p_4 = (h_4 / -h_2) < 0; \quad P_5 = (\pm h_5 / -h_2) < 0; \quad P_6 = (\pm h_6 / -h_2) > 0;$$
$$p_7 = (-h_7 / -h_2) > 0; \quad p_8 = (h_g / -h_2) < 0; \quad p_9 = (-h_9 / -h_2) > 0;$$
$$p_{10} = (h_{10} / -h_2) < 0; \quad p_{11} = (h_{11} / -h_2) < 0; \quad p_{12} = (-h_{12} / -h_2) > 0;$$

This gives a negatively sloped BOP curve (EE) under flexible exchange rates in the *(Y,Q)* space. Apart from variables for foreign prices, official interest rate policy and lagged investment, the rest of the parameter signs are either positive definite or negative definite. The sign on coefficient p_5 (for interest rate reform) may be positive or negative: orthodox effects suggest that investment expenditure is reduced through the demand for money, real incomes contract and foreign reserves improve; the McKinnon-Shaw effects suggest that diversion of funds out of cash into interest-bearing assets tends to depress the curb-market rate, and reserves are depleted. The sign for p_6 (lagged investment) is indeterminate: it depends on whether (or not) the negative wealth effects outweigh the positive investment effects on foreign reserves.

In general, therefore, the reduced-form model consists of a system of three equations under flexible exchange rates. Equation (11.31) represents an aggregate demand schedule (AD) which has as left-hand side variable real income. Equation (11.33) represents an aggregate supply schedule (AS) which has as left-hand side variable domestic prices. Equation (11.35) represents the foreign balance schedule (EE) which has the exchange rate as left-hand side variable.[7]

The novelty of our approach relates to the application of reduced-form modelling techniques in the sense that, starting from first principles, we are able to reduce the complete structure of a transition economy to just three equations that consist of the macroeconomic targets and policy instrument variables that are most pertinent to the policy reform programmes which are being undertaken in transition economies. The equations are straightforward to manipulate theoretically and empirically particularly in so far as data availability is a problem. The model does not impose excessively burdensome data requirements; and certain "difficult" variables, notably the informal market interest rate, are solved out of the system.

A further strength of the model developed here is that it can incorporate institutional assumptions that are pertinent to most transition economies. Consequently the results obtained are generally richer than, and differ in certain important instances from, those obtained in mainstream macroeconomic models. For example, the summary of the model in Table 11.2 contains predictions that may appear unconventional. Many of these can be traced to two simple, but key assumptions. First, we assume that money is endogenous. According to equation (11.13), the residual in the government budget identity is the supply of (high-powered) money. The second assumption is that we allow for the existence of parallel (informal) markets in loans and deposits, foreign currency, and goods; essentially, our specification of the main behavioural equations, and thereby the predicted signs of the model, are influenced by the dual markets. The official interest rate is a policy instrument and therefore appears as an exogenous variable in the model. The market clearing interest rate is assumed to be the curb market rate which in turn is "solved out" of the system in order to derive the aggregate demand curve. Both the curb market and official rates help determine the levels of interest-sensitive expenditures and demand for money. The exogeneity of `both the official interest rate and the quantity of domestic interest-bearing government debt, or "loans" (L), is made possible by the assumption that most banks are still heavily regulated, and credit is rationed to the private sector. Given the official interest rates, the government can sell more of its loans to the private sector by increasing the secondary reserve requirements of commercial banks. Clearly, these two assumptions incorporate important aspects of many transition economies.

The policy instruments in the model consist of budgetary and financial instruments. The budgetary instruments are real government spending, income tax rate and import tax rate; while the financial policy instruments are the official interest rate, loans from commercial banks, foreign reserves and foreign aid. The money supply can be made exogenous in simulations by considering shocks to government spending (say) which are financed by increased loans from commercial banks. The special role of these variables in the model relates to the Orthodox-Structuralist issues in the analysis of policy reforms in transition economies.

However, the model also has some important limitations. First, it is comparative static in nature, and second it is distinctively "short-run"; thus it only allows us to look at one period effects of policy changes. Clearly, we would not expect some of the more paradoxical results to carry over to the long run. However, they do illustrate the practical difficulties of managing an economy in the short-run with endogenous money and informal markets in goods, foreign currency and credit. Since the model is eclectic in structure, it would be reasonable to expect some of our counter-intuitive signs to show up in short-run empirical estimation; but, in the longer-run, fundamental relationships, such as the neutrality of money, should re-assert themselves. We do not however attempt to model the transition to the longer-run in this paper.[8]

11.4   The model comparative statics: system-wide predictions

11.4.1   Initial equilibrium

We proceed to perform comparative statics analysis of the model, as detailed in Appendix 11.1. The analysis yields system-wide predictions that can be applied to study policy reform issues.[9] Equations (11.31) for AD, (11.33) for AS and (11.35) for EE give the initial equilibrium of the model.

TABLE 11.2
A taxonomy of single-equation and
system-wide macro response predictions
of the model for single-shot policy actions

Flexible exchange rates	Macro targets		
	Real growth rate	Inflation rate	Exchange rate

All model variables

Endogenous variables

	Real growth rate	Inflation rate	Exchange rate
Y	n.a.	+	+
Q	-	n.a.	+
E	+	+	n.a.

Structural variables

I_{-1}	±	+	±
I_{-2}	±	n.a.	n.a.
$(M_{-1}+L_{-1}+F_{-1})$	+	-	-
Q^*	+	+	-

Policy variables

L	-(-)	+(±)	-(-)
R	±(±)	-(±)	±(±)
G	+ (+)	-(±)	+(+)
TY	-(-)	+(±)	-(-)
TZ	-(-)	+(+)	+(+)
Ko	+(-)	-(-)	-(-)

Note: For each variable, the single equation effects are indicated without parentheses while the system-wide effects are indicated in parentheses; ± denotes an indeterminate sign; n.a. = not applicable.

Source: Single-equation predictions are based on equations (11.31), (11.33) and (11.35); system-predictions are based on simultaneous solution of the model in Appendix 11.1.

On theoretical grounds, the EE schedule must be steeper than AD. The economics of this concerns the relative changes in domestic prices *(Q)* needed to restore equilibrium along the EE and AD curves. On the one hand, regarding AD, an increase in real income raises the demand for output and the demand for real cash balances. To restore equilibrium in the goods market, a fall in prices is required. Lower prices have two main effects; they improve the competitiveness of the economy and hence increase exports, they also reduce imports and thus increase output; they also have a monetary effect, increasing the supply of real cash balances, both directly through the fall in *P* and indirectly through improving the balance of trade. On the other hand, regarding EE, lower prices work only through the balance of trade effect. Intuitively therefore, for AD, there are two major forces at work; whereas for EE there is only one. Hence, a larger change in *Q* is needed to restore equilibrium along EE than along AD, and EE has a steeper slope.

11.4.2   Comparative statics

An increase in bank loans to government The single-equation effects are such that an increase in bank loans to government will induce a fall in real income. Since money is endogenous, an increase in *L* is equivalent to a contractionary open market operation. Hence the money-supply is reduced as is import demand as well as consumption expenditure. Thus the AD curve shift leftwards from AD to AD' in Figure 11.1 demonstrating a decline in aggregate demand. Not surprisingly, the system-wide effects of a rise in *L,* are contractionary. This is due to reduced money-supply and hence reduced aggregate demand; AD shifts further leftwards to AD*. With respect to aggregate supply, the single-equation effect of an increase in loans indicates an inflationary result. This effect operates via the money-market to the production function: "tight money" induces a rise in curb market interest rates, thus raising production costs and prices. However, the system-wide effects are indeterminate in the sense that they may either be positive or negative. If interest-rate effects on costs are relatively large, the stagflationary outcome shown in Figure 11.1 emerges. If, however, interest-rate effects on costs are relatively small, a more orthodox result of lower output *and* prices follows. McKinnon (1973) and Shaw (1973) argued that this is the more likely outcome.[10] Finally, an increase in *L* leads to an appreciation in the exchange rate irrespective of the outcome for prices. Lower output and real money balances both tend to improve the current account and/or appreciate the exchange rate.

Interest-rate reform effects   A rise in R (equivalent to an interest rate reform) has system-wide effects which are ambiguous. The key point is that a higher official interest rate improves the competitiveness of officially-channelled finance permitting an increase in the supply of funds to borrowers and reducing the free-market (curb) interest rate. Since the official rate rises and the free market rate falls, the overall effects are a combination of rising and falling interest rates. If in equation (A11.6) of Appendix 11.1 the restriction $(k_9 j_2 p_3 + p_6 j_2) > (k_9 j_3 + p_6 j_3 k_3)$ holds, meaning that the rise in the official interest rate triggers a low proportionate fall in the curb market rate, then the effects are "orthodox" and contractionary overall. If in addition the restriction $(k_9 j_2 p_1 + p_6 k_3 p_1 + p_6 k_2 p_1) > (k_9 + j_7 k_1 + j_7 k_3 p_1)$ holds, meaning that a rise in the official interest rate hardly triggers a fall in the curb market rate, then prices increase. Strictly, therefore, these two restrictions effectively imply that the official interest rate dominates the free market rate as the marginal cost of funds for investors, producers, and asset-holders. The reverse is true if the two inequalities are reversed, the curb market rate sets the marginal costs of funds. Since the curb market rate falls, McKinnon-Shaw effects dominate: output rises and prices fall as shown in Figure 11.2   Figure 11.3 shows yet another possibility if the first restriction holds and the second restriction does not; then the net result is a more orthodox overall deflationary outcome i.e. lower output and prices. This seems the most likely outcome in the present model as the above restrictions are relatively mild.[11]

A money-financed increase in government spending   The single-equation effects of a money-financed increase in G on AD are illustrated on Figure 11.4. The AD curve shifts rightwards to AD' showing a rise in real income. Given real taxes, an increase in G increases the budget deficit, increasing money supply and raising real income. In terms of expenditures, a rise in G directly increases AD. The system-wide effects are also expansionary as demonstrated by a further rightward shift of AD to AD* in Figure 11.4. However, prices may rise or fall, because of the inverse relationship of the two interest rates (corresponding to interest rate implications of the orthodox versus McKinnon-Shaw dichotomy). The single-equation and system-wide effects of a rise in G lead to a depreciation in the exchange rate of the transition economy. This is because a rise in G, by raising real income, induces an increase in import demand; this leads to depreciation of the exchange rate. Thus, the economy-wide effects of a rise in G are either expansionary and disinflationary (Figure 11.4), but they could be expansionary and inflationary; in either case, the exchange rate depreciates.[12]

An income tax surcharge The single-equation and system-wide effects of fiscal policy involving an income tax surcharge operate via the consumption function in the goods market, and via the government budget constraint in the money-market. Real disposable income falls as the income tax rate rises, and this reduces consumption and investment expenditures. The AD shifts leftwards, as aggregate demand falls.[13] Regarding AS, the single equation effects are such that a rise in income tax shifts the AS curve leftwards: real income falls and domestic prices rise. The system-wide effects are ambiguous. On the one hand, if a rise in income tax is internalised within the cost structure of firms, domestic prices are marked-up by the tax rate: an inflationary result will obtain. On the other hand, if a rise in income tax adversely contracts real disposable income, domestic prices fall following reduced demand. The single-equation and system-wide effects of a rise in income tax on the external sector induce an appreciation of the exchange rate. Specifically, a reduction in after-tax incomes reduces the demand for imports while the fall in domestic prices increases foreigners' demand for exports, so that the net effect on the foreign balance schedule is to appreciate the exchange rate.

A rise in import tax rates The single-equation effects of a rise in the import tax rate involve a shift of the AD curve leftwards, indicating a fall in aggregate demand. Import tax rate effects operate via the government budget constraint in the money-market. Real income falls since, under small country assumptions, the incidence of the import tax burden is on the importer and the consumer. The system-wide effects are still contractionary. With respect to AS, both the single-equation and system-wide effects show that a rise in the import tax rate is inflationary: it is a cost to the producer, pushing up production costs and finally the domestic prices. The effect of a rise in the import tax rate on BOP is to induce a leftward shift of the EE curve. The exchange rate appreciates, owing to contraction in real income and a fall in import demand, following the tax rise.

C.J. Green and V. Murinde

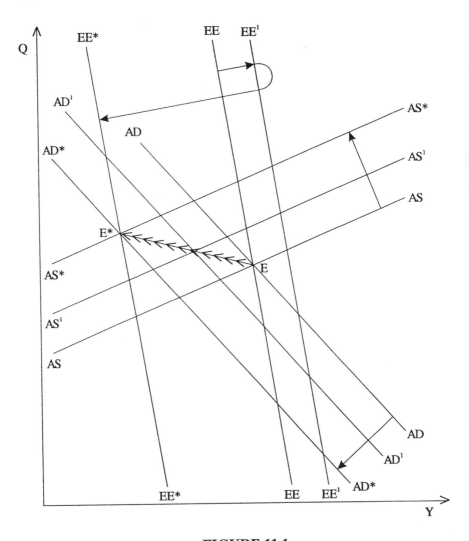

FIGURE 11.1
Stagflationary effects of a "tight money" policy
through open market operations

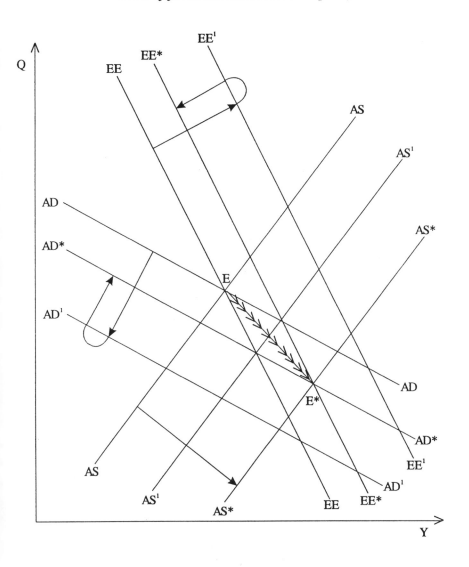

FIGURE 11.2
McKinnon-Shaw (type) effects of
an interest rate policy reform

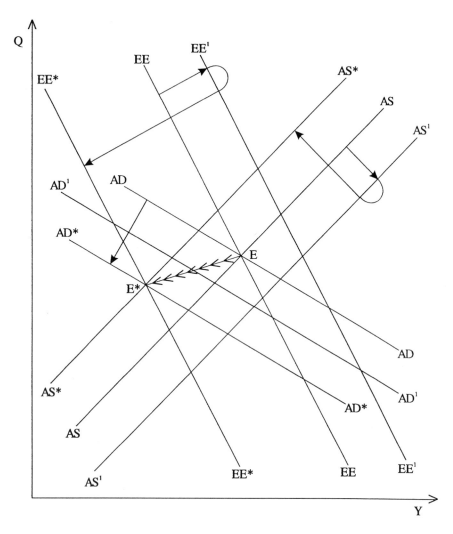

FIGURE 11.3
Semi-orthodox (type) effects of
an interest rate policy reform

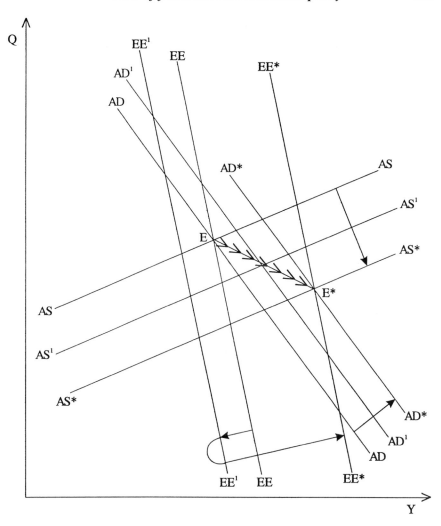

FIGURE 11.4
Effects of a controlled money financed
increase in government spending

An increase in external aid and capital inflows It is found that an increase in external aid is expansionary on aggregate demand, via the investment expenditure function. The increase in foreign aid and capital inflows complement locally available resources for investment expenditure; aggregate demand expands partly because the inflow in financial resources (if converted into domestic currency) induces a fall in the curb market rate. The results also suggest that on the whole, the exchange rate appreciates in the long run. This is consistent with the fact that foreign aid and capital inflows directly improve the foreign exchange reserves of the country and help stabilise the exchange rate in the short run.[14]

11.5 Summary of results and conclusion

We summarise the general results of our model in Table 11.2 and put forward three main results from the previous discussion (in Section 11.4) of the single-equation and the system-wide outcomes regarding the potency of the policy instruments for financial restructuring in transition economies.

Result 1 It is argued that the theoretical ambiguity of the single-equation effects on the demand side and the system-wide effects on both the supply and demand sides of a rise in the official (regulated) interest rate in transition economies, stems from the orthodox versus McKinnon-Shaw controversy. The ambiguity occurs because a rise in the official rate increases the supply of bank deposits and reduces the demand for bank loans thus reducing credit rationing. As credit rationing in the official market is gradually eliminated as part of ongoing financial restructuring, the unsatisfied demand that goes to the informal financial market is reduced; this induces a fall in the curb-market rate. Since one rate rises and the other falls, interest-sensitive spending, loan demands, and working capital demands may either increase or decrease on balance. Hence aggregate demand and aggregate supply and the exchange rate may each either rise or fall.

Result 2 We find that a rise in government borrowing from commercial banks *(L)* is stagflationary in its first-round (single-equation) effects, but its system-wide effects are indeterminate. In the first round effects, a rise in L is equivalent to a cut in money (or monetary targets) and thus induces a rise in the free (curb) interest rate; aggregate demand falls and prices (via mark-up pricing) go up; the second round effects are indeterminate as the official and curb interest rates may offset each other.

Result 3   We predict that the system-wide effect of a rise in government spending is expansionary but may generate either higher or lower inflation. The indeterminacy arises from the probable effect of a rise in government spending on money and the curb versus official interest rate. The transmission mechanism is such that if the curb market rate decreases, lower inflation will result (because of lower working capital costs) otherwise higher inflation obtains. The result contributes to the scepticism about McKinnon-Shaw optimism that financial reform which raises the official interest rate achieves higher output and lower prices. The result suggests the McKinnon-Shaw argument does not provide a special case for interest rate reform because, in the short run, a rise in government spending has comparable effects! In general, a budgetary policy consisting of an increase in government spending does just as well as a financial reform that involves interest rate liberalisation and monetary targets.

In general, the main contribution of this paper is that it demonstrates a novel application of flow-of-funds and conventional macroeconomic theory to underpin the policy framework for a transition economy in the form of a macroeconomic model.   The application of orthodox economic theory is consistent with elements of theoretical foundations of orthodox policy reform while explicit incorporation of the special features of a transition economy reflects elements of the New-structuralist approach.   For example, we argue that the single equation and system-wide model predictions, denoted by the theoretical signs of the coefficients, reflect the key elements in the Orthodox-Structuralist debate; and provide a useful base for estimation and testing as well as counterfactual simulations and policy experiments.[15]   It is on this basis that the model developed in this paper can be regarded as an overall framework for studying economic policy reform issues for transition economies.

Notes

We acknowledge useful comments from Clas Wihlborg and participants at a conference on "Restructuring Financial Institutions in Emerging Economies" held at Tallin-Lohusalu in Estonia on 17-18 October 1994; a conference on "Financial Reform in Emerging Market Economies" held at Poznan University of Economics in Poland on 20-21 January 1996; and a conference on "Financial Sector Reform" held at Tallin Technical University on 18-20 September 1996.   The research for the paper was undertaken with support from the European Commission's Phare / ACE Programme 1994 under contract number 94-0685-R. However, the interpretations and conclusions expressed in this paper are entirely those of the authors and should not be attributed in any manner to the European Commission.

1. We consider our approach to blend orthodox and structuralist macroeconomics. According to FitzGerald (1993, p. 22-23), the structural approach embraces three basic premises: (i) economies are built up from economic agents (e.g. firms and governments) as exemplified by our Table 11.1; (ii) product and factor markets clear through both quantity and price adjustments, as indicated in Section 11.3; (iii) the institutional structures condition the policy outcomes (as in our policy predictions).

2. We recognise the coexistence of formal and informal markets in goods, credit (loans), and foreign exchange. However, our insight is that the informal markets are parallel markets that are tolerated by government officials; they are not black markets in which the contraband is illegal as was the case during price controls and rationing under the central planning system. The informal (parallel) markets therefore clear either through price adjustment or through quantity adjustment (queues). In the discussion of financial assets, it is assumed that firms attract finance for investment from the official financial sector (e.g. banks) as well as the informal financial sector (e.g. we mention loans for working capital purposes). The existence of these dual markets reflects the main problems that economic agents face in obtaining domestic finance. For example, the official financial sector is repressed, credit is rationed, and with the attendant moral hazard and adverse selection problems, the unsatisfied demand spills over to the informal sector. Financial reform, signified by a rise in the official interest rate in our model, introduces the transition from financial repression. These arguments are reflected in the investment equation (11.7), the money demand equation (11.15) and the production function (11.8).

3. Equation (11.7) underscores two issues. One, given that the influence of the curb-market interest rate is assumed to be more operative via the investment function than the consumption function, we use the investment function to capture the curb-market effect; the consumption function may be relevant but at a great cost of being more cumbersome. Two, in the context of financially repressed transition economies, the official rate of interest is ineffective because of credit restrictions. An interest rate reform (a rise in R) enables the banks to garner private

savings and make funds available for investment; hence while credit restrictions exist, the reform affects investment positively, and thus the official interest rate is positively signed in contrast to the negatively signed curb rate.

4. Essentially, equation (11.7) could be represented by two equations for domestic and foreign investment, respectively:

$$I_d = ID\ (Y, NR - \hat{Q}^e, R - \hat{Q}^e, Q),$$
$$id_1 > 0;\ id_2 < 0;\ id_3 > 0;\ id_4 > 0$$
$$I_f = IF\ (Y, NR - \hat{Q}^e, R - \hat{Q}^e, Q* E, K_0),$$
$$i_1 > 0;\ i_2 < 0;\ i_3 > 0;\ i_4,\ i_5 > 0$$

However, the above would be more cumbersome without necessarily offering more insight than the specification in equation (11.7).

5. The specification of the government budget constraint ignores the interest on government and foreign debt. This is because, as characterised in most transition economies, under financial repression the interest rate is artificially pegged low and does not change in the short run.

6. This definition of K_0 is consistent with our specification of the investment function (equation 11.7): the inflow of overseas aid may be accompanied by the inflow of investment from overseas companies.

7. Our AD-AS-EE model offers more scope for analysing macroeconomic policy in transition economies than a standard IS-LM-BP model; essentially our model allows for endogenous determination of prices (or the inflation rate). In addition, in obtaining a reduced form of the model, we assume equilibrium holds. Although most transition economies experience macroeconomic disequilibrium, we argue that initial equilibrium assumptions make it possible to isolate policy effects meaningful.

8. By identifying the structural features of transition economies and underpinning the one-period policy effects, the model provides a useful point of departure for future research into dynamics analysis. In addition, most of the supply side issues highlighted here would be useful to incorporate into existing computable general equilibrium models that attempt to deal with income distribution (for example, Roberts and Zolkiewski, 1996).

9. We check whether there is a unique equilibrium which corresponds to a given set of exogenous parameters in the model. We also check whether a stable equilibrium is attainable for the entire set of endogenous and

exogenous parameters in the system. Although we are able to simplify the analysis and tie down the one period response of policy changes, our analysis of stability may appear incomplete in the sense that we do not explicitly consider the dynamics.

10. The developed economy analogue of commercial loans to government *(L)* is bond financing. Note that the system-wide results for transition economies obtained here differ from short-run results, but are similar to long-run results, for developed economies.

11. This result derives from the restrictions on the coefficients of the official and curb market interest rates in the money demand equation (11.15). To explore the relationship between these two rates more deeply, a more developed model of the behaviour of banks and firms and their dealings with the public sector is desirable. This microstructure analysis, however, would comprise a paper in its own right, and falls outside the scope of the present paper that addresses the broad macroeconomic framework.

12. More usually, the result is the other way round: $(\partial Q/\partial G) > 0$. What we obtain in the model is: $(\partial Q/\partial G) \gtrless 0$; most probably < 0. This is due to indeterminate short-run effects at work since in our model a rise in G is money-financed and has interest rate implications of the orthodox versus McKinnon-Shaw variety.

13. The corresponding diagrams for an income tax surcharge, a rise in import tax rates, and an increase in external aid and capital inflows (derived in Appendix 11.1) are configured on the same basis as Figures 11.1-11.4; they are not produced here but are obtainable from the authors on request.

14. More usually, however, an increase in *Ko* is associated with higher government spending. This should raise the money supply. In practice, therefore, whether *Ko* reduces or increases the money supply depends on how aid flows are integrated into the public finances of the economy in question.

15. A theoretical proof of rank and order conditions for identifiability of the model is obtainable from the authors on request.

References

Anton, I., D. Danciu and C. Mitu, 1996, The role of SMEs in the regional redevelopment of Romania, Eastern European Economics, 34, 2, pp. 65-95.

Borish, M. S., M. F. Long, and M. Noel, 1996, Lessons from bank and enterprise restructuring in the transition economies of Europe and Central Asia, World Economy, 19, 1, pp. 39-62.

Caprio, G., D. Folkerts-Landau and T. Lane, 1994, Building Sound Finance in Emerging Market Economies (IMF, Washington D.C.).

Dornbusch, R. and S Fischer, 1994, Macroeconomics (McGraw-Hill, New York), 6th Edition.

Fitzgerald, E. V. K., 1993, The Macroeconomics of Development Finance (St. Martin's Press, London).

Fry, M. J., 1995, Money, Interest and Banking in Economic Development, 2nd Edition (Johns Hopkins University Press, Baltimore).

Frydman, R., K. Pistor and A. Rapaczynski, 1996, Exit and voice after mass privatisation: The case of Russia, European Economic Review, 40, 5, pp. 581-588.

Griffith-Jones, S. and Z. Drabek, 1995, Financial Reform in Central and Eastern Europe (Macmillan Publishers, London and Basingstoke).

Hillman, A. L. and H. W. Ursprung, 1996, The Political economy of trade liberalisation in the transition, European Economic Review, 40, 5, pp. 783-794.

Khan, M. S., et al., 1991, Macroeconomic Models for Adjustment in Developing Countries (IMF, Washington D.C.).

McKinnon, R. I., 1973, Money and Capital in Economic Development (The Brookings Institution, Washington D.C.).

Montiel, P. J., P. Agenor and N. U. Haque, 1993, Informal Financial Markets in Developing Countries (Blackwell, Oxford).

Murinde, V., 1993, Budgetary and financial policy amid structural bottlenecks, World Development, 21, 5, pp. 841-859.

Patterson, D. M., 1996, Reform in Eastern Europe: A general equilibrium model with distortions in relative prices and factor markets, Canadian Journal of Economics, 29, 2, pp. 457-472.

Roberts, B. M. and Z. Zolkiewski, 1996, Modelling income distribution in countries in transition: A computable general equilibrium analysis for Poland, Economic Modelling, 13, 1, pp. 67-90.

Roe, A. R., et al., 1993, Instruments of Economic Policy in Africa (Heineman Educational Books, London).

Rondinelli, D. A. and J. Yurkiewicz, 1996, Privatisation and economic restructuring in Poland: An assessment of transition policies, American Journal of Economics & Sociology, 55, 2, pp. 145-160.

Ruggerone, L., 1996, Unemployment and inflationary finance dynamics at the early stages of transition, Economic Journal, 106, 435, pp. 483-494.

Rybczynski, T. M., 1991, The sequencing of reform, Oxford Review of Economic Policy, 7, 4, pp. 26-34.

Sachs, J. D., 1996, The transition at mid decade, American Economic Review, 86, 2, pp. 128-133.

Shaw, E. S., 1973, Financial Deepening in Economic Development (Oxford University Press, New York).

Svejnar, J., 1996, Enterprises and workers in the transition: Econometric evidence, American Economic Review, 86, 2, pp. 123-127.

Taylor, L., 1990, Socially Relevant Policy Analysis: Structuralist Computable General Equilibrium Models for the Developing World (The MIT Press, Cambridge).

Turnovsky, S. J., 1990, Macroeconomic Analysis and Stabilization Policy (Cambridge University Press, Cambridge).

World Bank, 1993, Estonia: The Transition to a Market Economy (The World Bank, Washington D.C.).

Appendix 11.1
Model comparative statics

Basing on equations (11.31), (11.33), and (11.35) we write the following implicit function form of the model:

$$FF^1(Y,Q,E; L,R,G,TY,TZ,K_0,F) = 0$$

$$FF^2(Y,Q,E; L,R,G,TY,TZ,F) = 0$$

$$FF^3(Y,Q,E; L,R,G,TY,TZ,K_o,F) = 0 \qquad \text{(A11.1)}$$

To carry out comparative statics, we totally differentiate to yield:

$$
\begin{bmatrix} 1 & j_3 & -j_2 \\ -k_1 & 1 & -k_3 \\ -p_1 & -p_3 & 1 \end{bmatrix}
\begin{bmatrix} dY \\ dQ \\ dE \end{bmatrix}
\begin{bmatrix} -j_6 dL - j_7 dR + j_8 dG - j_{11} dTY - j_{12} dTZ + j_{10} dK_0 - j_9 dF \\ k_7 dL - k_9 dR - k_{10} dG + k_{12} dTY + k_{13} dTZ + k_{11} dF \\ -p_4 dL - p_6 dR + p_7 dG - p_{11} dTY - p_{12} dTZ - p_8 dK_0 - p_{10} dF \end{bmatrix}
$$

$$\text{(A11.2)}$$

The above system yields the Jacobian
$j^* = 1 - k_3 p_3 + k_1 j_3 + j_3 p_1 k_3 - j_2 k_1 p_3 - j_2 p_1 > 0;$ since the Jacobian is non-vanishing, the system of equations has a locally unique solution. We therefore apply Cramer's Rule to yield the following system-wide multipliers.
Loans to Government (L)

$$\frac{\delta Y}{\delta L} = [-j_6(1 - p_3 k_3) + j_3(p_4 k_3 - k_7) + j_2(p_3 k_7 - p_4)] \, J^{*-1} \gtrless 0; \qquad \text{(A11.3)}$$

$$\frac{\delta Q}{\delta L} = [k_7(1 - j_2 p_1) - p_4(k_3 + j_2 k_1) - j_6(k_1 + p_1 k_3)] \, J^{*-1} \gtrless 0; \qquad \text{(A11.4)}$$

$$\frac{\delta E}{\delta L} = [-p_4(1 - j_3 k_1) - k_2(j_3 p_1 - p_3) - j_6(p_1 + p_3 k_1)] \, J^{*-1} > 0; \qquad \text{(A11.5)}$$

The official interest rate (R)

$$\frac{\delta Y}{\delta R} = [-j_7(1+p_3k_3)+k_9(j_3j_2p_3)-p_6(j_2-j_3k_3)]\ J^{*-1} \gtrless 0; \qquad (A11.6)$$

$$\frac{\delta Q}{\delta R} = [-k_9(1-j_2p_1)-j_7(k_1+k_3p_1)+p_6(k_3+j_2p_1)]\ J^{*-1} \gtrless 0; \qquad (A11.7)$$

$$\frac{\delta E}{\delta R} = [-p_6(1-j_3k_1)+j_7(p_1p_3k_1)-k_9(p_3-j_3p_1)]\ J^{*-1} < 0; \qquad (A11.8)$$

Government spending (G)

$$\frac{\delta Y}{\delta G} = [j_8(1-p_3k_3)+k_{10}(j_3-p_7k_3)-p_7(j_2-j_3k_3)]\ J^{*-1} > 0; \qquad (A11.9)$$

$$\frac{\delta Q}{\delta G} = [-k_{10}(1-j_2p_1)+j_8(k_1+p_1k_3)+p_7(k_3+j_2k_1)]\ J^{*-1} \gtrless 0; \qquad (A11.10)$$

$$\frac{\delta E}{\delta G} = [p_7(1+k_1j_3)+k_{10}(j_3p_1-p_3)+j_8(p_1+k_1p_3)]\ J^{*-1} < 0; \qquad (A11.11)$$

Income tax rate (TY)

$$\frac{\delta Y}{\delta TY} = [-j_{11}(1-p_3k_3)-k_{12}(j_3+j_2p_3)-p_{11}(j_2+j_3k_3)]\ J^{*-1} < 0; \qquad (A11.12)$$

$$\frac{\delta Q}{\delta TY} = [k_{12}(1-j_2p_1)-j_{11}(k_1+p_1k_3)-p_{11}(j_2k_1+k_3)]\ J^{*-1} \gtrless 0; \qquad (A11.13)$$

$$\frac{\delta E}{\delta TY} = [p_{11}(1-j_2k_1)-j_{11}(k_1p_3+p_1)-k_{12}(p_1j_3-p_3)]\ J^{*-1} > 0; \qquad (A11.14)$$

Import tax rate

$$\frac{\delta Y}{\delta TZ} = [-j_{12}(1+p_3k_1)-k_{13}(j_3-j_2p_3)-p_{12}(j_3k_3-j_2)]\ J^{*-1} < 0; \qquad (A11.15)$$

$$\frac{\delta Q}{\delta TZ} = [j_{12}(k_1+p_1k_3)+k_{13}(1-j_2p_1)-p_{12}(k_3+j_2k_1)]\ J^{*-1} > 0; \qquad (A11.16)$$

$$\frac{\delta E}{\delta TZ} = [p_{12}(1+j_3k_1)+k_{13}(p_3-j_3p_1)-j_{12}(p_1+k_1p_3)]\ J^{*-1} > 0; \qquad (A11.17)$$

External aid policy (Ko)

$$\frac{\delta Y}{\delta K_0} = [j_{10}(1+p_3k_3)+p_8(k_3j_3-j_2)] \ J^{*-1} > 0; \qquad (A11.18)$$

$$\frac{\delta Q}{\delta K_0} = [-p_8(k_3+j_2k_1)+j_{10}(-k_1+k_3p_1)] \ J^{*-1} > 0; \qquad (A11.19)$$

$$\frac{\delta E}{\delta K_0} = [-p_8(1+j_3k_1)-j_{10}(k_1p_3+p_1)] \ J^{*-1} < 0; \qquad (A11.20)$$

Part Four

Privatization and Foreign Investment

Financial Section Reform and
Privatization in Transition Economies
J. Doukas, V. Murinde and C. Wihlborg (Editors)
© 1998 Elsevier Science Publishers B.V. All rights reserved

283

3 2 7

(L. Europe)

Chapter 12

PRIVATIZATION IN POST-COMMUNIST ECONOMIES

P 21   L33   P3 l

Michael A. Goldstein
College of Business and Administration, University of Colorado at Boulder,
Boulder, CO 80309-0419, USA

N. Bulent Gultekin
The Wharton School, University of Pennsylvania, Philadelphia, PA 19104-6367,
USA

12.1   Introduction

Privatizing Central Europe is a daunting challenge for financial theorists and practitioners alike. Perhaps no other change in economic philosophy has occurred in such a short period of time. These changes are massive, both in absolute and relative terms. Unlike prior privatization in countries with developed or semi-developed capital markets, there is no history of capital market infrastructure or market-oriented accounting or reporting systems and a dearth of technologically advanced fixed assets such as computers. The very size and nature of such a change, the vast number of people and economic resources affected, the need to develop market structures, and the need to reach a new equilibrium as rapidly and efficiently as possible seem to demand new approaches and ideas.

To fill this demand, many proposals for privatization programs have been supplied by economists and practitioners to speed the privatization process. Each proponent claims that their proposal "solves" the privatization problem in a superior manner with a maximum of efficiency and a minimum of cost. These proposals fall into various categories. The general fund scheme calls for the creation of a single, large mutual fund containing all of the shares of the privatized companies with the public holding the mutual fund shares. Other proposals call for the distribution of vouchers to be used to bid for the shares or even direct distribution of shares to the public. Some limited forms of financing have also been suggested, such as debt financing of shares similar to the leveraged buy-out (LBO) concept or employee stock ownership plan (ESOP) financing. Some others recommend privatizing the pension fund system in conjunction with other measures, such as increasing the role of the banking system.[1]

Other authors have focused on specific privatization or general caveats as to the process of privatization.[2] To date, however, there has not been a theoretical analysis of the privatization process. This paper fills this gap by applying the rich body of knowledge contained in over fifty years of finance literature to the issues raised in the privatization process. More specifically, we reduce three generalized privatization schemes to their fundamental values and apply modern finance theory under a variety of assumptions. We then compare the results as predicted by finance theory with those claimed by the proponents of these schemes. Unlike much of the literature that proceeds it, this paper is predictive, as opposed to descriptive.

To this end, we have organized the paper as follows. Section 12.2 contains a brief description of the initial state of affairs in post-communist countries. Section 12.3 presents a brief discussion of the definitions and goals for privatization. Section 12.4 provides familiar theoretical underpinnings for why these goals will be achieved through privatization. The bulk of the paper is in Section 12.5, which contains the discussion of three privatization proposals reduced to their purest form: free distribution of actual shares, free distribution of vouchers with no nominal value that will be used to bid for shares, and distributing the primary securities to listed closed-end mutual funds. Section 12.6 discusses preliminary issues related to the market for control. Finally, Section 12.7 contains the conclusion and some policy recommendations for the privatization process.

12.2   The initial setting in post-Communist countries

Privatization consists of a complex interlocking set of operations which depend on the state of the economy. In a developed market economy such as the U.S. or the U.K., the emphasis is on the transfer of state assets into private hands to remove politics from business decisions, thereby making a more efficient use of assets. In developing market economies such as Chile or Latin America, this objective for privatization is still present, but the need to develop capital markets is also an important objective, as well as a constraint on the process. Although there are substantial differences in the privatization experiences of developed and developing countries, the private sector has typically been at least a modest component of the economy.

In contrast, the privatization process in post-communist countries takes a different definition. Here, privatization plays an integral role in the transformation of the entire current economy into one that is market driven. Privatization, therefore, as used to describe the process elsewhere, does not adequately describe the enormity of its role in post-communist countries, where it involves a total restructuring of the economy into an entirely different form with new institutions and management skills.[3] It requires the processing of a large stock of enterprises from state-owned to privately-owned, the development of the necessary elements and institutions of a market economy (including the human skills needed in this new structure), and the commercialization of companies before and after ownership changes.[4]

Substantial difficulties initially inhibit the rapid implementation of privatization programs, such as:

a)   the generally inefficient initial deployment of assets,
b)   an insubstantial private sector,
c)   a shortage of market-oriented professional managers,
d)   an inadequate financial structure,
e)   poor (non-financial) accounting and reporting practices,
f)   inappropriate corporate governance practices,
g)   a monopolistic market structure, and
h)   the large number of enterprises to be privatized.

A number of post-communist countries have begun their privatization process, while some others are now well on their way along the privatization path. However, it is useful to recall that the initial situation in many post-communist countries was quite bleak; and for some countries the situation has not changed dramatically. Capital markets are not fully developed, at least by Western standards. Moreover, the banking system does not have years of experience in operating under market discipline, nor does it have much experience in developing or exercising market discipline on its borrowers (although this is improving in certain countries). These institutions therefore could not initially or cannot currently be relied upon for governance, monitoring and capital allocation.[5] It is still true that for many companies accounting data is poor or non-existent.[6] Furthermore, most private individuals have very limited accumulated wealth and therefore face severely limited capital constraints due to the poor state of the capital market and banking sectors.[7] Privatization, therefore, needs to be considered in the context of a society and economy undergoing massive changes.[8]

Initially, almost all participants have almost no information. The government (the initial official owner of the assets) does not know the underlying value of the assets, and citizens have even less knowledge, having never seen an income statement or balance sheet. While the managers may have more information regarding the assets they control, even their information is not of very high quality as they have not been operating under market conditions.[9] Even relative prices are uninformative, as they are not market-driven.[10]

Due to the practically non-existent level of information on individual firms, extensive research will be necessary initially to determine what firms own and what they have earned, let alone determine what they are worth as an ongoing concern. In addition, the high level of uncertainty as to the eventual equilibrium make long-term analysis near impossible. All of this must take place in an environment with limited technological abilities, so that even the computers to undertake the analysis are not available.

This research will be extensive and costly, especially relative to the level of wealth in the society.[11] Until privatization occurs, information will not be produced because there is no ability to realize private returns on investment in information. With so little information available, information asymmetry will be low and almost all investors will be similarly uninformed.[12] Therefore, extensive and expensive information searches need to be undertaken for reasoned and accurate information to be included in market decisions and transactions.[13] Due to the high costs involved, this might not occur.

12.3   Privatization: definitions and goals

12.3.1. Definition

Before embarking on a discussion of privatization, it is useful to examine what the term means. It is apparent that privatization means different things to different people. To some, it is the re-establishing of the links from companies and factors of production to the capital markets. To others, it is a change in the corporate governance structure.

In fact, privatization is all of these and more. Privatization is a variety of measures and steps to change the way raw materials are converted into consumption goods. This process entails removing government control and interaction and replacing it with private actors. Merely changing one of the variables might not be sufficient. For example, if prices are still determined by government fiat, it will not matter if corporate governance is switched from public to private hands. Alternatively, if everything is owned by the government, it may not matter if prices are allowed to fluctuate.[14]

Therefore, privatization is a process, a method of changing production and pricing from public to private hands. To accomplish this result, many steps need to be taken in an orderly and systematic fashion. For example, a significant number of financial and governmental institutions need to be in place to ensure socially beneficial results. Stock exchanges do not arise overnight: laws need to be written; security and exchange commissions need to be established; accounting procedures need to be developed; clearing methods, brokerage houses and investment banks need to be created; and exchanges, physical or electronic, need to be arranged all before trading can take place. Many players in the privatization arena fail to recognize this necessity, offering privatization proposals or procedures, instead of detailed privatization plans.

1.2.2. Goals

An understanding of the goals of privatization is necessary before evaluating the merits of any particular privatization scheme. Unfortunately, there has been some confusion in the literature as to the goals of privatization. Some have seen privatization as an end itself, not as the means to an end. If this were so, then privatizing would simply be a matter of changing the ownership of the company from the state to private hands. Instead, privatization is undertaken to achieve a more important objective: the improvement of enterprise efficiency and a change in ownership sufficient to alter corporate governance.

Hence, privatization is of primary interest due to the implicit assumption that private control increases efficiency.[15] Thus, privatization has the ultimate goal of increasing societal consumption by increasing the output of vastly under-utilized assets and by a more appropriate allocation of resources across these assets. Restated, privatization attempts to:

a)   change the control of the factors of production to increase output; and

b)   reallocate resources across assets to maximize the value of the output.

These two changes occur in different markets. The first change, changing the control of the factors of production, occurs primarily in the labor markets.[16] The second change, the reallocation of resources across assets, occurs in the capital markets. This paper primarily focuses on the second issue, that of reallocation of resources through the capital markets. If trading is allowed to occur, then the capital market may both help reallocate resources across assets by indicating relative pricing and also provide a market for ownership rights, thereby allowing a market for control to be created as well. Since the markets of control and ownership of income streams are linked by the same instrument, i.e., shares, some attention is also placed on the ability of shareholders under the different scenarios to affect a change in the control of the factors of production.[17] Liquidity for individuals is also an important concern.

12.4   Meeting these goals in a competitive market

Before we analyze how well the proposals meet the goals of privatization, a reasonable question to consider is how these goals are met in a competitive market. The theoretical answer has been given by the First Welfare Theorem and the Second Welfare Theorem of economics, which relate a competitive allocation with pareto optimality.

From the First Welfare Theorem, we can see that an allocation that is the result of a competitive equilibrium (in which firms maximize profits, households maximize utility subject to a budget constraint, and markets clear) will result in a Pareto optimal allocation.[18] The Second Welfare Theorem indicates that any Pareto optimal allocation can be achieved through the competitive process by the appropriate assignment of property ownership rights or redistribution schemes.[19]

The underlying tenant of modern-day privatization is the Second Welfare Theorem. It indicates that by changing the endowment structure, any pareto optimal allocation may be achieved through competitive markets. Privatization in post-communist countries may be viewed as the redistribution of endowments across a populace such that, given the developments of markets and corporate structure, a desired pareto optimal solution will be achieved as the result of the competitive process. Since different privatization proposals will result in different distributions of wealth across the populace, different competitive equilibria will be achieved depending on which proposal is implemented.

Each of these results will have strong implications on social welfare. Since the Second Welfare Theorem implies that any competitive equilibrium may be reached if endowments are properly redistributed initially, and since privatization proposals seem to imply different initial distributions and different resulting competitive equilibria, the implementation of these proposals may result in significantly different levels of social welfare. As this aspect of privatization is quite important, this paper will develop the different distributional structures that will result from the implementation of these proposals. The implications for social welfare, however, are left up to the reader.

12.5   Privatization proposals

While there are a variety of privatization schemes, we analyze only three schemes that rely on capital markets for ownership changes and corporate governance which are the base cases underlying most privatization schemes in post-Communist countries: free distribution of shares directly to the people, the creation of mutual funds, and the distribution of vouchers.[20] These analyses provide insight into results for combination of these schemes.[21] Alternatives, such as private asset sales or privatizations through banks, are not the focus of this paper. As noted previously, political considerations inhibit private asset sales and the banking sector is/was not sufficiently developed to monitor companies effectively (as banks under centrally-planned economies were "banks" in name only). Therefore, the analysis has been limited to the three extreme cases noted above.

Privatization proposals may be analyzed on a myriad of levels and the criteria for their evaluation also depend on the objectives of the government. In this paper, privatization is assumed to have two essential goals: increasing the value of the output and reallocating resources across factors of production. This paper primarily looks at the latter of these two goals. It does so by analyzing the resulting distribution of shares and wealth and determining if trading in the underlying shares will occur.

While trading of securities is not essential for all forms of privatization, it is crucial to the success of the privatization processes analyzed in this paper which rely on capital markets for efficiency gains and changes of control. In these schemes, if trading occurs, then relative pricing across firms will be established and thus capital may be allocated more efficiently. In addition, the presence of trading will allow changes in corporate control. However, if in these schemes there is no trading, then there will be no price discovery and no valuation of assets, nor will external changes in control take place.[22] Finally, we predict and describe the most likely market and ownership structure and the competitive equilibria that will result from these basic proposals using the existing financial theory.

To develop this analysis, it is important to follow the historic train of thought through which these privatization proposals evolved. Each proposal builds upon its intellectual predecessors as each tries to address some of the problems in these mass privatization schemes. Therefore, we begin with a discussion of the most basic form of privatization, the free distribution of shares, and examines the benefits and pitfalls of this type of proposal. This proposal is then used as the base case against which other proposals are evaluated. We then proceed to look at free distribution of shares through mutual funds, which was the next step in the development of privatization proposals. After demonstrating the inconsistencies in this type of proposal, we examine the currently popular voucher scheme proposals, and demonstrate some of the pitfalls and difficulties inherent in these voucher schemes. (While each section may be read independently, the ideas build upon each other and are best understood in sequence.) It is to the base case of free distribution of shares that we now turn.

12.5.1 *Free distribution of shares directly to citizens*

Some form of free distribution is a part of almost every large privatization plan. The most basic form of privatization is to distribute actual shares in each company to each citizen as a form of an initial endowment without the provision of any additional information. It is viewed as one of the fairest ways to distribute initial endowments. The underlying assumption is that the populace, on its own, will exercise the rights contained within these shares to control the underlying assets and increase the productivity of the nation. In addition, it is assumed that market participants will trade such shares with each other on the market in such a way that prices are established and that the underlying value of such firms may be revealed. Implicit in this assumption is that the market, on its own, will engage in information gathering and attempt to price the securities on a semi-informed basis, and, at the same time, will exercise its rights of ownership to increase the earnings and dividend stream potential of the underlying assets by exerting control over management. The proposal assumes that the market would act on its own to establish valuation and price discovery.

Trading in this setting will be necessary for control changes, information accumulation and intertemporal transfers of wealth. However, high brokerage, information, and organizational costs will hinder trading.[23]

Transaction costs and trading Each individual will receive a collection of shares that may be a large proportion of his/her overall wealth. The value of the endowment the individual receives in any one firm will be very small. This level of smallness, as we shall see, may result in a no trade situation, and therefore inhibit price discovery and/or changes in control.

Trading would involve incurring brokerage and transaction costs. These brokerage and transaction costs are likely to be large compared with the underlying value of the shares to be traded.[24] In fact, depending on the eventual market structure that evolves, it is likely that the brokerage and transaction costs would exceed the value of the shares themselves. No trading will occur as a result. Even if the agent wished to intertemporally transfer *any* wealth from the future to the present, the costs of transacting will prevent this from occurring.

For trade to occur requires the value of a share be at least twice the cost of brokerage. The cost of transacting has some minimum fixed costs that must be met, regardless of volume. These costs are large, relatively speaking, even on modernized U.S. exchanges. Presumably, they would be prohibitively expensive in underdeveloped exchanges. Therefore, it is likely that we get **no trading in individual securities due to high brokerage costs**.

These size problems do not occur only on the first day of trading. In fact, after the initial round of trading, it will be necessary that the expected return from trading -- and not merely the expected value of the share -- will exceed the transaction costs. If transaction costs are high, such a discrepancy in beliefs will occur only infrequently, inhibiting the development of a secondary market and resulting in thin capital markets.[25]

Of course, it is possible that exchange could occur if transactions costs were reduced. One way that this could occur is by informal, non-centralized trading. However, this would lead to the result of wide and dispersed trading, which would result in non-effective price discovery. Without centralized reporting of transactions, prices would vary from location to location and participants would be unable to learn from each other's trades. Centralized, liquid capital markets will not arise, preventing price discovery and thus proper resource allocation. Therefore, **informal, non-centralized trading will develop to reduce transactions costs. While price discovery may begin, it will be inefficient.**

Demands for current consumption are likely to cause unorganized selling of shares across the country without any form of publicly disclosed price information. Given the strong desire for current consumption by the average citizen, it is possible that a few capital rich individuals will travel the country purchasing shares from citizens anxious to convert their shareholdings into cash. With the lack of information as to fair competitive prices, it is likely that many of these sales will take place at prices significantly below those that would occur on more organized markets. In these countries, there is a social and political concern that this would result in the nomenklatura owning the majority of the shares at bargain prices.[26]

It follows that if no trading occurs due to excessive brokerage costs, there will not be any incentive to accumulate information, as the cost of acting on that information would exceed the value of that information itself due to brokerage costs alone.[27] Therefore, another implication is that **information accumulation will not occur** if high brokerage costs prevent trading or cause non-centralized trading. Such **uninformed disperse trading may lead to speculative behavior**, resulting in high uncertainty and volatility. There is a risk that this may ultimately undermine investor confidence in the system itself.

Information costs inhibit information accumulation   In Grossman and Stiglitz (1980), the number of informed traders is endogenously determined based on the cost of acquiring such information. The cost of information could be very high and its quality low. Therefore, with the possible exception of management, it is likely that there will be few, if any, informed traders in the market. More accurately, the relative asymmetry in information between market participants will be low since the quality of information is so poor and the cost of accumulating information is so high. Thus, there will be **little information accumulation, price system will not be informative and the markets will be very thin due to high information costs**.

A key assumption in this and many other privatization proposals is that the market, *on its own*, will accumulate information and value the securities, thereby relieving the government of its responsibility to do so during the privatization process. As is noted above, such a reliance on the market could *hinder* the development of capital markets and the privatization process itself.

Information is, in many ways, a public good. As such, economic theory predicts it will be underproduced in a competitive economy. Therefore, reliance on the market for the production of information seems shortsighted. In addition, if one assumes risk averse investors, firms will be valued below their true value if there is an underproduction of information. Many schemes purport to "solving" the privatization problem by leaving information accumulation to the private sector. As has been shown, this more likely exacerbates the problem.[28]

Control changes blocked An investor would also want to increase the value of his/her holdings by increasing the value of the underlying assets. In this case, it will be necessary to remove or change management, or at least management controls and incentives.

Changing managements require the collective action of individual investors, who must be united and organized. As noted by Jensen and Meckling (1976), diffuse ownership inhibits shareholder control over management. If organizational costs are so large that they exceed the expected return the investor will receive as a result of the organization, then no one will undertake such an organization as the costs outweigh the benefits. With a diverse shareholder base, it is likely that the costs of organization will be very large. In addition, no one shareholder has any incentive to incur such costs, since, as Grossman and Hart (1980) note: "The proper management of a common property is a public good to all owners of the property ... If one small shareholder devotes resources to improving management, then all shareholders benefit." (p. 59)

Since each investor was given such a small endowment of each firm initially, the relative benefit of organization for any particular individual will be small.[29] Given shareholders that are widely dispersed and the difficulty of collective action, it is unlikely that the relative benefit of organization for any particular individual will exceed the cost. Thus, **wide dispersion of shareholders results in no organizational activity or control**.[30]

Therefore, it will not be in any individual's interest to initiate or complete any organizational activity unless he/she can accumulate enough shares to overcome organizational costs. However, as Grossman and Hart (1980) point out, it will also be necessary that the investor receive some form of extra compensation or private benefit to induce the investor to incur such costs.

If, due to capital constraints or brokerage costs, the individual cannot accumulate sufficient shares or if a market does not exist for trading, then no such action will take place. However, this in turn prevents the accumulation of shares and thereby external changes in control. If so, there will neither be trading nor will there be an increase in efficiency in the use of the underlying assets, and thus both of the aims of privatization will have been thwarted. Thus, if there is **no trading of individual securities, then external changes in control are blocked.**[31]

Implications Infinite divisibility of a firm is not necessarily a good thing. The unbundling of the economy into such small pieces will cause transaction costs to take on unusual significance. Transactions costs will prevent trading, information accumulation and control changes. Organizational costs are always high with an atomized shareholder base. Information accumulation costs will also take on new importance as they will be quite high due to the poor level of information available. Lack of liquidity in the marketplace will hurt many investors looking for intertemporal transfers and hurt the economy in preventing price discovery and control changes.

It appears important that trading be allowed and that control not be overly dispersed. There is probably an optimal level of concentration of ownership which is likely to be dictated by the eventual brokerage costs of trading. These costs are likely to be such that they imply one share per firm per person is not a tenable solution. One instinctive alternative to this vast dispersion of shares is the distribution of shares via a small number of mutual funds, to which we now turn.

12.5.2   Free distribution of shares through mutual funds

Perhaps in recognition of the problems associated with a wide dispersion of shares, others such as Sachs et al. (1990) have proposed creating a small number of mutual funds, which will each be given shares in a large number of state-owned enterprises (which have been converted into joint-stock company form).[32] It is assumed that these funds will invest resources in information accumulation and trade these underlying securities among themselves so as to enhance the performance of their fund. Shares of these mutual funds will be distributed to the citizenry and can be traded. Each citizen will receive an equal endowment of shares in each mutual fund, thereby maintaining a sense of overall fairness and equity. This proposal assumes that the mutual funds will price the underlying securities and trade among themselves so that citizens will be able to determine the value of their mutual fund shares by noting market value of the fund's portfolio. Furthermore, the plan assumes that capital market discipline will force the mutual funds to be effective managers of the firms in their portfolios.[33]

No trading in underlying securities There will be no trading of shares of the underlying firms among a few large mutual funds with identical endowments if the underlying securities themselves are not traded among small investors. This result occurs because the small investors, who, because of their intertemporal consumption preferences, differing utility functions, or other reasons, may act like the liquidity traders. Without liquidity traders there will be no trading.

Grossman and Stiglitz (1980) noted that there will be no trading if agents have homogeneous beliefs and endowments. Each fund manager will have the same belief structure, since no fund manager will invest in information accumulation in these markets due to the high cost of information, the existence of asymmetric information, and the lack of liquidity traders. If fund managers expend resources on information gathering, it will rapidly be known by the other fund managers due to the small number of funds. Since there are no liquidity traders to absorb trading losses, the other fund managers will assume that the first fund manager has superior information and will therefore not trade in that market.

The classic free rider problem described in Grossman and Hart (1980) will also prevent information accumulation. Any increased profits due to better management due to information accumulation will be shared with the other funds as they each own equal endowments. The first manager will be worse off than each of the other funds, as he/she expended resources but will receive the same return. Therefore, fund managers will not expend the resources on information accumulation, resulting in no trading or information accumulation.

If, instead of identical endowments, the funds are given random endowments, the mutual funds will restructure their portfolios in single trades of large blocks of shares so that each fund ends up with majority control in the enterprises in which its endowment is the largest relative to the other funds. Trading will stop once they reach equilibrium optimal portfolio weightings.[34]

Once a fund has majority control in a firm, it will be advantageous for that fund to expend resources to restructure the firm's underlying assets to improve its efficiency since the fund will receive the benefit of such an investment of resources. It seems possible, therefore, that funds will rapidly strive for control.[35]

The fund that owns a majority of shares will now be an insider, or an "informed" investor, and will have superior information as compared with the other funds, which, comparatively, are "uninformed" investors. At this point, asymmetric information theory indicates that there will no longer be trading in such shares. There has to be two sides to the trade for there to be trading and for prices to be established. Due to the asymmetric nature of the information and the lack of liquidity traders, both sides of the transaction will not wish to trade at the same time. Grossman and Stiglitz (1980) prove that if there is no liquidity traders, there can be no equilibrium.[36]

These funds have no liquidity needs, and therefore will not be liquidity traders. Nor will anyone else. With **no liquidity traders, there will be no trading.**[37]

Bundling: mutual fund shares become primary securities Without trade, information about the value of individual firms will not be known. Values of individual assets cannot be determined from the price of a portfolio of assets if the individual assets are not also traded. The value indicated by the market for the mutual fund shares will be for the assets as a group, and it will be impossible to separate out the value of the individual non-traded units. The problem is that the mutual funds are not redundant securities. Markets are not complete; the trading of each firm's share would expand the market and provide new information.

So, if financial markets are to provide signals, or information about individual stocks, the securities themselves must first be traded among a large number of investors. Otherwise, trading shares of closed end mutual funds when the underlying securities are not traded does not complete the markets. In this case, **funds themselves become primary securities rather than redundant securities and cannot be easily priced.**

In addition, due to the wide dispersion of ownership of mutual fund shares and the extraordinarily high information costs in evaluating the value of the mutual fund share (since, to value a mutual fund share one would have to determine the value of *each* underlying asset and determine how its value covaries with the entire portfolio), **trading in the mutual fund shares would be merely speculative, and not information driven.**

Implications It seems that care needs to be taken to insure that exogenously imposed structures do not inhibit capital market development or hinder the development of a market economy overall and the ability to change the corporate governance structure. This scheme could hinder the development of capital markets and might result in even more serious consequences.

While mutual funds seem to reduce the dimensionality of the problems associated with the direct free distribution of shares noted earlier, they create worse problems of their own. The lack of liquidity traders rapidly produces the result of no trading which has undesirable consequences. First, no trading results in no price discovery. Second, the lack of trading prevents the creation of a market for control, which could directly prevent optimal changes in the corporate governance structure. As Grossman and Hart (1980) point out, it is only the threat of removal by an outsider which will force a manager to act on behalf of the shareholders.

If the underlying securities themselves are not traded, trading of the shares in mutual funds does not provide any information about the underlying security valuation. Schemes that only allow trading of closed-end mutual funds that purport to solve the issue of valuation in this fashion are erroneous. Furthermore, without trading in the underlying securities, it will be hard to price the assets in the fund, and therefore it will be difficult to value the mutual funds. Given the difficulty in valuing these funds, price discovery will be limited even in the mutual fund shares themselves. The lack of information will result in speculative trading. Speculative trading will distort price formation, undermine financial stability and investor confidence, and could lead to fraud.

The economy will suffer from the random grouping of firms into closed-end funds because these companies will not be grouped optimally to take advantage of natural synergies. Assuming that a market structure exists, societal resources would be used to regroup them if necessary. Even worse, these groupings cannot be undone easily if the underlying securities are not traded.[38] Thus, optimal groupings would be prevented, potentially causing large inefficiencies. The inability to undo these groupings make this proposal worse than direct free distribution, as society is at best equally as well off as with free distribution (if groupings are random), and potentially worse off (if unnatural monopolies stifle growth and competition).[39]

These results hold assuming that there is a sufficiently large number of mutual funds to create a competitive market and industrial structure. If only a handful of funds are formed, as proposed by Sachs et. al. (1990), then the mutual fund scheme creates an economy with five giant holding companies, either conglomerates if companies are distributed randomly or giant structural monopolies if the groupings are specialized. Those who advised the use of five mutual funds unknowingly recommended an economy that will be more centralized than it was under communist rule. While these authors seem to imply that distributing shares through five mutual funds would instantly create a market system, actually such a scheme would have been an excellent mechanism to nationalize a market economy.[40]

It is apparent that artificially grouping firms into funds may cause significant problems. Neither extreme dispersion nor extreme concentration of shares seems appealing. As an alternative to the two previous free distribution of shares proposals, some have proposed auction processes using vouchers, to which we now turn.

12.5.3 Distribution of shares using vouchers

In both of the previous proposals, actual shares were initially distributed to citizens. Under voucher schemes, however, vouchers instead of shares are distributed and are used in auctions for shares of state-owned enterprises to determine the initial distribution of shares. Therefore, while in the previous proposals each citizen received the same endowment in shares, in this proposal they will receive the same value of endowment in vouchers.[41] However, by using the vouchers in auctions, the actual composition of their ultimate initial endowment of shares will differ based on their bids during these auctions.[42]

Auctions, of course, do not require vouchers for their operation.[43] Shares of state-owned enterprises could be sold in auctions where cash is used for payment. However, voucher auctions are frequently proposed in lieu of cash auctions due to the perceived fairness of voucher auctions. In voucher auctions, every citizen receives the same initial endowment of vouchers and therefore everyone starts off equally. However, the few individuals which currently have sufficient capital to participate in cash auctions are viewed suspiciously by the remainder of the public as it is perceived that this capital was accumulated illegally and unfairly under the previous regime. In addition, there is also concern that foreign investors will purchase the nation's assets at bargain prices if cash auctions are used.

As voucher schemes allow for the exclusion of these groups, many feel that the *ex post* results from voucher auctions are likely to be more politically acceptable than those of cash auctions.

We will therefore analyze voucher schemes in which auctions will take place where only vouchers may be bid.[44] The results of these auctions are not dependant on whether these vouchers are sold or given away freely.[45] The general example of voucher auction schemes calls for the distribution or sale of books of vouchers, with no nominal value. Auctions of state-owned enterprises will take place, with only vouchers accepted as payment. Prior to the auction, vouchers can be traded for money. After the auction, a secondary market for shares will develop.[46]

On the surface, the voucher and auction mechanisms of this scheme appear to create a vastly different proposal than the previous schemes such as the free distribution of shares. However, as we shall see, this method brings us to the same results as previous methods, differing only in the path taken and the cost of getting there.

Free distribution vs. voucher systems The privatization proposals discussed in this paper are actually different distribution mechanisms implying different methods and forms for distributing endowment initially. However, it is not the initial endowment which is of concern, but the competitive equilibrium that results.[47] While different initial endowments appear to imply different resulting competitive equilibria and different distributions of wealth across the populace, this is not always the case.

Many believe that the use of vouchers result in superior and different competitive equilibria than the free distribution of shares. While it is true that voucher systems will likely result in a different initial endowment of shares immediately after the auction takes place, it is not necessarily true that the resulting competitive equilibria will be any different than the one which results from the free distribution of shares. After the auction of shares for vouchers, a normal trading market for shares will be in place, which is simply an auction market denominated in cash. While voucher auctions are competitive markets, so too are equity markets.

To see this, assume a frictionless world with perfect information and no brokerage or transaction costs in either the voucher auction market or in the equity market that follows. As the auction allowed investors to adjust their portfolio holdings costlessly, at the end of the auction they will hold their optimal portfolio. Now consider the first day of trading. While it is true that before the opening of the equity market on the first day the portfolio holdings of a investor in the voucher scheme will be different than the holdings of the same investor who received a free distribution of shares, at the end of the day both will have the same holdings. This analogous result occurs because both may costlessly readjust their portfolio holdings in the equity market during the day. The only difference is that under the voucher scheme the investor is initially able to adjust his portfolio in the voucher auction market, while under the other scenario, the readjustment takes place in the equity market. In either case, both investors end up with the same portfolio holdings (subject to some constraints on the form of the auction described below). The only difference is how the ultimate endowments are achieved.

Of course, in the real world, transaction costs are a significant issue. However, since both markets can get investors to the same result, the only relevant question is which can achieve the result at the lowest cost to society. While both schemes require the development of equity markets, the voucher scheme also requires the creation of an entirely new additional market, the voucher auction bidding market, which is a sunk cost and is worthless as soon as the auction process ends. Even if both systems had no brokerage costs, there is an expensive additional fixed cost under voucher schemes. The variable transaction costs to the investor under a voucher scheme will have to be significantly less than under a free distribution scheme for the voucher scheme to be optimal.[48]

Vouchers and auction design   The design of the auction greatly affects the results of the voucher auction.[49] Perhaps the most disruptive auction would be a one-time single auction in which all state-owned enterprises are auctioned simultaneously. In such a system, the relative prices in vouchers are not relevant for pricing securities in currency. Instead of imparting information as to the relative value of the underlying good, the voucher prices merely impart the relative expectations of what others will bid.[50] The information useful in such an auction is how many vouchers are other investors expected to bid which requires an investment in information to determine how much to bid. Therefore, the relative prices of shares in vouchers will provide little information as to the relative value of these shares in money. This information is necessary for proper capital allocation in the future. Any investment in information used to determine the value of shares in vouchers would be an investment in information on how much others are going to bid and not the relative value of the shares. Since such information will not impart useful information for society, it would be a deadweight loss.

Another problem with one-time auctions is that it is possible that an investor will consistently bid too low and thereby be closed out of the bidding process. For example, imagine everyone has 10 points and there are 10 firms. Individuals 1 to 9 bid eight points on firms 1 through 9, respectively, and two points on firms 2 through 10. Individual 10 bids one point per firm. In the end, individual 10 receives nothing. He has been effectively closed out of the bidding process. Therefore, demand and supply are not matched.[51]

An iterative process can be used to solve the mismatching of demand and supply, but this will still not solve the problem of the lack of relative pricing.[52] In an iterative process, the vouchers are returned and the process is begun anew. Therefore, even though the market may eventually clear and demand may equal the outstanding stock, relative prices do not emerge as there is no penalty for overbidding or future benefit from underbidding. This occurs because vouchers are not the numeraire for consumption. If the outstanding capital stock is subdivided into manageable units and the auction process is repeated with different voucher books so that again a certain voucher book is only valid for a certain auction, then the above results still hold because the above scenario has merely been repeated multiple times.

A necessary condition for vouchers to reveal relative prices is the same book of vouchers be valid for more than one auction in the series. These relative prices will impart some information, as the expected value of a voucher should be worth its proportion of the overall market value of the firms in the auction.[53] Unlike the previous example, over-bidding in early auctions will cause under-bidding later and under-bidding earlier will force over-bidding later, encouraging bidding as accurately as possible.[54] In general, however, voucher auctions will not lead to efficient price discovery.[55]

The emergence of financial intermediaries An interesting feature of the voucher systems is the possibility of endogenously created mutual funds. One can consider the endowment of vouchers as an initial endowment of one unit of capital. While we can also consider the endowment of shares received under the free distribution of shares scheme as a unit of capital, transactions costs of handling so many shares are mitigated if single voucher packets can be tendered as they are smaller in unit size and are more fungible. More importantly, as vouchers are used before the auctions, they allow for the *ex ante* investment decision as well as *ex post* monitoring which is present in both cases. (The financial intermediary will need to undertake similar monitoring functions on its ultimate endowment of shares, whether this endowment is the result of the deposit of shares under the free distribution scheme or the results of auctions under voucher schemes.)

Research on financial intermediation, such as Leland and Pyle (1977) and Boyd and Prescott (1986) discuss the creation of mutual funds under this scenario. Campbell and Kracaw (1980) extend this work to argue that these funds would also need to provide other services as well for their existence to occur.

Perhaps the most applicable work is by Diamond (1984), which points out that a financial intermediary will minimize the cost of monitoring information (or, in this case, gathering information or exercising control). Diversification within the intermediary helps lower these costs. He also notes the optimality of debt contracts within his model and that the intermediary will hold **illiquid** assets. He notes "The centralization of monitoring each loan by a single intermediary will mean that there are not active markets for these assets" (p. 410). Boycko, Shleifer and Vishny (1994) note that such intermediaries will be forced to monitor effectively as, due to illiquid markets, they cannot trade effectively.

The benefit to vouchers, therefore, is the ease with which financial intermediaries may be created to mitigate the cost of transacting and monitoring. While mutual funds may also be endogenously created if shares are freely distributed to citizens directly, the transaction costs of handling so many shares may inhibit their growth. Thus, while the creation of a voucher auction market creates additional fixed costs, it may reduce the cost of financial intermediation sufficiently to make voucher schemes less costly than other methods.[56] Boycko, Shleifer and Vishny (1994) note that the creation of such financial intermediaries were encouraged by the Czech and Russian privatization programs. They note that one benefit of such financial intermediaries is that they will accumulate sufficient shares to become a core investor, and thus help alleviate corporate governance concerns that accompany diverse ownership.[57]

However, the ease with which financial institutions can be created may also be a potential source of trouble for voucher schemes. The key to Leland and Pyle (1977), Campbell and Kracaw, and Boyd and Prescott (1986) is that the monitor must invest his own capital, and will suffer losses for non-compliance.[58] Likewise, the key to Diamond (1984), is the non-pecuniary penalties incurred by the monitor, such as jail or having his legs broken, if he fails to honor his obligations to his investors. Fund managers will over-promise if they suffer no losses for non-performance.

Diamond (1984) predicts that a single intermediary will prevail, owning the entire share of assets. If a single fund owns all the assets, the value of the fund will approximate the wealth of the society. The results implied by Diamond (1984) are extreme, but it demonstrates that when there are no penalties for non-performance, funds will compete for size, inducing fund managers to make promises that may only be fulfilled by achieving size alone. There is no disincentive to make such promises as there are no penalties for non-performance. Only a few funds, however, will achieve sufficient mass to fulfill their promises. The rest will default. Apart from the political problems that may result, we have replaced state-ownership with a most a handful of funds. The same problems with over-concentration still apply.

Implications Auctions with voucher systems is essentially a different mechanism to redistribute the endowment of shares. Equivalent results under voucher auctions occur in the cash-for-share auctions inherent in equity markets. The only differences will be due to brokerage and set-up costs.

One-time auctions do not allow price discovery or relative pricing. Citizens should receive a one-time allocation of vouchers which can be used in sequential offerings. This enables vouchers to have money-like qualities, and the resulting prices will be close to relative prices because over- and under-bidding will be penalized. Designing such schemes is theoretically difficult and operationally expensive. While voucher auctions may be intuitively appealing because the process seems competitive, the emerging results are not necessarily relative prices. Establishing relative prices still requires an investment in information and creating ingenious auction schemes that mimic the role of money. Short of this, voucher auctions become an arbitrary allocation scheme. The problems associated with a low level of information continue to apply to voucher auctions as they do to any other distribution mechanisms. Unless there is substantial investment in information, auctions do not solve the problem of valuation.[59]

Vouchers may lead to the endogenous creation of financial intermediaries due to lower transaction costs. On the other hand, enforcement mechanism are also required for financial intermediaries to function appropriately. No losses for non-performance encourages an inherent tendency to compete for size by over-promising, possible defaults by small funds, and concentration of ownership by a few large funds.

The experience with the voucher system in the former Czechoslovakia proves enlightening. As predicted, many mutual funds have been created. These mutual funds have not been required to invest their own capital, nor are they being monitored effectively by the government. Most appear like the Diamond model, offering guarantees of fixed returns as high as 1000% for the deposit of vouchers, and only a handful of funds attracted a large portion of the outstanding vouchers. Given the lack of infrastructure and regulations, many mutual funds do not fear legal redress for non-performance of their contracts. This structure is prone to investor disappointment.[60]

12.6   The market for control: one final concern

In developed markets, shares of a firm are the instrument through which a variety of investment, ownership and control issues are determined. Shares give the shareholder specific rights and claims in the financial world that are unique and are tied together as a bundle in the typical common share. A typical common share gives the holder the following:

a)   the ownership right to the underlying physical and intangible assets of the firm;

b)   a residual claim on the future earnings that result from the use of these assets; and

c)   the right to control the underlying physical and intangible assets.

Although obvious, these items are important in the study of privatization methods, as they each indicate different areas of concern. Most, if not all, privatization methods incorporate the use of shares in their proposals. However, many of the concerns that privatization proposals wish to address deal with only a subset of the three areas that a typical share encapsulates. For example, the primary goal of privatization is the increase in societal output. Therefore, it is the **control** feature of the share with which most privatization plans are concerned, as it is hoped that changing the control of the assets will result in a change in the use of the assets in such a way that an increase in the quantity and quality of goods will be realized. The other features of a share are there to provide the proper incentives for the use of such control, although in actuality these incentives may not result in the desired outcome.

The market for corporate control may also be affected by the voting structure of securities.[61] Grossman and Hart (1988) note the free rider problem inherent with an atomized shareholder base. If shares are widely held such that the holdings of any individual agent are small, individual shareholders will not have the proper incentives to exercise their control and remove inefficient incumbent management. Within their model, the authors show that the allocation of ownership and control across securities helps determine the cost and success of removing incumbent management.

Their model is highly dependant on the distribution of private benefits of management across various management teams. Within their model, allocation of control is unimportant if private benefits to both parties are small, and so separate securities for ownership and control may exist, or they may be contained in the same security with one vote per share. If both parties value control because both parties will receive private benefits, then one vote per share is not optimal as there will be differing markets for ownership and control. Finally, if one party has private benefits, the optimal mix of ownership and control are different, depending on who receives the private benefits.

It is in the development of the capital market structure that these issues are of most concern. Trading of shares is desired as it will impart information to the market which will increase efficiency by improving the allocation of resources from one area to another. The goal of privatization is not the creation of a stock market but the increase in efficiency and output. Thus, the creation of a stock market is a means to a desired outcome, and not an end in of itself. Note, however, that the price of a share and the volume of trading will be a function of the aspects of the share listed above. There will be a market for control, as well as a market for the residual claim on the earnings, as well as a market for the underlying value of the assets. Unfortunately, there will only be one instrument, the common share, for each of these markets. Therefore, certain desired outcomes, such as an effective change in the control of the firm, may not result if the market for trading shares is blocked.

For example, Grossman and Hart (1980) argue that the possibility of takeover bids will encourage existing management to realize higher values of the firm. If a takeover is impossible, however, due to the lack of trading, such an increase in the realization of the firm's value may not take place.

Bagwell and Judd (1989) consider control issues relating to payout and investment decisions. They note that transactions costs of rebalancing portfolios are an important factor in the optimal decision rule. If transaction costs are small, then majority rule is optimal. If, however, trading is blocked due to high transaction costs, then a different rule is optimal. Their model indicates both that blocked trading affects the market for control and that control is important for issues beyond takeover situations.

Conversely, if the market for control reaches equilibrium, it is possible that trading will cease and therefore although optimal control may have resulted, information as to the allocation of resources may not result as there may not be revealing prices. This is the case when there is a complete merger or takeover or buyout. At this point, the shares of the initial firm are no longer available on the market, and therefore the resource allocation information contained in the price of these shares will not be made available to the general market.

12.7 Conclusion

As is often the case, reality meshes with theory imperfectly. Individuals in Central Europe are certainly more varied in beliefs, information levels, endowments, wealth, risk parameters, and preferences than most theories allow. However, a reasonable case can be made for many of the simplifying assumptions made above.

Most likely, any of the privatization proposals will, over time, result in the development of capital markets. The key question, however, is how long and at what cost, and who will profit along the way. The search for the optimal privatization program is a search to find the most rapid, least costly method of fully transforming an economy to maximize its output efficiently, but at the same time to find a method that is equitable, fair, and politically acceptable.

It appears that, like it or not, there is no getting around the process of information gathering and price discovery when offering securities in such undeveloped capital markets as exist in Central Europe. To rely on the market system to invest on its own in such information gathering is unrealistic and wasteful of societal assets. First, the cost of acquiring information makes such investment unlikely in a competitive market. Second, to the extent that this process is undertaken by more than one firm, it is an expensive waste of societal resources. Basic information on a company, such as assets, revenues, etc., is and should be a public good. As it is a public good, such tasks should be undertaken by the government on behalf of the entire citizenry.

In addition, to the extent investors are risk averse, they will value assets at lower than their expected value. To the extent that investors are very unsure about the quality of their information, all assets in the economy will be valued at lower than their worth on an expected value basis. At an extreme case, the relative values that arise may be more of an indication of the relative certainty of information provided than an accurate assessment of the relative productive capacity of these assets. As a result, efficient allocation of capital and resources across assets might not occur.

To avoid such problems, the government should invest in the costs of an IPO process for each large firm in order to establish some benchmark from which investors, acting competitively, can use as a starting point for their own analyses. Information accumulation will take time and money, but having a credible, public starting point will both reduce price uncertainty and prevent a redundant waste of resources.

As a result, vouchers with no nominal value do not seem to provide much additional information to a privatization process, but do significantly increase the cost and difficulty. Therefore, such a process does not seem optimal. Likewise, the creation of a limited number of mutual funds is not a good idea as it is difficult to see why trading will occur and it subverts the market's natural tendency to create such funds. In fact, it may prevent the optimal grouping of assets. Given the implicit assumption inherent in the privatization process that the market can allocate resources better than the government, it does not seem optimal for the government to attempt to replicate the market's actions. Unfortunately, solely relying on the free distribution of the physical securities may not be much better due to the high transaction costs involved. In addition, it does not provide for the opportunity for citizens to opt to purchase small companies in their entirety instead of purchasing shares in large corporations. As Winton (1993) and others have shown that at times such a structure might be optimal, it seems optimal to insure that this possibility exists.

It seems obvious, therefore, that different privatization methods should be used for different companies with different needs. Most agree that the smaller sized companies be given or sold to individuals or small groups as rapidly as possible. The trick is what to do with the larger concerns. As we have seen, there is an inherent tension between too much concentration and too little. Free distribution of shares will inhibit price discovery due to transaction considerations and will have control problems. Oddly enough, the same problems exist for too much concentration; control problems also result from trying to manage a company that is one-fifth the entire economy and simply is too big.

The solution seems to be in the appropriate bundling of securities. The package should be valued highly enough that it will overcome transaction cost problems, yet small enough to allow for effective control. These packages should be sufficiently specialized that it makes economic and managerial sense for the pieces to be together. Intelligent bundling of companies to achieve vertical integration or economies of scale will also allow for managerial economies, thereby spreading a scarce human resource in those markets more efficiently and will *create* value. The result is that fewer shares will be distributed with greater per unit share value, enabling trading to occur. At the same time, these companies will be sufficiently small that they may be unbundled later, by external forces if necessary. Great care needs to be taken in creating the market structure to avoid setting up industry monopolies to ensure competition. However, it seems likely that such a bundling can occur without necessarily creating undesirable monopolies so that optimal trading structures, corporate governance and economic efficiency will result. While these efforts will take time and energy, the results will surely be worth it.

Notes

Background research was prepared in part for the Ministry of Finance of the Polish Government during the summer of 1990 to evaluate the privatization proposals for the Polish economic reform program. The project was supported by the International Finance Corporation. N. Bulent Gultekin served as the Chief Advisor to the Ministry of Privatization by a grant from U.S.A.I.D. during 1990-91. Michael Goldstein served as Research Director for this project during the summer of 1990. Additional research help was provided by Sondra Baron, Ian Murray and Elizabeth Palmer. This paper was partially funded by Weiss Center for International Research and appeared in its working paper series. Goldstein also gratefully acknowledges generous financial support for this paper from the Geewax-Terker Foundation and the Rodney L. White Center for Financial Research at the Wharton School. An earlier version of the paper was presented at the 1991 AFFI Conference in Belgium. We would like to acknowledge extensive discussions on the matter of privatization and privatization processes with Gavin Wilson of the International Finance Corporation during Summer 1990 in Washington and Warsaw. We are also particularly indebted to Anthony Santomero for his support. In addition, we would like to thank Franklin Allen, Nancy Davis, Hidemi Fujiwara, Michel Habib, Bruce Kogut, Christopher Leach, Roger Leeds, Ananth Madhavan, James Mahoney, Morris Mendelson, Greg Van Ingwen, Clas Wihlborg and Andrew Winton. All remaining errors are, of course, ours.

1. For example, Sachs et. al. (1990) propose creating five closed-end mutual funds. See Frydman and Rapaczynski (1990) or Nellis (1990) for voucher and direct distribution systems. LBO-style debt financing can be found in Jedrzejczak (1990) or see Gates (1990) for ESOP financing. Mendelson (1991, 1992) suggests a variety of methods including using pension funds and the banking system.

2. Luders (1990) contains detailed description of the Chilean privatization experience, along with an analysis of the consequences of privatization and the lessons learned. Hinds (1990) considers various problems in privatizing Central European economies and recommends that a mixed strategy of a variety of privatization processes be pursued. Vuylsteke (1990) also notes the various procedural changes needed for privatization in Central Europe and recommends a multi-faceted strategy.

3. Sappington and Stiglitz (1987) note that the costs of government intervention in firm's decisions is affected by privatization. While this should be true for all countries, emerging economies have special concerns. Vickers and Yarrow (1991) note that results from developed countries may not hold for developing or emerging countries. In addition, many have debated the appropriate speed that this transition should take place. Dewatripont and Roland (1992a,b) and Roland (1993) suggests gradualism due to political considerations and to prevent government reversal. Wyplosz (1993) argues that governments will "avoid actions that generate strong minority objections" in following privatization reforms. Aghion (1993) argues that large unemployment may result from rapid privatization, due to the speed of new job creation. He feels that "a complete reliance on privatisation and the operation of market forces may be an untenable restructuring strategy." On the other hand, Murphy, Shleifer and Vishny (1992) note that partial reform does not always provide optimal results. Boycko, Shleifer and Vishny (1994) note that privatization methods are determined by political forces but that, properly structured, privatization may achieve desirable economic results as well.

4. See Lipton and Sachs (1990). Aghion (1993) notes that privatization has moved slowly due to administrative problems, costs and lack of managerial resources. Some note that the question is whether the market or the public sector has failed, such as Prager (1992). De Fraja (1993) has a theoretical model which indicates that, in good states of the world, the public firm is more efficient than the private one, due to consumers' welfare function entering the government's utility function. He notes that although it is Western opinion that " ... state-owned enterprises are less productively efficient than their private counterparts ... in the long run, the allocative efficiency disadvantages of private firms are more than compensated by their superiority in productive efficiency [over public firms]", his paper and others fail to find confirmation.

5. It is for this reason that this paper does not consider privatization schemes that require active monitoring by the banking sector. (Tellingly, none of the proposed privatization schemes for Poland relied on the banking sector for their success.)

6. As Bouin and Michalet (1991) note, such poor accounting data may increase the *ex ante* risk of ownership. Blanchard, Dornbusch, Krugman, Layward and Summers (1991) note that poor accounting data may also affect the use of mass scale public offers.

7. Aghion (1993) notes that efficiency may be overridden by initial wealth constraints in Eastern Europe. Calvo and Frenkel (1991) note privatization difficulties caused by underdeveloped credit markets.

8. As noted in Yeaple and Moskowitz (1995), some have argued that privatization will help develop capital markets, although academic literature has not yet determined this definitively for countries with existing capital markets.

9. One concern that arises due to the low level of information available to outsiders, including the government, is that managers, who currently have control of the assets, may misuse such control for their own profit. As a result, the government will need to protect against fraud. Indications of this situation may be shown by the recent rescinding of a sale organized by the managers of a large hotel chain due to the huge underpricing of the sale.

10. This lack of accurate information is the result of two factors. First, accounting standards and reporting systems over the past 45 years were not designed for a market system, leading to a lack of accurate market-oriented historical information on which to base investment decisions.

Even if this information were available, the prevalence of government subsidies, control and intervention limit the relevance of such data for imparting market information. Finally, the system, as it changes from a communist to market controlled economy, will be undergoing a change in fundamental values and prices as it adjusts to reach a new equilibrium. It is uncertain what future cash flows and interest rates be, especially in the near term. These factors combined yield a situation in which there is little information provided to the decision-makers in the marketplace, and the value and reliability of existing information is low.

11. For example, one estimate of the typical cost of privatizing one company in Poland came to approximately $500,000.

12. Managers, who might have more information overall, may not have useful information regarding the actual market value or potential for their firms as their external environment is changing rapidly and it is uncertain how they will adapt. In any case, due to concerns about fraud, insider trading, and political unrest, it will be likely that managers will be barred legally from acting upon their information. Even if they could do so, wealth and borrowing constraints may prevent them from being able to use their information in the marketplace.

13. Of course, some members of society may be able to accumulate information on a limited number of companies via a variety of means (outside of official channels). Most, however, will not be able to do so. Under classic asymmetric information theory, a knowledgeable few would be sufficient to achieve a number of societally beneficial results (such as accurate pricing); however, this requires that the individuals have easy access to large amounts of capital, which is or was not the case in the initial stages of privatization in post-communist countries.

14. Kay and Thompson (1986) and Vickers and Yarrow (1991) argue that efficiency is more affected by competition in the product markets than ownership.

15. The underpinnings of this assumption begin by assuming that private ownership of the factors of production results in more effective control of these assets. More effective control in turn implies more efficient use, which in turn increases the overall net production of society. If ownership of the factors of production can also be traded, then relative prices may be established which will allow for more efficient allocation of resources across assets, increasing the overall net production of

society yet again. These increases in production enable a society to increase consumption.

16. Some may argue that the change in control also occurs in the capital markets. This is only true to a limited extent. The capital markets do control the ownership of the assets. However, for most assets, the "control" that matters is not as much the ownership but the management of the assets. These changes occur more often in the labor market, where laborers and managers are hired and fired. Most of the time, changes in control of the factors of production occur due to the firing of the CEO or other managers and the hiring of others. It is rare that a direct change in ownership is required, and even when ownership does change, the end result is usually the changing of one manager for another. A takeover is not required to change control of the assets, just a change in the number and type managers and/or laborers. (This presumes, however, that the current owners are also interested in efficiently managing the assets -- a tenuous assumption under communism.)

17. Fama (1980) notes that separation of ownership and control may be efficient in large corporations.

18. A competitive allocation is an allocation a and a price system p such that:

Firms maximize profits, i.e., y_f is the optimal solution to:

$C_f(p) = \max p * y_f$ s.t. y_f is an element of Y_f
for firms $f = 1..N$

Households maximize utility, i.e., given initial shareholdings s_{hf} and $C_f(p)$ and endowments e_h, consumption x_h is the optimal solution to:

$\max u_h(x_h)$
s.t. $p^*x_h = p^*e_h + \text{sum } \{s_{hf}^*C_f(p) \text{ from } f = 1..N\}$
for households $h = 1.. M$

and markets clear, i.e., for goods $i = 1 .. L$,

sum over h $\{x_h^i\}$ <= sum over h $\{e_h^i\}$ + sum over f $\{y_f^i\}$

19. One implication of these theorems is that it is necessary to have a full price system such that markets clear. This requires that the markets be complete, so that all items may be priced. Therefore, capital markets are necessary to indicate the price, or value, of a factor of production.

20. Each of these methods call for the free distribution of assets by the government. Roland (1993) notes that the free distribution of assets may alleviate important political constraints. As noted in Boycko, Shleifer and Vishny (1994), while privatization in Western Europe and North America is usually for by sale, the methods proposed or tried in post-Communist countries all involve the free distribution of assets, although these methods are usually combined with sales of some assets. (Sales of companies were tried in Poland, but this method was eventually abandoned.)

21. An extensive set of summaries and evaluations of a wide variety of privatization schemes submitted to the Minister of Privatization of the Republic of Poland in 1990 may be found in Gultekin and Wilson (1990).

22. In such cases, the end result may be privately-held firms which are initially monitored by banks. While this may not be all bad (the German system, for example), two caveats are in order. First, if this was the desired result initially, there are more direct and efficient methods than a failed mass privatization to achieve it. Second, this result will only be beneficial if the banks themselves are sophisticated monitors. While that is true in Germany, it is less true in previously centrally planned economies, as the "banks" did not work, act or lend money in a privately competitive system, but instead were directed from above.

23. We should note a number of corner solutions to start which relate to intertemporal consumption. First, if the communist regimes were completely successful in their experiment in that all individuals have the same wealth, information and utility functions, then we get that no trading will occur as everyone will value everything equally, as noted in Grossman and Stiglitz (1980). If, however, they have different intertemporal demands for consumption, they will trade with each other to meet their intertemporal demands, as per Hirshleifer (1970) or Barro (1974). But what will they trade intertemporally? If they are in the CAPM world of Sharpe (1963, 1964), they will hold the market portfolio, which was their initial endowment. Therefore, there once again will not be any trading across securities but trading of the entire

314 M.A. Goldstein and N.B. Gultekin

market portfolio across individuals depending on their intertemporal marginal rates of substitution of consumption. Another area to note is the limitations on foreign ownership that many countries have imposed as part of their privatization plan. These limitations follow naturally from the above theory in that foreigners are likely to have more wealth than the indigenous population. Barring any legal constraints, it is likely that there would be a massive intertemporal transfer of wealth and consumption from the local population to the foreign population, resulting in foreign ownership of the majority of assets in the country. While there are many potential benefits of such a structure (due to more effective management techniques, industry expertise, information acquisition abilities, and optimal intertemporal transfer opportunities), the political cost of such a transfer is deemed to outweigh such benefits.

24. For example, at the beginning of the privatization process in 1990, Poland had 38 million citizens. Using annualized earnings for the first quarter of 1990 and an estimated price/earnings ratio of 4, collective market value of the 484 largest firms is $24.6 billion at a translation rate of 9,500 zloty/$. Assuming that every Pole gets one share of every firm, we get an average value per share of only $1.34 per share. It is important to note that this number is likely to be artificially high as it is based upon estimated earnings which are to a large degree fictitious because of the hyper-inflation toward the end of 1989. See Gultekin and Wilson (1990) for further estimates. The transactions costs of trading a single share would be higher than that, given the cost structure in the U.S., which is more advanced and should have some scale economies.

25. Another danger is volatility and market thinness. Pagano (1989) also warns of market breakdown due to the mixture of high volatility and high transaction costs. He notes "thinness and the related price volatility may become joint self-perpetuating features of an equity market, irrespective of the volatility of asset fundamentals."

26. We hasten to point out that such an equilibrium, although perhaps not desirable, will be pareto optimal once achieved. As Varian (1984) points out in illustrating the First Welfare Theorem in the Edgeworth Box, if there is $100 to be distributed, one solution is to give me all of it and you none of it. While this result may be pareto optimal (in that we cannot make one person better off without making the other worse off), you may not like it very much.

27. In fact, as Grossman and Stiglitz (1980) point out, the very existence of brokerage costs will prevent trade if traders have the same endowments and beliefs since they would end up with their original endowments in a competitive equilibrium but will still incur trading costs if they trade. What if beliefs are different? Grossman and Stiglitz (1980) note that: "... when initial endowments are the same and peoples' beliefs differ slightly, then the competitive equilibrium allocation that an individual gets will be only slightly different from his initial endowment. Hence, there will only be a slight benefit to entering the competitive market. This could, for sufficiently high operating costs, be outweighed by the cost of entering the market." (p.402)

28. Furthermore, if it were optimal to leave initial information production up to the market, then we would see more of it in developed capital markets. Instead, even in developed markets, we see new firms go through an expensive IPO process to provide information to potential investors at the expense of the firm as a whole. Surely if it were cheaper and better to leave such information accumulation up to the market firms would do so, as they would achieve a competitive advantage. Instead, firms produce information once for all investors to see, implying it is cheaper for the firm to do it once than for each investor to undertake these costs on their own. As the government is the current owner of the firm in post-communist countries, the analogy still applies.

29. This presumes, of course, that individuals did not sell their shares *en masse* to those few capital rich individuals combing the country-side as described earlier. If those capital rich few accumulated enough shares, many of these problems would vanish, although a number of other problems (such as political backlash) may occur. This result is unlikely, however. Due to initial limitations on the wealth of individual citizens and the large dispersion of the populace, it would be very costly and difficult to accumulate enough shares this way to overcome the problems stated above. It is also not obvious that these capital rich few are the best owner/managers society has to offer. Again, if the desired result was the concentration of shares in the hands of a few, this method of privatization is not the best or most efficient way to go about it.

30. In fact, the problem with public ownership as noted in Alchain and Demsetz (1972) -- that each citizen is an owner of a public firm and thus does not feel much individual responsibility -- would remain the

same if each citizen receives one share of every firm. Nothing in this case would have changed.

31. Not all aspects of the potential for changes in control are good, however. Franks and Mayer (1990) note that with the possibility of takeovers, employees may reduce their firm-specific human capital investment and managers may shy away from long-term investment.

32. Poland's plan is most similar to this form. Ten mutual funds will be given shares of firms by the government, with one fund receiving 33% of the shares of a firm, and the other nine receiving 3% each. (Only 60% of the firm will be distributed, leaving the government as the largest holder of shares.)

33. The description here is only a general outline of the intent of the proposal. More detailed information relating to the operational aspects of this plan may be found in Sachs et. al. (1990) as appraised in Gultekin and Wilson (1990). Operational problems with this scheme as in all others are ignored here. For example, finding and appointing board members to a very large number of companies is non-trivial, assuming sufficient skills exist.

34. There may be a very short period of trading initially as the funds restructure their portfolios. Grossman and Stiglitz (1980) and Grossman and Hart (1980, 1988) provide some indication that this result will occur. One could, for example, assume that the cost of obtaining information in the Grossman and Stiglitz (1980) model is the cost of gaining control. Due to the problems noted earlier regarding the lack of market-oriented accounting standards or financial reporting mechanisms, etc., it may be impossible for outsiders to acquire information effectively. Insiders, however, may have access to information due to the very nature that makes one an insider. The only way to become an insider in this case is to gain control. These trades would be undertaken without information as no fund would find it advantageous to complete extensive research on a company prior to obtaining control. The high information costs involved in such research would not necessarily be offset by potential gains since the cost of attaining such information is fixed regardless of the number of shares owned. In addition, the sheer magnitude of the number of firms to be analyzed would likely inhibit such research until a fund has a majority share. Furthermore, the cost of information acquisition in an economy where there is no tradition of external reporting is more costly than many people realize. More important, this cost is invariant,

whether the acquisition of information is done by merchant bankers or mutual funds. In addition, the worldwide supply of individuals or firms capable of completing such research is sufficiently small that the task could not be completed without the other funds knowing which funds have evaluated which enterprises. A fund will not wish to trade with a fund that has superior information; therefore, the potential gains of getting such information will not be realized. As each fund is rational and assumes all other funds are also rational, no fund will expend significant resources on analyses which require expensive information gathering. Therefore, initial trading prices will not reflect information, but merely preferences for a redistribution of endowments.

35. In fact, such an event is expected in Poland. As noted in Boycko, Shleifer and Vishney (1994), " ... funds will then be allowed to trade shares, but mostly they will be expected to oversee the restructuring of firms and to attract foreign investment."

36. This result occurs because the expected value of the returns achieved by an uninformed investor when trading with an informed investor is negative. To see this, note that the informed investor knows how much the firm is worth and will not overpay when buying or underprice when selling so his expected value of trading will always be positive. The expected values of returns on trading between uninformed investors is zero, since neither party has better information so neither party will do better on average. Since the uninformed investor has a positive probability of trading with an informed investor on any given trade (since he does not know the identity of the counterparty to the trade), the expected value of trading for the uninformed investor is negative. The uninformed investor, on average, loses when trading in a market with informed investors, and so will not trade with them, unless there are the presence of liquidity traders who will trade in sufficient quantity to subsidize the losses of the uninformed investors. Since there will be no liquidity traders, there will be no trading, and, as a result, information will not be reflected in the prices. The lack of trading occurs because of the lack of liquidity traders present to compensate the uninformed investor for trading in a market with asymmetric information. Liquidity traders trade not for informational reasons, but for exogenous ones, such as intertemporal switching from investment to consumption, due to unexpected sudden needs for cash (such as medical emergencies, car troubles, etc.). Since these liquidity traders no longer want to hold the securities, they will trade regardless of price.

As a result, the expected value for an uninformed trader of trading with a liquidity trader is positive. Liquidity traders, therefore, subsidize the uninformed traders for trading in a market which also includes informed traders. Without liquidity traders, no trading will exist.

37. Even if we relax the lack of liquidity traders somewhat, we do not improve the situation significantly. For example, assume that a small proportion of the shares of the underlying securities are distributed directly to the populace, for example, to the workers of each firm. In this case, the workers may act as liquidity traders, should they choose to trade their shares (which may be unlikely due to control considerations and high brokerage costs). However, Grossman and Stiglitz (1980) show that the percentage of trades undertaken by liquidity traders directly affects the level of prices, because it induces trading by the uninformed traders. If there are very few trades by liquidity traders, it becomes increasingly likely that an uninformed trader will be trading with an informed trader, and so the uninformed trader will be less likely to trade. Uninformed traders will also require substantial inducements to trade in such an environment, which will cause large spreads to occur, as shown in Glosten and Milgrom (1985). Grossman and Stiglitz (1980) also show that the level of trading and the information content of prices depends on the number of liquidity traders. Thus there will be very few liquidity traders and extremely thin trading, which could cause market breakdown, as noted in Pagano (1989).

38. While the entire mutual fund could be taken over, sheer size would prohibit such a massive undertaking without governmental assistance, which is exactly the opposite of what privatization is attempting to achieve.

39. In fact, as there is always the possibility to mimic the groupings that result in this scheme if free distribution is used, a degree of freedom is lost and society is surely net worse off, as under the free distribution scheme it could always mimic any grouping occurring in this instance.

40. Boycko, Shleifer and Vishny (1994) note that there is a danger that such funds, instead of overseeing and monitoring managers, could instead become "lobbyists for state credits and subsidies" for the firms.

41. Boycko, Shleifer and Vishny (1994) note that this method has been used by a number of countries, such as the former Czechoslovakia, Mongolia, Lithuania and Russia.

42. Aghion (1993), Bolton and Roland (1992) and Van Wijnbergen (1992) have called for non-cash auctions.

43. Likewise, voucher schemes do not require auctions. For example, distributing vouchers which can only be tendered one-for-one for specific shares is identical to simply distributing the shares themselves with one additional step in the process. If vouchers with a nominal value are distributed which may be tendered for a variety of shares which will be offered without an auction process, the government is actually attempting a typical initial public offering (IPO) process. Such IPO processes may accept either both cash and vouchers or just vouchers alone. In either case, the government will need to price the shares prior to the IPO and over- and under-subscriptions may result from under- or over-pricing. For this reason, distribution methods using auctions have been suggested in order to avoid the necessity of developing a mechanism to determine share allocation.

44. There are a variety of permutations of voucher schemes. One option is to give the vouchers nominal value and both cash and vouchers to be used to purchase shares during the auctions. If the vouchers are sold to the public for their exact face value, it is difficult to see why vouchers would be purchased. Cash can be used to purchase many goods, while vouchers can only be used for privatization auctions. Since cash can also be used for privatization auctions and the price of a share in cash is the same as it is in vouchers, cash would dominate vouchers and no one would hold vouchers. As a result, proposals with vouchers with a nominal value that are to be used in auctions along with cash often suggest that the vouchers are to be sold for less than the face value or even given away freely. Such vouchers include the "privatization bonds" in Poland or convertible bonds which may be exchanged for shares in other countries. However, the sale of these vouchers at a discount create interesting arbitrage opportunities, the outcome of which depend on the ability to trade the vouchers on secondary markets prior to the auction.

45. Before beginning, it is important to note that any nominal value on the voucher is irrelevant as it merely determines the number of "points" the voucher is worth. Unlike money, vouchers have no intrinsic value and cannot be converted into consumption. Therefore, the price rationing system is not functioning as it would be in typical financial markets. In financial markets, the price of the share and the return on the share are in the same units, i.e., money or a direct substitute. However, in a

voucher bidding process, the cost of the share is a unitless voucher, while the return is in money. Vouchers, since they cannot be converted into consumption with certainty, have an indeterminate value. Their value is dependant in many ways on the eventual prices of the securities in terms of vouchers, which is unknown prior to the auctions.

46. Such a scheme is presented in Frydman and Rapaczynski (1990). The basic premise of this proposal is that ownership of industry will be transferred to the masses of the population, but at the same time, control of industry will be vested in highly efficient institutions (investment funds) that will bring modern knowledge, skills and technology to the industry. This supporters of this plan have assumed that the individual investor will not make their own decision regarding the use of vouchers, but instead will delegate that decision to large, competitive mutual funds, which will be managed initially by foreign banks and investment houses. This plan assumes that the funds themselves should have different general strategies in terms of risk profile or industry weightings. They will charge management fees, which will be determined by the level of competition among the funds. Fund performance will be monitored by the investors' movement assets among the funds. The funds should be sufficiently large so that there is incentive for them to do research and perform well; also, they will have an incentive to acquire large blocks of shares, in order to exercise control over management and implement appropriate changes in the enterprise. An inherent assumption in this plan is that the market will monitor the funds, and the funds will monitor the privatized enterprises. The funds could develop similar to the German system in which the banking sector plays an important role in the monitoring of the productive sector.

47. Boycko, Shleifer and Vishny (1994) argue that initial distributions, or at least the method of initial distributions matter, as providing the populace choices provides more interest (and thus political support *ex ante*) than "a simple assignment to people of pieces of paper that are allegedly claims to assets."

48. The high fixed costs included in the voucher system -- including the cost of designing such a system, educating the populace, creating the proper infrastructure for the bidding process, etc. -- could make it likely that the total societal costs will be greater under a voucher scheme. In addition, society members unused to capital markets will have to learn one system only to discard it and learn another.

49. See Boycko, Shleifer and Vishny (1994) for a discussion of voucher design, including whether vouchers should be denominated in points vs. currency, whether vouchers should be tradeable or not, etc. They also discuss the benefits of voucher auctions and voucher auction design in political and economic terms.

50. For example, many business school MBA programs in the United States have installed elaborate auction systems for students to select courses or interview slots. Their admissions offices assure us that these students are talented and highly educated. Therefore, these students should act as good proxies for the actions of others in what essentially is a voucher scheme. Each student is endowed with the same number of points, and the interview slots surely have value, albeit an uncertain one (especially in a declining economy), as they are a necessary but not sufficient condition for an eventual job. It almost always turns out that, out of 100 points, certain courses or interview slots tend to cost approximately 96 points, with the remainder going for one point or less. According to participants, they bid this number of points because they expected that others would as well and they knew that if they bet less, they definitely would not receive the course or interview. They also noted that over the years, the number of points bid converged, as they had access to the cost in points of last year's winning bid. Finally, they noted that it was certainly not true that those jobs were 96 times more valuable than the other jobs. (This was even more true for the courses.) Instead, it was simply that they felt that the cost in points for certain jobs would be around 96 and for others around one or two and so they bid accordingly. In other words, they bid points not on the relative value of the interviews themselves, but on what they believed others would be bidding. Schools which prevent disclosure of previous results of auctions show very high variability in the price in points for the same course with the same professor from one semester to the next, indicating such structures do not lead to price discovery.

51. In general, voucher systems encourage specialization, since, as shown above, those who concentrate their bidding will be more likely to receive the shares, or, in fact, any shares at all. This will increase investors idiosyncratic risk. On the other hand, voucher schemes may be appropriate for privatization which include all state-owned assets, and not just the largest of the state-owned enterprises, as some individuals may use their vouchers to purchase a small store or enterprise in its entirety. This action may be privately optimal for the

individual involved if he/she receives some additional benefit, as in Grossman and Hart (1980), as it is, in effect, a takeover of the small enterprise. Winton (1993) indicates that for certain firms large investor claims will provide optimal monitoring and control, resulting in optimal managerial effort. In fact, Winton (1993) shows that under certain conditions, unlimited liability ownership forms, such as a sole proprietorship or a partnership, are more optimal than limited liability forms, such as a corporate form with limited liability. While one benefit of this method of privatization is that it will allow optimal ownership of small businesses, and will allow governments to structure such ownership in an optimal manner, other methods of privatization do this as well. In particular, privatization schemes which use vouchers with a fixed nominal value would also work, as well as schemes which incorporate ESOPs or LBOs. As noted by Vuylsteke (1990) and Hinds (1990), a mixed strategy calls for separate privatization forms for large and small companies are optimal as they would also achieve this result. The auction process itself is not a necessary component of deriving the benefit noted in Winton (1993).

52. Versions of iterative processes were used in Czechoslovakia and Russia. In Czechoslovakia, fixed-price auctions were held in which there were multiple rounds, with winning bidders receiving shares (with the price being reduced in the next round for the remaining shares) in undersubscribed issues, *pro-rata* distributions in slightly over-subscribed issues, and with no shares distributed and the fixed price increased in the next round for grossly oversubscribed issues. In Russia, privatization was voluntary, with auctions only occurring when firms agreed to them.

53. For example, if there are 100 vouchers in existence and the total value of the firms to be auctioned in this sequential auction is $500, then the expected value of each voucher is worth $5.

54. The final auction in a sequential auction will resemble a one-time auction. Overbidding will no longer be penalized and underbidding will not reap future benefits.

55. Hillion and Young (1995), in an empirical study of the Czechoslovak auction, find that updating rules used in that auction injected noise and inhibited efficient price discovery.

56. A problem with arguments for the development of financial intermediaries is that non-tendering shareholders will also benefit from any steps that the financial intermediary might take to improve the

earning potential of the firm, as noted in Grossman and Hart (1980). As the investors already own shares in the firm at no cost to themselves, they can "mimic" the holdings of the financial intermediary in the sense of Campbell and Kracaw (1980) merely by following a buy-and-hold strategy. Therefore, as noted by Grossman and Hart (1980) or Campbell and Kracaw (1980), it is necessary that financial intermediary owners receive some private benefit from owning the financial intermediary, either due to management contracts of the financial intermediary with the firm or due to other services the financial intermediary can provide. Otherwise, no one will tender their shares to a financial intermediary and will instead simply hold their portfolio, partially because brokerage costs prohibit them from selling their shares. However, the use of vouchers should allow the low cost development of financial intermediaries if one can assign them before the auction takes place.

57. Boycko, Shleifer and Vishney (1994) also note that governments can encourage outsiders to get large blocks so as to alleviate the governance problem, as was done in Czechoslovakia and Russia.

58. In the event that financial intermediaries are capitalized in hard currency, the monitor may purchase vouchers and bundle securities so as to avoid transaction costs problems that may arise and will allow investors that prefer immediate consumption to liquidate their holdings, as discussed previously in the section on the free distribution of shares. The same results apply.

59. An earlier version of this paper, presented in 1991, predicted that voucher auctions would not lead to efficient price discovery. In fact, this is what happenned in Russia. As noted in Boycko, Shleifer and Vishny (1994), "... large investors just brought in suitcases of vouchers, and tendered them to get whatever shares they could get in an auction. Evidently, even large investors had no idea what the companies were worth, and felt that shares were cheap enough not to bother with complicated bids."

60. See Goldstein (1998) for a discussion of the promises of mutual funds in the Czech Republic and Albania.

61. See Allen (1989) for an excellent survey.

References

Aghion, Philippe, 1993, Economic reform in Eastern Europe: Can theory help? European Economic Review, 37, pp. 525-532.

Alchain, Armen and Harold Demsetz, 1972, Production, information costs, and economic organization, American Economic Review, 62 (December), pp. 777-795.

Allen, Franklin, 1989, The Changing Nature of Debt and Equity: A Financial Perspective, Conference Series No. 33, Federal Reserve Bank of Boston.

Bagwell, Laurie Simon and Kenneth L. Judd, 1989, Transactions Costs and Corporate Control, Working Paper 67, Kellogg Graduate School of Management, Northwestern University.

Barro, Robert J., 1974, Are government bonds net wealth?, Journal of Political Economy, 82, 6, pp. 1095-1117.

Blanchard, Olivier, Rudiger Dornbusch, Paul Krugman, Richard Layward and Lawrence Summers, 1991, Reform in Eastern Europe (MIT Press, Cambridge, MA).

Bolton, P. and G. Roland, 1992, Privatization in Central and Eastern Europe, Economic Policy, 15, pp. 276-309.

Bouin, O. and A. Michalet, 1991, Rebalancing The Public and Private Sectors: Developing Country Experience, Development Center Studies, Organization for Economic Development and Cooperation, Paris.

Boycko, Maxim, Andrei Shleifer and Robert W. Vishny, 1994, Voucher privatization, Journal of Financial Economics, 35, pp. 249-266.

Boyd, John H. and Edward C. Prescott, 1986, Financial intermediary-coalitions, Journal of Economic Theory, 38, pp. 211-232.

Campbell, Tim S. and William A. Kracaw, 1980, Information production, market signalling, and the theory of financial intermediation, Journal of Finance, 35, 4, September, pp. 863-882.

Calvo, Guillermo A. and Jacob A. Frenkel, 1991, Credit markets, credibility, and economic transformation, Journal of Economic Perspectives, 5, 4, Fall, pp. 139-148.

De Fraja, Giovanni, 1993, Productive efficiency in public and private firms, Journal of Public Economics, 50, pp. 15-30.

Dewatripont, M. and G. Roland, 1992a, The virtues of gradualism and legitimacy in the transition to a market economy, Economic Journal, 102, March, pp. 291-300.

Dewatripont, M. and G. Roland, 1992b, Economic reforms and dynamic political constraints, Review of Economic Studies, 59, pp. 703-730.

Diamond, Douglas W., 1984, Financial intermediation and delegated monitoring, Review of Economic Studies, 51, pp. 393-414.

Fama, Eugene, 1980, Agency problems and the theory of the firm, Journal of Political Economy, 88, 2, pp. 288-307.

Franks, Julian and Colin Mayer, 1990, Capital markets and corporate control: a study of France, Germany and the UK, Economic Policy, 10, April, pp. 189-232.

Frydman, Roman and Andrzej Rapaczynski, 1990, Privatization in Poland: A New Proposal, Working paper, Ministry of Finance, Poland.

Gates, Jeffrey R., 1990, ESOPs and Privatization in Poland, Privatization proposal.

Glosten, Lawrence R. and Paul R. Milgrom, 1985, Bid, ask and transaction prices in a specialist market with heterogeneously informed traders, Journal of Financial Economics, 14, 1, March, pp. 71-100.

Goldstein, Michael A., 1998, Privatization success and failure: finance theory and regulation in the transitional economies of Albania and the Czech Republic, Managerial and Decision Economics, forthcoming.

Grossman, Sanford J. and Oliver D. Hart, 1980, Takeover bids, the free-rider problem, and the theory of the corporation, Bell Journal of Economics, 1, 1, Spring, pp. 42-64.

Grossman, Sanford J. and Oliver D. Hart, 1988, One share/one vote and the market for corporate control, Journal of Financial Economics, 20, pp. 175-202.

Grossman, Sanford J. and Joseph E. Stiglitz, 1980, On the impossibility of informationally efficient markets, The American Economic Review, 70 3, June, pp. 393-408.

Gultekin, N. Bulent and Gavin Wilson, 1990, The Polish Privatization Program: Background Information, working paper, August, Ministry of Privatization, Warsaw, Poland.

Hillion, Pierre and S. David Young, 1995, The Czechoslovak Privatization Auction: An Empirical Investigation, Social Science Working Paper, No. 921, California Institute of Technology, August.

Hinds, Manuel, 1990, Issues in the Introduction of Market Forces in Eastern European Socialist Economies, Working paper.

Hirshleifer, J., 1970, Investment, Interest, and Capital (Prentice-Hall, New York).

Jedrejczak, G., 1990, The Role of Leveraged Buyouts in Polish Privatization, working paper, February, Ministry of Finance, Warsaw, Poland.

Jensen, Michael and William Meckling, 1976, Theory of the firm: Managerial behavior, agency costs, and ownership structure, Journal of Financial Economics.

Kay, John and David Thompson, 1986, Privatization: A policy in search of a rationale, The Economic Journal, pp. 18-32.

Leland, Hayne E. and David H. Pyle, 1977, Informational asymmetries, financial structure, and financial intermediation, Journal of Finance, 32, 2, May, pp. 371-387.

Lipton, David and Jeffrey Sachs, 1990, Creating a market economy in Eastern Europe: The case of Poland, Brookings Papers on Economic Activity 1, pp. 75-147.

Luders, Rolf J., 1990, Privatization in Chile: Lessons from a Massive Divestiture Program in a Developing Country, Working Paper.

Mendelson, Morris, 1991, Privatizing Eastern Europe, Journal of International Securities Markets, Autumn.

Mendelson, Morris, 1992, Strategic considerations for privatizing Central Europe, Journal of International Securities Markets, Spring.

Murphy, Kevin M., Andrei Shleifer and Robert W. Vishny, 1992, The transitions to a market economy: Pitfalls of partial reform, The Quarterly Journal of Economics 107, August, pp. 887-906.

Nellis, J., 1990, The Czechoslovakian Voucher Scheme, Working Paper.

Prager, Jonas, 1992, Is privatization a panacea for LDCs? Market failure versus public sector failure, Journal of Developing Areas, 26, April, pp. 301-322.

Pagano, Marco, 1989, Endogenous market thinness and stock price volatility, Review of Economic Studies, 56, pp. 269-288.

Roland, Gerard, 1993, The political economy of restructuring and privatization in Eastern Europe, European Economic Review, 37, pp. 533-540.

Sachs, Jeffrey, et. al., 1990, Memos regarding privatization, Ministry of Finance, Poland.

Sappington, David and Joseph Stiglitz, 1987, Privatization, information and incentives, Journal of Policy Analysis and Management, 6, pp. 567-582.

Sharpe, W. F., 1963, A simplified model for portfolio analysis, Management Science, January, pp. 277-293.

Sharpe, W. F., 1964, Capital asset prices: A theory of market equilibrium under conditions of risk, Journal of Finance, September, pp. 425-442.

Van Wijnbergen, S., 1992, Economic Aspects of Enterprise Reform in Eastern Europe, Mimeo, World Bank.

Varian, Hal R., 1984, Macroeconomic Analysis, Second edition (W. W. Norton & Company).

Vickers, John and George Yarrow, 1991, Economic perspectives on privatization, Journal of Economic Perspectives, 5, 2, Spring, pp. 111-132.

Vuylsteke, Charles, 1990, Privatization and Ownership Changes in East and Central Europe, World Bank Group Conference Proceedings, June.

Winton, Andrew, 1993, Limitation of liability and the ownership structure of the firm, Journal of Finance, 48, 2, pp. 487-512.

Wyplosz, Charles, 1993, After the honeymoon: On the economics and the politics of economic transformation, European Economic Review, 37, pp. 379-386.

Yeaple, Stephen and Warren Moskowitz, 1995, The Literature on Privatization, Federal Reserve Bank of New York Research Paper 9514, June.

Financial Sector Reform and
Privatization in Transition Economies
J. Doukas, V. Murinde and C. Wihlborg (Editors)
© 1998 Elsevier Science Publishers B. V. All rights reserved

3 9

Chapter 13

REDUCING POLITICAL UNCERTAINTY
AND MORAL HAZARD IN EAST-WEST
FINANCIAL RELATIONS

P33 P34
P31

D82 6415

Gunnar Eliasson
The Royal Institute of Technology (KTH), 10044 Stockholm, Sweden

13.1   Introduction

Western business firms are subjected to significant political uncertainty
when engaged in investment in the formerly planned economies. Most of
this uncertainty is of such a character that there will be no spontaneous
creation of insurance coverage in the market. The unertainty, furthermore, is
so large that even *very* large firms would not dare to take them on if
investments involve substantial irreversible, or "sunk costs". Involvement
would, therefore, be restricted either to *very* short-term investments, or to
reversible investments with small or no commitments of human and
specialized capital. Economic growth in the formerly planned economies,
however, requires long-term commitments and technology transfer on the
part of investors. Hence, long-term investments and growth will not take
place unless these political uncertainties are eliminated. In the formerly
planned economies with (still) rudimentary legal protection of property
rights this uncertainty reduction cannot be engineered without some
domestic or foreign government involvement in the form of guarantees or
some other kind of coverage.

   It is in the interest of western industrial nations to see viable growth
economies emerging out of the formerly planned economies. There should,
hence, be a strong interest in instituting an "insurance" system that would
reduce the political uncertainty created by the absence of the political
stability and the institutions necessary for the dynamic functioning of a
market economy. This insurance system should furthermore be organized
such that incentives to develop these necessary institutions are strong.

Above all the insurance system should be capable of bridging the period of social instability that might otherwise abort the reindustrialization process of the formerly planned economies.

One difficult problem for the organization of such an insurance system is that reindustrialization will take a very long time. Another problem is the moral hazard problem both on the part of firms and of support receiving countries.

This paper sketches an insurance system that significantly reduces the moral hazard problems and places business investment decisions where the competence to take them resides; in the firms (even though it is based on large government equity contributions).

In what follows, we first discuss the distinction between political uncertainty and business risks, and then suggest an "insurance system" capable of reducing, or converting, political uncertainty into calculable risks. This insurance arrangement can be seen as a political business deal between a formerly planned economy and the rich western nations. The paper concludes with a discussion of how to control two political problems always involved in these kinds of arrangements: moral hazard and a final settlement of disputes between the insurance system and its client investors. The solution is to make the receiving formerly planned economy hostage of the system, i.e. making incentives dependent on good political behavior.

13.2   The nature of political uncertainty and business risks

Theoretically we should be talking about the elimination of political uncertainty - using Knight's (1921) terminology - to create a situation of subjectively computable business risks[1] that investors would dare take on. There are three elements to consider when organizing an insurance system that converts political uncertainty into manageable political risks:

(1)   the *nature of uncertainty* – the insurance principles
(2)   an *incentive system reducing the moral hazard* propensity of *receiving* Eastern nations
(3)   an *incentive system* boosting political support of *political uncertainty reduction*

The guiding principle of the proposal to be expounded below is that the insurance system created to reduce political uncertainty should not distort market incentives. In addition it should be designed to be effective for supporting long-term investment commitments. Since the formerly planned economies not only lack the institutions of the West that minimize political uncertainty, but also resources to invest, the uncertainty reduction should apply to indigenous as well as foreign direct investment.

The task thus assigned to this insurance system or insurance company becomes similar to Frank Knight's (1921) notion of the nature of the firm.[2] The firm, in Knight's (1921) way, can be seen as a specialist competent in transforming uncertainty into subjectively computable business risks. The East-West Insurance Corporation (EWIC), to be introduced here, will be assigned the task to make a business out of political uncertainty.

Rents from long-term investments are typically obtained only after some time. The insurance we are talking about is the probability of not being able to capture these rents because of government opportunistic behavior, and not to recover the original investment, because of uncertainty beyond those technical and commercial risks a normal business should be expected to take against its own equity. The time dimension is critical. The insurance coverage needs to be sustainable in time and up to large limits.

An important aspect of political uncertainty as described below is that it cannot be identified for each country by known or subjectively estimable distributions. The uncertainty depends both on the investor and on the national authorities. Hence, it is important that the insurance arrangements incorporate incentives to reduce moral hazard not only on the part of investors but also on the part of the national authorities, to keep the political opportunism low.

Investments in any economy are subject to the five sources of uncertainty listed in Table 13.1. The three first kinds of uncertainties originate in political sources and refer to uncertainty about rules. Their nature is such that risk averse actors would consider them very large. Even large firms would potentially risk total failure. Many of these uncertainties, furthermore, originate in such sources that no business firm would consider their assessment as part of their normal professional competence. Neither would this be the case for a regular insurance company, as we know them. Hence, any viable insurance arrangement would require very special competence and/or some kind of government guarantee. But badly designed, such a guarantee will induce serious moral hazard. In the short term the ability to influence and even bribe the authorities selectively would be such a special competence. In the long run the ability to influence the writing, interpretation and enforcement of law is what matters. Some private party might think itself capable of assessing the political uncertainty and taking it on as a "calculable" risk. Even if most investors would consider themselves capable in this respect we would then not be looking at an efficiently functioning economy. One reason is that the magnitudes involved usually require government intervention from outside the host country. The first two force majeure categories in Table 13.1 are obviously sources of huge potential losses.

Another reason why the existence of political uncertainty as described here is associated with inefficiently functioning investment incentives is that the uncertainty - especially the third kind in Table 13.1 - implies that the rule system in the host country is not applied in a predictable way. Most of the formerly planned economies exhibit more or less of this unpredictability, and the cases, reported in Eliasson (1997) illustrate how.

Investors in Western countries have to face as well the second group of uncertainties in Table 13.1. There are business risks in the conventional sense and there are risks of private opportunistic behavior. Legislation in the West is often designed to minimize opportunistic behavior on the part of agents, on the presumption that political uncertainties do not exist. Contract law, antitrust law and bankruptcy law are examples of such legislation.

The practical problem for the insurance system is to draw a clearly defined line between the risks that firms should take as part of their business and those where extraordinary political uncertainty beyond the competence and capacity of the firm to cover is present. If this extraordinary uncertainty can be removed many investment projects in the formerly planned economies will not look unfavorable compared to the corresponding investments in the West. This means drawing the line between political uncertainty and business risks in Table 13.1. To draw that line I will use the contract defining the proprietary rights to future profits (or the real assets), the equity contract.

The equity contract specifies the holder's right to influence the management of his or her investment, to access the rents accruing from the same investment and the right to trade in the contract (the share). In the western market economies these rights are well defined and fairly liberal. An important task of the investor or the management of the investing firm is to assess the business risks associated with achieving an expected rate of return from the invested assets and their management. The political uncertainties in Table 13.1, however, mix with the business risks. These sources of uncertainty (first and second order) influence the earnings capacity of the firm or affect directly the property rights making them ill defined. In other words, the possibilities to freely manage, access and to trade in the entitlement to future profits are uncertain (Eliasson 1993).

TABLE 13.1
Risk hierarchy

	Political uncertainty (uncertainty about rules)
(1)	Force Majeure — first order uncertainty — military etc.
(2)	Force Majeure — second order uncertainty — collapse of monetary system
(3)	Institutional Deficiencies-controllable by political authorities — third order uncertainty
	Business risks (uncertainty about behavior)
(4)	Monitoring and controlling opportunistic behavior on the part of business agents
(5)	Business risks

Source: Eliasson, Rybczynski and Wihlborg (1994).

While the assessment of business risks defines the competence of a firm's management, this is not so for political risks. The political uncertainties (1), (2) and (3) in Table 13.1 are outside the range of professional experience of business managers and tend to result in a prohibitive "risk premium" or discount factor in their investment decisions. This problem becomes especially acute, if the investment involves significant sunk costs. Even though some (large) firms may consider themselves capable of assessing political uncertainties the same way they do with business risks, this is something one would not even consider a desirable professional competence of business managers. Whatever the view on this matter, business managers cannot be as professional in converting political uncertainty into manageable political risks as they are in managing business risks. Hence, the investment decisions will have to be evaluated using high discount rates, resulting in less, and short-term investments.

The objective of the proposal to follow is to remove the assessment of such political uncertainty from the business investment problem, by either instituting a specialist political insurance system or other type of insurance system, where such risks are covered by a third party. Our perspective is that of western governments who want to see the formerly planned economies rapidly transformed into industrial economies. It is assumed that western governments are willing to cover those risks, if an incentive system that minimizes opportunistic behavior on the part of the receiving countries can be organized. Such political opportunistic behavior would include collusion between business interests in the East and political authorities there to harass the foreign investor, once the investments have been sunk, such that the investors eventually give up and sell out cheap. Another example of host country opportunistic behavior is a change in the tax rules, once significant foreign investments have been sunk to extract more tax income, and to block the repatriation of profits to the investing parent by imposing exchange controls, citing extraordinary macroeconomic problems.[3] Part of the design, of course, also has to be to prevent opportunistic collusion between the politicians of the receiving country and the foreign investor to swindle the East-West Insurance Corporation.

13.3   The East-West Insurance Corporation (EWIC)

The objective of the East-West insurance arrangement is to make (1) the host country politicians concerned with getting their market institutions in order, (2) the firms willing to invest and (3) the insurance company management concerned with the equity value of the insurance operation.

The EWIC could be created in the following way:

(1)   A group of western nations assess the extent of political uncertainties in the East, and where in the East they would be willing to underwrite such uncertainty on behalf of its potential business investors. They thus determine the equity stake in the "East-West Insurance Corporation" domiciled in a western country. These equity stakes are apportioned to the different host countries it is willing to support.

(2)   Each formerly planned economy is allotted an equity stake in the EWIC in proportion to the willingness of the western countries to support risktaking in the particular countries. It becomes a share owner responsible for the proper management of that stake such that it grows in value, as if it were invested by a 100 percent commercial investor, according to market principles. The equity stake is not available, tradable or mortgageable until the formerly planned economy has attracted a sufficient number of investors and reached a certain minimum level of development and/or per capita income. The equity is there to protect the potentially profitable investments of western

companies and not to finance any development programs. If misused the receiving country loses its stake. The equity is reduced if western companies investing in that country claim and receive compensation for losses occurred due to political uncertainties in terms of Table 13.1. The awarding of such compensation has to be entirely non-political according to a preset legal procedure, on which the receiving eastern country has no say. Thus, the politically uncertain countries hold the equity financed by western countries who retain control over the procedures for payment of insurance.

If properly managed the equity stake will grow in pace with the management of the assets of the EWIC and the success of the insurance business; that in turn depends on the political behavior of equity holders.

The charter of the EWIC would - to the extent possible - prespecify the three political uncertainties covered by insurance. In case a firm contemplating investment in a covered country is uncertain about coverage of the particular political risks it envisions, it can enter negotiations with the EWIC in order to determine whether coverage would be accepted or obtainable at an extra charge.

The principle for pricing of the insurance service would, however, be based on each host country declaring its level of political uncertainty under categories 1, 2 and 3 in Table 13.1 to attract foreign investment. If it underdeclares, its equity holding will decrease when insurance is paid out. For a reasonable commercially determined premium the foreign investor is covered by the EWIC equity for these risks.

Since the business firm is always facing uninsurable risks (market failure, uncertainty, as explained above), an investing firm would always be willing to pay something for insurance, either in the form of an agreed upon voluntary excess[4] or a charge. Hence, the EWIC, to the extent it develops a professional political risk assessment capacity, should also be able to earn an extra return on its equity and this return would go to the host countries holding equity. The receiving nations would thus be concerned about reducing the political uncertainty. If not, claims on the same equity would increase. This is the moral hazard control mentioned above.

The western supporting countries, by agreement, will get nothing directly. Their contributions, hence, are to be regarded as gifts, but these gifts are investments in future trading opportunities with the formerly planned economies that are politically and commercially well behaved by western standards. The EWIC can therefore be looked upon as a particularly effective form of western financial assistance to an industrially developing country.

13.4   The nature of the moral hazard problem and EWIC

As noted the purpose of the insurance arrangement is to make (1) the politicians in formerly planned economies concerned with getting their institutions in order, (2) the firms willing to invest and (3) the insurance company management concerned about increasing the equity of the insurance operation. There are two types of moral hazard problems to consider in this context. First of all, a viable transition from a planned to a market economy subjects the citizens of the formerly planned economy to social adjustment pressure that they may resist under a western type democracy   favoring the currently voting population. The short-term interests need, however, not be in the long-term public interest, i.e. in the interest of future generations.

The second type of moral hazard is more serious. Foreign investors and the insurance company can earn money in different ways. Many of these ways will, however, not contribute to long-term economic growth. The politicians of the receiving country may rather pocket some money than taking care of the future public interests of the country. Such corruption appears to have been common in the underdeveloped countries receiving foreign aid. Hence, the problem for the western countries is to prevent the forming of coalitions among foreign investors, insurers/donors and local politicians. Such coalitions are not beneficial for the long-run development of the economy. Such "bad" behavior on the part of political authorities also includes social concerns that are detrimental to long-run growth. One should not assume, in forming this arrangement, that the political regimes of the receiver country are informed and non-corrupt. If they are badly informed and corrupt it is not in the interest of the West to support them. Resources are then, for the time being, invested more efficiently elsewhere. Neither should one expect foreign investors to take responsibility for the long-run development of the receiving country. Hence, the monitoring of bad coalition forming will have to be the task of the insurance corporation. Efficient performance of the insurance corporations, however, requires well defined, simple and strict goals. The worst thing that can be done would be to make EWIC responsible for solving short-term social problems in the receiving country. Therefore, the management of EWIC must be responsible for its own equity growth and avoid underwriting risks for investments in the politically wrong markets. Countries with excessive welfare programs will most likely obtain less insurance coverage for investment. Thus the insurance corporation would de facto be vested with a political power that has been resisted by many developing nations for a long time.

The western offer must, therefore, be on a take it or leave it basis. Only countries willing to accommodate will receive support. Hence, by organizing competition among the formerly planned economies for good long-term behavior long-term growth in the region will be maximized. This amounts to making management of the insurance corporation responsible for its own long-term equity development and protected from political pressure, and restrict its operations, such that it only engages in insurance activity that promotes its long-term equity development.

13.5   A court of last resort

One important problem is how disputes between the EWIC and its client investors should be settled. Again, the appropriate legislation for conflict resolution could be made to reduce the moral hazard problem further. Whenever a dispute arises referring to political uncertainties, there should be a well defined procedure to run it through the local courts. But the risk taking foreign investors should always have the option to take it out of the local court and place it in front of an international court to judge according to a well defined foreign law and/or be treated in a non-discriminatory manner. The verdict so obtained determines the EWIC adjudication role.

Since the EWIC is domiciled in a western country and subject to western legal procedures, there is no way for the receiving country to politically misappropriate the "gift" until it has fulfilled its obligation after many years. The procedures would create a strong deterrent to arbitrary political rule changes in the receiving country. They would also provide a strong incentive to establish local conventions (and precedents) including the enactment of "enabling" laws (Wihlborg 1996, Eliasson 1997) that are compatible with western market principles in order to avoid the embarrassing attention that would reduce the inflow of foreign capital.[5]

It is important to note that the insurance arrangements discussed here mean that the inflow of capital is dependent on private, profit motivated decisions on the part of firms and banks, not on political decisions by governments. Those countries that move fast to establish orderly domestic institutions will reduce political uncertainty the most and both receive a proportionately larger volume of foreign investments and keep a larger part of the equity share in the EWIC.

The incentive scheme is very business like. The countries that manage their economy most successfully in the end receive the most in the form of equity value. The cost for this foreign aid to the donating country would be the same. The rules would be well defined and clear and involve a minimum of negotiations and bureaucratic procedure at the national levels. Incentives would be high on the part of the receiving country to do its best to organize a viable growth economy.

Notes

This paper was presented to the workshop on *Currency and Financial Sector Reforms in Eastern Europe* in Tallinn December 10-11, 1992. A revised version appeared as No. 388 (1993) in the Working Paper series of the Industrial Institute for Economic and Social Research (IUI), Stockholm.

1. Technically the political uncertainty makes investors apply such high-risk premia in their business assessments as to make the investment unprofitable. For some reason the distinction of Knight (1921) between *uncertainty* and *risk* has been removed from modern finance literature, with the peculiar consequence that technical and market risks are treated as calculable and predictable insurable phenomena, something Knight (1921) regarded as fundamentally and empirically wrong. With political discretion involved the need to bring back the original concept of uncertainty becomes clear.

2. As it can be interpreted. See Eliasson (1990), and LeRoy and Singell (1987).

3. It must be noted, however, that some mature industrial countries, like Sweden, also did this now and then during the postwar period through a large part of the 1980s.

4. The maximum amount the insured is willing to cover himself.

5. Eliasson, Rybczynski and Wihlborg (1994), Eliasson (1997) and Wihlborg (1996) discuss enabling law in more detail. *Enabling* law, as opposed to *mandatory* law, implies that parties to contracts and stakeholders in firms are able to develop details of contracted arrangements by mutual agreement. Such laws contribute to the development of economically efficient contractual arrangements and laws that allow business practices to develop over time in response to technological and institutional change. To deal with this in the formerly

planned economies, lacking a constitutionally guaranteed respect for certain basic principles of individual rights, also the problem of the enforcement of enabling law has to be solved. Eliasson (1997) and Wihlborg (1996) here discuss a second kind of enabling law as a set of constitutionally dominant legal principles defined in terms of not desired or desired outcomes, that overrule all existing or new laws and regulations. Unconditional principles written into the constitution and enforced by a politically independent Supreme Court guarantee property rights in terms of management rights, access to profits and tradability (see Table 1 in Eliasson 1997).

References

Day, Richard H., Gunnar Eliasson and Clas Wihlborg (eds.), 1993. The Markets for Innovation, Ownership and Control (North Holland, Amsterdam).

Eliasson, Gunnar, 1990, The firm as a competent team; Journal of Economic Behavior and Organization, 13, 3, pp. 275-298.

Eliasson, Gunnar, 1993, A Note: On privatization, contract technology and economic growth, in: R. Day, G. Eliasson and C. Wihlborg, eds., The Markets for Innovation, Ownership and Control (North-Holland, Amsterdam).

Eliasson, Gunnar, 1997, Investment incentives in the formerly planned economies, in: T. Haavisto, ed., The Transition to a Market Economy; Transformation and Reforms in the Baltic Countries (Edward Elgar, Cheltenham).

Eliasson, Gunnar, Tad Rybczynski and Clas Wihlborg, 1994, The Necessary Institutional Framework to Transform Formerly Planned Economies – with special emphasis on the institutions needed to stimulate foreign investment in the formerly planned economies (Industriens Utredningsinstitut (IUI), Stockholm).

Knight, Frank, 1921, Risk, Uncertainty and Profit (Houghton, Mifflin).

LeRoy, S.F., and L.D. Singell, Jr, 1987. Knight on risk and uncertainty. Journal of Political Economy, 95, 2, pp. 394-406.

Wihlborg, Clas, 1996, Economic Efficiency with Enabling and Mandatory Law. Paper presented to the 6th International Joseph A. Schumpeter Society, Stockholm June 2-5, 1996.

Index